THE CLASSIC
ZUCCHINI COOKBOOK

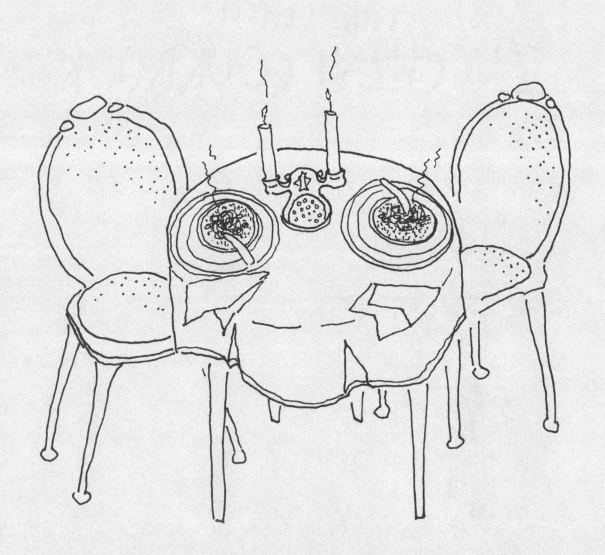

THE CLASSIC ZUCCHINI COOKBOOK

225 Recipes
for All Kinds of Squash

Nancy C. Ralston, Marynor Jordan, and Andrea Chesman

Illustrations by Laurie Hadlock

Storey Publishing

The mission of Storey Publishing is to serve our customers by publishing practical information that encourages personal independence in harmony with the environment.

To Richard, Rory, and Sam

Edited by Dianne M. Cutillo
Creative direction by Wendy Palitz
Art direction and cover and text design by Cynthia N. McFarland
Text production by Jennifer Jepson Smith
Indexed by Nan Badgett / word•a•bil•i•ty

Recipe Credits: Recipes on pages 40, 43, 44, 78, 160, 167, and 176 from *The Joy of Gardening Cookbook* by Janet Ballantyne, Storey Publishing, 1994. Recipes on pages 252 and 263 from *Desserts from the Garden* by Janet Ballantyne, Storey Publishing, 1983.

Printed in the United States by R.R. Donnelley
10 9 8 7 6 5 4

Library of Congress Cataloging-in-Publication Data

Ralston, Nancy C.
    The classic zucchini cookbook : 225 recipes for all kinds of squash / Nancy C. Ralston, Marynor Jordan, and Andrea Chesman ; illustrations by Laurie Hadlock.-- 3rd ed.
        p. cm.
    Includes index.
    ISBN 978-1-58017-453-4 (alk. paper)
    1. Cookery (Zucchini) I. Jordan, Marynor. II. Chesman, Andrea. III. Title.
TX803.Z82 R33 2001
641.6'562--dc21
                            2002001139

Contents

Preface

I don't know when I've had more fun in the kitchen. Making up recipes for zucchini is almost like child's play. You can do anything with zucchini and get good results.

So when I received a phone call asking me if I was interested in taking on a revision of *Garden Way's Zucchini Cookbook* 25 years after its original publication, I was happy to say yes. Immediately, contracts were signed, zucchini was planted, and meetings were arranged. At one of those meetings, I happened to mention to a sales manager at Storey Books that I thought zucchini was basically a boring, bland vegetable, and his jaw dropped. But that's a good thing, I hastened to add. Because it means that you can do a lot with it — and many people will be glad to buy a cookbook that presents new ideas for preparing this versatile vegetable.

That an overabundance of zucchini can be a problem is uncontestable. Every article I have ever read about zucchini mentions a New England joke: Why do Vermonters (or Bay Staters, or Mainers, or whatever — you supply your favorite state) have to lock their car doors every August?

To keep people from filling their cars with zucchini, of course! I can't verify that a car filling has ever occurred, but I have driven past many driveways that feature an overflowing bushel basket of zucchini and a sign reading "Free. *Please* take one."

Last summer, when I tested recipes for this cookbook and fed my family zucchini just about every single day, I supplied almost all of my testing needs with three plants of zucchini. That's a lot of zucchini for a minimal amount of gardening effort.

My breakthrough moment in the kitchen occurred about a week after attending a zucchini festival, where I heard tales of "mock apple pies" made with zucchini instead of apples. I followed the directions I was given and was amazed. If you peel zucchini and cook it in lemon juice with enough sugar and spice, you get something very much like apple pie filling. I took the pie to a picnic and completely enjoyed the incredulous looks I received when I told my friends the pie was made with zucchini, not apples. I had fooled everyone.

My son looked up from his slice and told me I should call it "Zapple Pie." After the Zapple Pie, we started thinking up titles for other recipes. Zapple Pie was swiftly followed by Zesto Pizza (pesto plus zucchini) and Zingerbread (gingerbread plus zucchini). The naming was fun, and the recipe-testing results were delicious. We moved on to Zesto Pasta Salad and Zapple Strudel, as well as Squoconut Pie, coconut custard pie made with yellow squash and coconut flavoring, but no coconut.

Pesto, pasta, pizza — these dishes weren't even on the distant horizon when Marynor Jordan and Nancy Ralston wrote the first edition of this book 25 years ago. That was a time when we were still eating an awful lot of ground beef, chicken was mostly roasted on a Sunday, and quality fresh fish was rarely found away from the coast. Whole wheat and bran were tossed with abandon into desserts, healthy eating often meant a punishing lentil loaf, and dinner for the rest of us was a casserole in which cream of mushroom soup featured prominently.

Much has changed since then. Our cooking is very much influenced by the foods of the Mediterranean, of which zucchini was an early example. A wider range of fresh vegetables and herbs is available from local supermarkets year-round. These days, we eat a lot more chicken, fish, and vegetarian meals. When we hunger for a change of pace, we don't think twice about whipping up a Thai curry or a Tex-Mex platter of enchiladas. We grill vegetables all summer, and we roast them all winter. In between, we sauté in heart-healthy olive oil, and we are generous with the seasonings, especially garlic. The new recipes in this edition reflect these changes. Of course, many of the old favorites have been retained as well.

I've heard it said that a true test of friendship is a willingness to accept extra zucchini in September. It is my hope that armed with this cookbook, you will have as much fun in the kitchen as I have had, and that your friendships are always enriched and never strained by an abundance of zucchini and other squash.

Andrea Chesman

1. Becoming Acquainted with Squash

Squash has a history of causing confusion. While Europeans were still cultivating only various types of inedible gourds, New World natives had been enjoying squash and pumpkins for at least 7,000 years. The confusion arose when the first European explorers visited the Americas and reported that the native people were cultivating a type of melon. It was a mistake made again and again; because Europeans had never seen anything like squash, they had no word for it. Nonetheless, the first European settlers in North America, who couldn't be too choosy given their circumstances, readily adopted squash as a food.

Native Americans introduced the first European settlers in New England to beans, corn (maize), and pumpkins, "the three sisters." They treated them to a seafood chowder made with "Indian squash" that at least one writer condemned as "the meanest of God's blessings." But after experiencing the New England winter, the Pilgrims came to appreciate pumpkin and squash for their prolific harvests that staved off starvation.

Native Americans showed the settlers how to bake whole pumpkins by burying them in the ashes of a fire, then cutting them open and serving them with animal fat and maple syrup or honey. The Pilgrims "improved" on this recipe: They opened the pumpkins up; scooped out the seeds and fibers; filled the cavities with milk, sweetener, and spices; replaced the tops; then baked the pumpkins. In addition, a recipe for "Pumpkin Pie" appeared in Amelia Simmons's 1796 cookbook. Ever since, pie has been the predominant use for pumpkins in

North America, despite a plethora of pumpkin recipes dating from those early days, including stews and soups, sauce for meat and fish, pancakes, breads, and butters. One can only imagine the flavor of early "pumpkin beer," brewed from a combination of pumpkin, persimmons, and maple syrup. Thus, winter squash became and remains a staple in New England.

It turns out, however, that botanists don't agree on a firm line dividing pumpkins from winter squash, or winter squash from summer squash. Scientists have identified four basic types of edible squashes. *Cucurbita pepo* is noted for its pentagonal stems with prickly spines. This group includes pumpkins and acorn squash, all summer squashes, spaghetti squash, and numerous gourds. Butternut squash, which is one of the best replacements for pumpkin in any recipe, is considered another species entirely (*C. moshata,* which has pentagonal stems without spines). *Cucurbita maxima* (those with round stems) includes buttercup, Hubbard, and turban squashes. *Cucurbita mixta* includes white and green cushaws and the Tennessee sweet potato squash.

From a culinary perspective, the relevant difference among these squashes is how mature they are when we eat them. Summer squash is eaten when immature, before the seeds have developed. Winter squash and pumpkins are eaten fully mature, after seeds and a hard shell have developed.

Although winter squash and pumpkin rapidly became staples in New World kitchens, summer squash was not common until the 1950s, when zucchini was reintroduced from Italy. It came via a circuitous route. In the 1820s, a South American squash called the Valparaiso was introduced to Europe. As its use became more widespread, this long, thick, meaty squash became known as "vegetable marrow" in England and "cocozelle" in France and Italy. Increasing travel in the post–World War II era slowly broadened American palates, and refrigerated rail cars and other improvements increased the availability of a wider range of foods. Home gardeners were the first to pick up the zucchini, which was accepted rapidly. Today zucchini and other summer squash are supermarket staples.

Summer Squash Varieties

Most summer squash recipes are interchangeable. All summer squash have tender, edible skins and flesh that ranges from mild and nutty to buttery or cucumber-like. But the shape and appearance of these squashes vary considerably. More and more varieties are available from garden seed catalogs, farm stands, and supermarkets, and it is fun to grow and cook new types. Many summer squash go by several different names.

Chayote. This squash breaks all the rules, starting with having one seed, which is edible.

Chayote looks like a pale green mango with fur-rowed skin. Because the skin is quite tough, it is usually peeled, although this is not necessary if the chayote is young and fresh. Once peeled, it can be used in any summer squash recipe. Chayote is also known as *mirliton*.

Cocozelle. This heirloom type of zucchini from Italy has raised ribs or stripes. The flavor is supe-rior when the vegetable is young.

Crookneck Yellow Squash and Yellow Summer Squash. The crook is being bred out of yellow summer squash, as are the warts that make the skin bumpy. Most yellow summer squash is straight and smooth-skinned, but the older, bumpy-skinned varieties may have better flavor.

Middle Eastern–Type Zucchini. These zucchini are typically rounder than most zucchini and pale green in color. They may be called *Lebanese, Egyptian, Cousa, Kuta,* or *Magda* squash. Use them in any zucchini recipe. Because of their shape, they are good for stuffing.

Pattypan. Shaped like flying saucers, these scal-loped squash are best when small, 2 to 3 inches in diameter. Their interesting shape makes them particularly appealing for slicing and grilling, roasting, or sautéing. They are also wonderful stuffed. Pattypans come in colors ranging from cream to green. These squash may be found under the name of *scallopini* or *cymling*.

Round Zucchini. These may be called *globe zuc-chini, Ronde de Nice,* or *apple squash.* Buy them when they are small. They are excellent stuffed.

Zephyr. A favorite among growers because it keeps well, zephyr squash looks like a smooth-skinned yellow crookneck squash half dipped in green paint. It has excellent flavor and texture.

Zucchini. The classic zucchini is a dark green cylinder with mild flavor. Golden zucchini are increasingly common.

Buying Summer Squash

Zucchini and summer squash are best when young and small. Baby squash should be about 2 to 4 inches long and weigh less than 6 ounces. Small squash are 4 to 6 inches long and weigh 7 to 11 ounces. Medium-sized squash are about 8 to 10 inches long and weigh 12 to 16 ounces. Large squash are anything above 16 ounces; these are generally best stuffed or used in dessert recipes.

When buying summer squash, look for firm specimens without gashes or dents in the skin. They can be kept in a perforated plastic bag in the refrigerator for 3 to 5 days.

Cooking Summer Squash

Summer squash is at its best when it is cooked briefly. It can be served plain or with butter or herbs, to emphasize its delicate flavor. Or it can be combined with bold flavors to make a more exciting dish. Squash cooked by using a dry-heat method — frying, grilling, roasting, or sautéing — usually has more flavor than squash cooked by steaming or boiling.

To prepare summer squash, wash it thoroughly. Trim off the blossom and stem ends. Then slice, chop, or grate as the recipe suggests.

Draining Summer Squash

Some recipes call for draining summer squash. The most effective way to do this is to slice or grate the squash and toss with salt. Set it aside for about 30 minutes. The squash will lose about one-quarter of its volume as excess moisture is released from its cells. Wring the squash dry in a clean kitchen towel, or squeeze by hand. The squash is now ready to cook with. A less effective method that can be used with grated squash is simply to wring it dry in a clean kitchen towel.

Many cooks find that salting summer squash before sautéing greatly improves its taste and texture. Other cooks are content to sauté squash without draining first. Try it both ways and see which you prefer. In this book, salting appears in sautéing recipes as an optional step, where appropriate. Salting and draining is not optional in recipes for baked goods.

Unless you are preparing squash to masquerade as apple, don't peel it; the peel is where most of the nutrition, fiber, and flavor lie.

Cooking Methods

Summer squash can be prepared by just about any cooking method. The goal is usually to bring the squash to the tender crisp stage — tender, but with some resistance to the tooth. Mushy summer squash is unappealing at best.

Baking. Baking is a slow-cooking method that can be used to combine squash with other ingredients, usually producing flavor that is greater than the sum of its parts. Layer the squash with flavorful ingredients, such as onions, leeks, garlic, and tomatoes. Sprinkle with herbs and salt and pepper, and drizzle with oil or melted butter. Bake for 1 to 1½ hours at 350°F. The squash will be transformed into a tender, flavorful dish.

Squash can also be stuffed before it is baked. Steam or blanch a whole or halved squash until barely tender. Scoop out the pulp and combine it with a filling. Put the filling back into the squash shell and bake until heated through (15 to 30 minutes) at 350°F.

Blanching. Summer squash is sometimes briefly immersed in boiling water to set the color and eliminate its slightly bitter flavor. It is a good idea to blanch summer squash before adding it to salads. To blanch, immerse whole or halved baby squash, or diced, sliced, or cubed squash, for 1 to 2 minutes in boiling salted water. To stop the cooking process, immediately drain the squash and immerse in ice water, then drain and pat dry with clean kitchen towels.

Deep-Frying. Doesn't everything taste better fried? Cut the squash into rounds or strips. Salt and drain to eliminate excess moisture and pat dry. Dredge the pieces in flour or coat in a batter. Fry in oil preheated to 365°F for 2 to 3 minutes, until golden.

Grilling. Summer squash is an excellent candidate for the grill. Leave baby squash whole or halve them; cut larger squash into ⅜-inch rounds or steaks. Brush with oil, vinaigrette, or salad dressing and place over a medium-hot fire. Grill until tender and grill-marked, 4 to 5 minutes per side.

What's in a Name?

The English word *squash* comes from the Narragansett word *askútasquash,* meaning "eaten when raw or green."

Microwaving. Summer squash can be microwaved, though it does little to enhance the flavor of the squash. Allow 3 to 4 minutes per pound.

Roasting. Roasting is an excellent way to bring out the flavor of summer squash. Leave baby squash whole or halve it; cut larger squash into rounds or spears. Coat the squash with oil and roast in a 450°F oven until lightly browned, about 15 minutes. Roasted squash is delicious served with a sprinkling of coarse sea salt or a drizzle of balsamic vinegar.

Sautéing and Stir-Frying. A very flavorful way to cook squash is to sauté or stir-fry it in butter or oil. If the squash is salted and drained first, it will brown better and the flavor will be somewhat enhanced. Melt the butter or heat the oil in a large skillet or wok over medium to medium-high heat. Add the squash and cook, stirring frequently, until the squash is tender crisp, about 5 minutes. Do not cover the pan while the squash is cooking. Do not overcrowd the pan, or the squash will steam rather than brown.

Steaming. Steam whole or halved baby squash or diced, sliced, or cubed squash over boiling water just until tender crisp, 4 to 5 minutes. Because steaming does not enhance the flavor of squash, a pat of butter, a sprinkling of herbs, or a sauce is often a welcome addition.

Sweating. A flavorful way to cook squash is to sauté it in butter or olive oil for 1 to 2 minutes. Cover and let the squash "sweat" out its juices for another 3 to 5 minutes, creating a delicate sauce. Sweating works especially well for sliced, diced, and cubed summer squash.

Winter Squash and Pumpkins

Whereas summer squash is briefly cooked, most cooking methods for winter squash are long and slow. Most winter squash varieties have inedible skins, but the seeds can often be toasted and eaten out of hand or used to garnish.

Winter Squash Varieties

Winter squash varieties differ greatly in size, flavor, and texture. Although most varieties can be used interchangeably, some squash require special preparation.

Acorn. Shaped like an acorn, this squash comes in green, orange, or white. Its flesh is somewhat drier and stringier than that of other varieties. Acorn squash is a convenient size for stuffing and for serving as baked or roasted wedges.

Banana. A monster of a squash, this can grow up to 100 pounds. It has mild, sweet, and very creamy pink flesh. Banana squash is more commonly found on the West Coast than in the eastern states. When banana squash shows up in the supermarket, it is usually sold in pieces.

Buttercup. Fans of buttercup squash claim that it is so naturally sweet, it doesn't need a sweet glaze. (Take that advice with a grain of salt.) It is dark green, with a round shape and a pale green "cap."

Butternut. The one winter squash that can be peeled easily, butternut squash has moist, rich, smooth flesh. It makes a delicious purée, and cubes and slices can be grilled or roasted. Butternut squash can be grated raw and used as a stand-in for grated carrots in baked dishes. This good all-purpose squash is usually available year-round.

Calabaza. Caribbean recipes that call for "pumpkin" are actually referring to the calabaza. This squash is usually rounded or pear-shaped and fairly large, with mottled skin that may be green, orange, amber, or cream, and speckled or striped. It is one "winter squash" that is grown year-round in warm climates.

Delicata. Also known as *sweet potato squash*, delicata is shaped like a long, ridged tube and has cream, orange, and green stripes. Delicata should be sliced in half lengthwise, seeded, and cut into crescent-shaped pieces. The peel is edible. One delicata squash serves two.

Hubbard. Hubbard squash presents a grand challenge in the kitchen. It can weigh anywhere from 8 to 40 pounds, and its skin is extremely hard to cut through. But once the squash is wrestled into manageable pieces, its light orange flesh is sweet and moist. Hubbard squash makes excellent baby food.

Pumpkin. Pie pumpkins, also known as "sweet" pumpkins or "cheese" pumpkins, are smaller than those cultivated for jack-o'-lanterns. They can be cooked like any other winter squash.

Red Kuri. You can recognize red kuri by its distinctive brilliant deep orange color. Its flesh is bland compared with that of other winter squash, but its color makes it very attractive on the plate. Red kuri is often used to make soup.

Spaghetti. Yellow and football-shaped, spaghetti squash has taken the distressing tendency of winter squash to be stringy and turned it into a virtue. When cooked, the flesh of the spaghetti squash turns into long, spaghetti-like strands. Although many suggest serving spaghetti squash as a pasta substitute, it is probably better to acknowledge its sweet flavor and work with it as a winter squash.

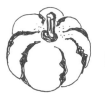

Sweet Dumpling. Small and pumpkin-shaped, sweet dumplings are cream colored with dark green stripes. Like that of delicata squash, the skin of the sweet dumpling squash is edible. The flesh is smooth, sweet, and moist. One sweet dumpling squash serves one.

Turban. As much prized for its decorative appearance as its flavor, the turban squash is indeed shaped like a turban. It can be cooked like any other winter squash. Its skin is tough and difficult to cut into.

Buying Winter Squash

When buying winter squash, look for firm, heavy fruit with no blemishes or soft spots on the skin. The stem should be intact. Store it in a paper bag in the refrigerator for up to 1 week or in a cool (50°F), airy place for up to 3 months. If you can, avoid presliced winter squash, as their color and flavor deteriorate rapidly. Because cooked winter squash freezes well, it is better to buy a large, whole squash and freeze the leftovers (that is, if you don't have to walk home from the supermarket).

Preparing Winter Squash for Cooking

Most recipes call for cutting winter squash into halves, quarters, or serving-sized pieces. This may be easier said than done. Some winter squash, such as blue Hubbard, require a heavy cleaver (or an ax) to do the job, while others, such as delicata, have skins that are easily cut or even edible. Butternut squash has a skin that is readily removed with a swivel-bladed vegetable peeler; when a recipe calls for peeled and diced squash, choose butternut. If you are faced with a winter squash you just can't saw through, the best thing to do is wrap it in a plastic grocery-store bag and drop it on a concrete floor (I've heard that is what they do at supermarkets). Another way to tame a winter squash is in the microwave. Place the whole squash in the microwave and cook on high for 2 minutes. Allow the squash to stand for several minutes, then cut in half for further cooking. After cutting the squash, remove the fibers and seeds.

Cooking Methods

Winter squash is usually cooked until it is completely tender. You can't really overcook winter squash (unless you are serving it stuffed, in which case you want the shell to remain intact). Test with a fork through the skin. The fork should meet with little or no resistance.

Baking. Place halved squash in a baking dish, skin-side up. Add an inch or so of water or juice to the pan. Bake at 350°F for 45 to 90 minutes, depending on the size of the squash. In a recent experiment, a whole 16-pound Baby Blue Hubbard took 3 hours to bake. You can bake a winter squash whole if you have trouble cutting it into pieces; just be sure to prick the skin in several places to allow steam to escape.

If you want to serve the squash stuffed, bake the halves skin-side up for about 45 minutes. Then turn the squash skin-side down. Loosen the squash pulp with a fork and add the stuffing ingredients, or remove the squash flesh and combine it with the filling ingredients, then return it to the squash shell. Bake for another 15 minutes, until the filling is heated through.

Deep-Frying. Although not a typical preparation in the United States, the Japanese sometimes deep-fry kabocha squash in tempura batter. Cut the squash into rounds, wedges, or strips and coat with batter. Fry for 2 to 3 minutes, until golden, in oil preheated to 365°F.

Grilling. Winter squash should be steamed before it is grilled. Steam slices until tender, then brush with oil. Grill until tender and grill-marked, about 5 minutes per side.

Microwaving. Place squash pieces skin-side up in a microwave-safe container. Cover with plastic wrap. Microwave on high for 4 minutes. Turn the squash over and rotate the dish. Microwave for 4 more minutes, until the squash is fork tender. Continue to microwave, if necessary, until the squash is completely tender.

Roasting. Roasting is an excellent way to bring out the flavor of winter squash. Peel and cut into slices, dice, or cube. Coat the pieces with oil and roast at 425°F until lightly browned, 20 to 30 minutes, turning frequently. To roast halves or quarters, place them skin-side down in a roasting pan and roast at 425°F, until tender, 45 to 60 minutes; baste occasionally with butter or apple cider, if desired.

Steaming. Steam halves or pieces over boiling water, until tender (about 15 minutes, depending on the size of the pieces). Usually steaming is done in combination with another cooking method.

Growing Squash

Although squash is readily available in the supermarket year-round, there are plenty of good reasons to grow your own. First, squash is an almost foolproof garden plant, perfect for the novice gardener. The weather has to be extreme to destroy a squash plant; mere human errors of judgment are not enough. Most important, fresh, recently harvested summer squash are superior in flavor and texture to supermarket specimens.

To avoid a ridiculous embarrassment of riches (a harvest you can neither eat yourself nor give away), figure that two summer squash plants will provide sufficient zucchini, yellow summer squash, or pattypans to satisfy a household of four. Four winter squash plants will provide enough for four people for most of the year.

There are more than four seeds in a packet, so plan to share the seeds with a friend. Or buy the right number of plants already started at a nursery.

Most summer squash are "bush" types, meaning that the plant has a fairly compact shape. Summer squash will start producing young fruit in 45 to 55 days and will keep producing until the first frost, as long as they are harvested frequently. Winter squash, along with pumpkins and edible gourds, must reach maturity before the flesh is at its prime and require a huge amount of garden space for 75 to 120 days.

Most winter squash are "vining" plants. Unless a seed packet or catalog specifically identifies a winter squash as a bush type, the plant will be a space grabber. Vines may extend to 20 feet or more. If adequate garden space is a problem, vining squash can be trained to grow on a trellis or tepee. The expansive growth of vining squash can be curtailed by pinching back.

Bush types, although prolific, have less of a tendency to play octopus and overtake other planted areas of your garden. They can even be grown in containers on a sunny porch or deck. They require plenty of water and do best in the heat.

Squash Nutrition

All squash contain vitamin A, though the deep colored ones have the most. A 1-cup serving of winter squash provides more than 7,000 I.U. of vitamin A, while a cup of summer squash contributes a measly 520 I.U. But winter squash is more caloric than summer squash: 1 cup of winter squash contains about 80 calories (before you add the butter), while 1 cup of summer squash contains only 35 calories. Both squashes also contain vitamins B and C and fiber.

Harvesting

Zucchini and other summer squash hide under their foliage, where they can grow to unbelievable dimensions. Generally, the surplus of squash creates enough of a problem without having to deal with monster specimens. Small summer squash are preferable to those that have been allowed to grow until they are beyond their peak in size. Large summer squash are seedy, tough-skinned, and well past their peak of flavor or texture.

Winter squash must be allowed to reach maturity before they are harvested. At that point, their thick, tough skin makes them ideal for winter storage. Winter squash sweeten with age as the starches turn to sugars. If picked before reaching their prime, the squash will be watery and less flavorful.

After harvest, winter squash should be allowed to cure at room temperature for a couple of weeks to harden the skin. They should be stored in a cool airy space; 50°F is the ideal temperature for storage. Winter squash will keep for several months at this temperature. Should you be the beneficiary of an overly bountiful harvest, the preserving ideas in chapter 9 will help.

2. Starters, Salads & Soups

Sometimes I think every good meal begins

with squash. The recipes collected here — little

dishes, salads, and soups — can make a meal or

be served as a first course.

Zesto Bruschetta

Pesto plus zucchini makes "zesto" to top these delicious toasts. Serve them as an hors d'oeuvre, an accompaniment to soup, or just as they are for a light lunch.

10 slices of baguette or 5 slices of Italian bread, halved

1 clove of garlic, cut in half

1 cup grated zucchini or other summer squash

½ cup pesto (page 27)

10 tomato slices

Salt and freshly ground black pepper

⅓ cup freshly grated Parmigiano-Reggiano cheese

1. Preheat the broiler.

2. Arrange the bread on a baking sheet. Toast under the broiler until golden, 2 to 3 minutes per side.

3. Rub the cut halves of the garlic clove on the toasted bread.

4. Mix together the zucchini and pesto. Cover each toast slice with a heaping tablespoon of the pesto. Broil for 1 minute.

5. Top each toast with one tomato slice. Sprinkle the tomato slices with salt and pepper. Sprinkle the cheese over the toasts.

6. Return the baking sheet to the broiler and broil just long enough to melt the cheese, 1 to 2 minutes.

7. Bruschetta is best served immediately, but it holds up well on a buffet table.

Serves 5–10

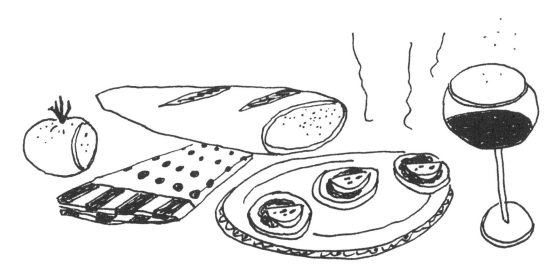

Zucchini Pizza Bites

Zucchini slices replace pizza dough in these little appetizers.
They are fun snacks to make with children.

2–3 medium-sized zucchini or yellow summer squash, cut into ½-inch rounds (24 slices)

Extra virgin olive oil

Salt and freshly ground black pepper

⅔ cup well-seasoned tomato sauce

¼ cup grated mozzarella cheese

¼ cup freshly grated Parmesan cheese

4–6 mushrooms, sliced

6–8 black olives, sliced

1. Preheat the oven to 425°F.

2. Brush both sides of the zucchini slices with the oil and arrange on a baking sheet. Sprinkle with salt and pepper to taste.

3. Roast for 7 minutes, or until the slices are just tender when pierced with a fork.

4. Meanwhile, in a small bowl, combine the tomato sauce, mozzarella, and Parmesan. Add salt and pepper to taste.

5. Spread one spoonful of the tomato sauce mixture on each zucchini slice. Top each zucchini slice with one mushroom slice and one olive slice. Return the baking sheet to the oven and roast until the cheese is melted and the sauce is heated through, 2 to 3 minutes.

6. Serve hot.

Serves 4–6

Zucchini Crudités with Three Dips

Have you let any zucchini get oversized? Or have you grown any round zucchini? Use them as the bowls in which you serve the dips. Slice overgrown zucchini in half lengthwise (or slice the top third off a round zucchini) and scoop out the flesh, leaving a shell with ¼-inch walls. If necessary, cut a thin strip from the bottom so that the bowls sit level. Fill the bowls with the dips and arrange raw vegetables around them.

SIMPLE CURRY DIP
1 cup plain yogurt
1 tablespoon curry powder
Salt and freshly ground black pepper

BLUE CHEESE DIP
½ cup buttermilk
6 tablespoons crumbled blue cheese
¼ cup mayonnaise
¼ cup chopped fresh parsley
2 small cloves of garlic

COTTAGE CHEESE DIP
1 carton (12 ounces) cream-style cottage cheese
1 tablespoon chopped fresh chives
½ teaspoon hot pepper sauce

CRUDITÉS
3 pounds assorted bite-size fresh vegetables

1. To make the curry dip, combine the yogurt and curry powder and mix well. Add salt and pepper to taste. Transfer to a serving bowl.

2. To make the blue cheese dip, combine the buttermilk, blue cheese, mayonnaise, parsley, and garlic in a blender or food processor. Process until smooth and thickened. Transfer to a serving bowl.

3. To make the cottage cheese dip, combine the cottage cheese, chives, and hot sauce in a blender or food processor. Process until smooth and thickened. Transfer to a serving bowl.

4. To serve, arrange the bowls of dips and raw vegetables on a serving platter.

NOTES: If you are not serving the dips immediately, cover them and refrigerate for up to 8 hours.

Good vegetable choices for the crudités are small zucchini, cut into spears; baby carrots; celery sticks; and cherry or grape tomatoes.

Serves 12

Zucchini Cheese Squares

Biscuit mix, zucchini, cheese, and seasonings make a quick and satisfying party appetizer that can double as a fine accompaniment to soup or a salad.

3 cups thinly sliced zucchini or other summer squash

1 cup buttermilk baking mix

½ cup chopped onion

½ cup freshly grated Parmesan cheese

2 tablespoons chopped fresh parsley

1 teaspoon chopped fresh oregano, or ½ teaspoon dried

1 teaspoon seasoned salt

1 clove of garlic, minced

Freshly ground black pepper

½ cup canola or olive oil

4 eggs, beaten

1. Preheat the oven to 350°F. Butter a 9- by 13-inch baking dish.

2. In a large mixing bowl, combine the zucchini, baking mix, onion, Parmesan, parsley, oregano, salt, garlic, and pepper to taste. Mix to combine. Make a well in the center.

3. In a small bowl, combine the oil and eggs; mix well. Pour into the well in the zucchini mixture and mix just enough to combine. Spread in the baking dish.

4. Bake for about 25 minutes, until golden.

5. Let cool on a wire rack for 5 minutes. Cut into squares and serve warm.

Serves 8–20

A Better Zucchini?

"I've always thought that someone should come up with a way to burn zucchini instead of firewood. Someone should invent a way of drying them, or genetically modifying them so they can dry well, and then people could burn them in their fireplaces. You know, zucchini grows so fast and they get big so fast, gardeners just don't know what to do with them. Well, I think you should be able to dry 'em and then throw them in your woodstove. And growers, they would plant so many cords per acre. Cords per acre, that's how you should grow it."

— Mike Merrill
Middlebury, Vermont

Mushroom Strudel

Phyllo dough produces impressive results considering how easily
it is handled. The zucchini largely disappears under the
dominant mushroom and feta cheese flavors.

2 tablespoons extra virgin olive oil

3 cups sliced mushrooms

2 shallots, minced

1 medium-sized zucchini, grated

4 ounces feta cheese, crumbled

¼ cup dried bread crumbs

Salt and freshly ground black pepper

12 sheets (each 17 by 12 inches) phyllo dough, thawed if frozen

¾ cup (1½ sticks) butter, melted

1. Heat the oil in a large skillet over medium-high heat. Add the mushrooms and shallots. Sauté until the mushrooms have given up their juice, about 10 minutes.

2. Wrap the zucchini in a clean kitchen towel and squeeze to eliminate as much moisture as possible. Add the zucchini to the mushrooms and sauté for 1 minute. Remove from the heat and stir in the feta cheese and bread crumbs. Season to taste with salt and pepper.

3. Preheat the oven to 400°F.

4. Open one sheet of phyllo on a work surface. Brush with some of the butter. Top with five more sheets of phyllo; brush each sheet with butter before adding another sheet on top. Spoon half of the filling along the short end of the phyllo, leaving a border of about 1½ inches on each end. Fold the long sides in to partially enclose the filling. Roll the phyllo and filling over onto itself to form a roll. Place on a baking sheet, seam-side down. Brush with more butter. Repeat to make a second strudel.

5. Bake for about 25 minutes, until golden. Set the pan on a wire rack to cool.

6. To serve, use two spatulas to transfer the strudels to a cutting board. With a sharp serrated knife, cut the strudels into 1-inch slices. Serve warm or at room temperature.

Makes 16 slices

Ratatouille Relish

The vegetables that make up the famous Provençal dish ratatouille are given
a sweet-and-sour treatment. The result is a piquant relish that can be served on
a relish tray or spread on crackers or toasts. Note that the vegetables
are salted and left to stand overnight, then cooked very briefly.

2 medium-sized zucchini,
   chopped

2 green bell peppers, chopped

2 tomatoes, chopped

1 small eggplant, peeled and
   chopped

2 tablespoons salt

1 cup sugar

1 cup distilled white vinegar

1 teaspoon mustard seeds

¾ teaspoon celery seeds

1. Combine the zucchini, bell peppers, tomatoes, eggplant, and salt
   in a large bowl. Toss to mix. Cover and let stand for 12 hours.

2. Drain the vegetables in a large colander. Rinse under cold
   running water; drain well.

3. In a large nonreactive saucepan, combine the vegetables with
   the sugar, vinegar, mustard seeds, and celery seeds. Mix well.
   Bring to a boil. Reduce the heat and simmer for 5 minutes, stirring frequently.

4. Cover and refrigerate for at least 2 hours.

5. Serve cold.

Makes 4 cups

Winter Squash Cheese Spread

Here's an unusual spread to serve with crackers — and it comes with its own serving dish! The combination of winter squash, dates, and chutney in a cream cheese base makes a sweet spread that complements a cheese board.

1 **medium-sized acorn squash, 1 large sweet dumpling squash, or 1 small turban squash**

1 **package (8 ounces) cream cheese, softened**

4 **tablespoons butter, softened**

¼ **cup chopped pitted dates**

2 **tablespoons drained and chopped cranberry or mango chutney**

1. If necessary, cut a 1-inch slice from the bottom of the squash so that it sits upright. Remove the stem end. Scoop out and discard the seeds and fibers.

2. Fill a saucepan with about 1 inch of water. Bring to a boil. Set the squash upside down in the saucepan.

3. Reduce the heat to medium, cover the pan, and simmer until the squash flesh is tender when pressed with a fork but the shell is still firm, about 20 minutes. Transfer the squash to a colander to drain and cool.

4. In a medium bowl, beat together the cream cheese and butter until thoroughly blended. Mix in the dates and chutney.

5. Scoop the flesh from the cooled squash shell, leaving about ¼ inch of shell. Add the squash flesh to the cream cheese mixture and blend well. Spoon the mixture into the shell. Cover and chill.

6. Serve chilled.

Serves 8–12

Winter Squash Snack Chips

Winter squash and pumpkin make great-tasting French fries, and they provide much more nutrition than conventional fries because they are rich in vitamin A. For snack chips, slice the squash as thin as possible; a mandoline is the best tool for this job.

1 **pound winter squash or pumpkin**

Oil, for deep-frying

1½ **tablespoons curry powder**

½ **teaspoon garlic salt**

Salt

Deep-Frying Tip

A deep-fry thermometer is essential for monitoring the temperature of the oil.

1. Peel and seed the squash. Slice as thin as possible; if desired, use the waffle-cut attachment on a food processor. Place the slices in a large bowl of ice water; refrigerate for 45 minutes.

2. Drain well. Thoroughly pat the squash slices dry between clean dish towels or paper towels.

3. Pour about 3 inches of oil in a deep-fryer or deep, heavy saucepan. Heat to 365°F.

4. Drop a handful of the chips into the oil. Stir several times with a long-handled wooden spoon to prevent them from sticking to each other. Fry until golden, 2 to 3 minutes. Using a slotted spoon, remove to paper towels to drain. Add another handful of chips to the oil and continue frying until all the chips are cooked.

5. Sprinkle the chips with the curry powder, garlic salt, and salt to taste. Serve immediately.

VARIATION: Some people prefer their chips sweet, in which case cinnamon and sugar can replace the curry powder, garlic salt, and salt.

Serves 4

Curried Toasted Pumpkin Seeds

A little cayenne adds heat to these curry-flavored pumpkin seeds.
Add as much as you want — as long as you serve them with lemonade or beer.

3 **cups hulled pumpkin seeds**

3 **tablespoons peanut, canola, or olive oil**

1 **tablespoon curry powder**

1 **teaspoon salt**

½ **teaspoon ground cayenne pepper, or more to taste (optional)**

1. Preheat the oven to 300°F. Line a baking sheet with parchment paper, or lightly oil the baking sheet.

2. Place the pumpkin seeds in a medium-sized bowl. In a small bowl, combine the oil, curry powder, salt, and cayenne, if using; stir well. Pour over the pumpkin seeds and toss to coat well. Transfer the pumpkin seeds to the pan and spread out into a single layer.

3. Roast for 25 to 30 minutes, until the seeds are lightly browned and crunchy. Shake or stir the seeds occasionally for even cooking. Check frequently during the last 5 minutes; do not allow the seeds to become scorched.

4. Transfer the seeds to a medium-sized bowl to cool completely. The seeds will become crisp as they cool. Store in an airtight jar for 1 week at room temperature or for up to 1 month in the refrigerator.

Makes 3 cups

Pumpkin Cider Bowl

For your next fall party, consider serving cider from a pumpkin cider bowl. Use a well-shaped 5- or 6-pound pie pumpkin. Preheat the oven to 350°F. Cut the lid from the pumpkin and scoop out and discard the seeds and fibers. Score the inside flesh several times. Place the pumpkin and its top flesh-side down in a large shallow pan. Add about 1 inch of water to the pan and bake for about 30 minutes.

Remove the pan from the oven and drain off the water. Turn the pumpkin right-side up, rub the interior with butter, and return to the pan, right-side up.

In a small saucepan, combine ½ cup sugar or honey, ½ cup apple cider, 1 cinnamon stick, and ¼ teaspoon ground nutmeg. Pour into the pumpkin and baste the insides of the pumpkin with this mixture. Return to the oven to finish baking, about 30 minutes.

Fill the pumpkin with warm cider — mulled or plain — and serve.

Once the cider has been served, the pulp can be scraped from the shell and used in any recipe calling for cooked pumpkin.

Spicy Pepitas

Roasted pumpkin seeds are a popular snack in Mexico. They can be enjoyed roasted and salted or flavored with ground chili powder. These wonderful fall snacks cry out for beer — perhaps a Corona or a Tecate — to accompany them.

3 **cups hulled pumpkin seeds**

3 **tablespoons canola oil**

1 **tablespoon chili powder or pure ground chile**

1 **teaspoon ground cumin**

1 **teaspoon salt**

Grow Pumpkins with Hull-less Seeds

If pumpkin seeds are your weakness, you may want to grow a variety that produces hull-less seeds. Johnny's Seed Company (see Sources, page 301) offers Kakai, a small black-striped pumpkin that is particularly prized for its seeds. You can also find hull-less green seeds in most natural food stores. To prepare seeds for roasting, wash them in a bowl of water to separate them from the stringy fibers to which they are attached. Pat dry. In addition to the recipe above, see page 23.

1. Preheat the oven to 300°F. Line a baking sheet with parchment paper, or lightly oil the baking sheet.

2. Place the pumpkin seeds in a medium-sized bowl. In a small bowl, combine the oil, chili powder, cumin, and salt; stir well. Pour over the pumpkin seeds and toss to coat. Transfer the pumpkin seeds to the pan and spread out into a single layer.

3. Roast for 25 to 30 minutes, until the seeds are lightly browned and crunchy. Shake or stir the seeds occasionally for even cooking. Check frequently during the last 5 minutes; do not allow the seeds to become scorched.

4. Transfer the seeds to a medium-sized bowl to cool completely. The seeds will become crisp as they cool. Store in an airtight jar for 1 week at room temperature or for up to 1 month in the refrigerator.

Makes 3 cups

Zesto Pasta Salad

Can you taste the zucchini in this dish? Probably not; the concentrated basil flavor of pesto camouflages the zucchini. However, the zucchini allows you to extend the pesto and creates a pleasing texture. It also keeps the salad moist. This pasta salad is as good on the second day as it is on the first.

2 cups grated zucchini

Salt

3 cups chopped broccoli

1 pound rotini, shells, twists, or other small pasta shape

1 tablespoon extra virgin olive oil

1 cup pesto (recipe follows)

¼ cup fresh lemon juice, or to taste

1 red bell pepper, diced, or 1 cup halved cherry tomatoes

Freshly ground black pepper

1. Begin heating a large pot of salted water for the pasta. Bring to a boil.

2. While the water heats, combine the zucchini and 1 teaspoon salt in a colander. Toss to mix and set aside to drain for 30 minutes.

3. Fill a medium-sized saucepan with 2 inches of water. Bring to a boil. Steam the broccoli over the boiling water until it is barely tender crisp, about 3 minutes. (Alternatively, place the broccoli in a bowl with about 1 inch of water, cover, and microwave until just tender, about 2 minutes.) Plunge the broccoli into cold water to stop the cooking; drain well.

4. Cook the pasta in the boiling water until al dente. Drain and rinse thoroughly to cool. Place in a large bowl and toss with the oil.

5. Squeeze the zucchini to eliminate excess moisture. Combine with the pesto in a medium bowl; mix well.

6. Add the pesto mixture to the pasta and toss to coat. Add the broccoli, pepper, and lemon juice and toss to mix. Taste and add salt, pepper, or more lemon juice, as needed.

7. Serve immediately, or cover and refrigerate for up to 1 day.

Serves 6–8

Pesto

Making pesto every summer is my favorite food preservation task. There's no boiling water to fuss with, no steaming hot stove to worry about. The food processor takes the labor out of making pesto. If you have a garden, or if you can buy basil in quantity from a farm stand, it's worth setting aside some time to make pesto in quantity for the freezer.

1½ cups fresh basil leaves, tightly packed
2 cloves of garlic
3 tablespoons pine nuts
¼ cup extra virgin olive oil
3 tablespoons freshly grated Parmesan cheese
Salt and freshly ground black pepper

1. Combine the basil, garlic, and pine nuts in a food processor fitted with a steel blade. Process until finely chopped. With the motor running, slowly pour in the oil and continue to process until a paste forms. Add the Parmesan and salt and pepper to taste; pulse to combine.

2. Let the pesto stand for at least 20 minutes before serving to allow the flavors to develop. Store in an airtight container in the refrigerator for up to 1 week or in the freezer for up to 4 months.

NOTE: To preserve the light green color of the pesto once you have transferred it to a storage container, cover the pesto with a film of olive oil to seal out the air.

Makes about ⅔ cup

Garden Macaroni Salad

Before pasta salads, there was macaroni salad, an all-American favorite made of elbow macaroni and diced crunchy vegetables and dressed with mayonnaise. This salad pays homage to that old-fashioned picnic standard, but with a twist. Zucchini replaces the expected celery, and the crisp vegetables — rather than the macaroni — play the starring role.

2 **cups diced small zucchini**

3 **cups cooked shell or elbow macaroni (from 6 ounces dried pasta)**

2 **cups shredded cabbage**

1 **cup grated carrots**

½ **cup diced green bell pepper**

½ **cup sliced red radishes**

3 **tablespoons minced onion**

1 **cup mayonnaise or sour cream**

2 **tablespoons fresh lemon juice**

1½ **teaspoons dry mustard**

1½ **teaspoons sugar**

Salt and freshly ground black pepper

Dill seed (optional)

1. Bring a small saucepan of salted water to a boil. Add the zucchini; blanch for 1 minute, until barely tender crisp. Drain, plunge into cold water to stop the cooking, and drain again. Pat dry.

2. In a large bowl, combine the macaroni, zucchini, cabbage, carrots, bell pepper, radishes, and onion.

3. In a small bowl, mix together the mayonnaise, lemon juice, mustard, and sugar. Season generously with salt, pepper, and dill seed, if using. Add the dressing to the salad and mix well.

4. Adjust the seasonings to taste. Serve immediately.

Serves 6

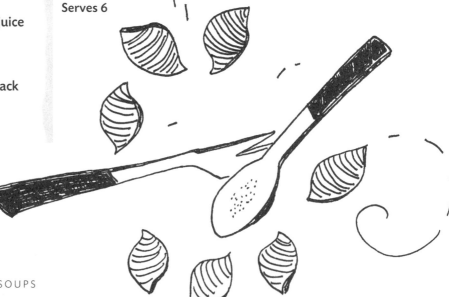

Lemon-Mint Couscous Salad with Grilled Zucchini

I recommend cooking the zucchini on a grill rack, which is a flat metal plate with holes in it that lets you grill small pieces of food without losing them in the fire. If you don't have a grill rack, slice the zucchini into long ¼-inch-thick steaks and chop after grilling. This hearty salad can be served as a vegetarian main course or side dish.

1½ cups instant couscous

½ teaspoon salt

2¼ cups boiling water

2 medium-sized zucchini, quartered and sliced

⅓ cup extra virgin olive oil

3 tablespoons fresh lemon juice

Salt and freshly ground black pepper

¾ cup crumbled feta cheese

½ cup black olives

¼ cup chopped fresh mint

1. Lightly oil a vegetable grill rack. Prepare a medium-hot fire in the grill with the rack in place.

2. Combine the couscous, salt, and boiling water in a large mixing bowl. Cover and let stand until the couscous is tender and the water is absorbed, about 10 minutes. Fluff with a fork.

3. Meanwhile, in a medium-sized bowl, combine the zucchini, oil, and lemon juice. Season to taste with salt and pepper and toss to coat.

4. Lift the zucchini out of the marinade with a slotted spoon and grill until tender, turning occasionally, 8 to 10 minutes.

5. Add the grilled zucchini to the couscous, along with the feta cheese, olives, and mint. Add salt and pepper to taste. Toss to combine.

6. Serve at room temperature.

Serves 4–6

Avocado Salad in Zucchini Boats

Be sure to use young, tender zucchini for this salad. Sometimes large zucchini are used as serving bowls, but here, the zucchini is meant to be eaten and enjoyed along with the luxurious avocado salad.

6 small zucchini, halved lengthwise

2 small ripe avocados, peeled and diced

1 small onion, minced

¼ cup extra virgin olive oil

1 tablespoon red wine vinegar

1 clove of garlic, minced

1½ teaspoons salt

¼ teaspoon freshly ground black pepper

6 cups torn mixed lettuces and greens

2 tomatoes, cut into wedges

1. Bring a large pot of salted water to a boil. Add the zucchini to the boiling water and blanch for about 3 minutes, until barely tender crisp. Drain. Plunge into cold water to stop the cooking; drain well.

2. Scoop the center pulp out of the zucchini, leaving about ¼ inch of flesh to support the skins. Drain the shells upside down on paper towels.

3. Dice the zucchini pulp. In a medium-sized bowl, combine the zucchini, avocado, and onion.

4. In a small bowl, combine the oil, vinegar, garlic, salt, and pepper. Mix well. Pour the dressing into the avocado mixture. Toss gently to mix. Taste and adjust the seasoning. Spoon into the zucchini shells. Cover and chill thoroughly, about 4 hours.

5. When you are ready to serve, arrange the lettuce on individual salad plates or one large serving platter. Arrange the zucchini boats on top. Garnish with the tomato wedges and serve immediately.

Serves 6

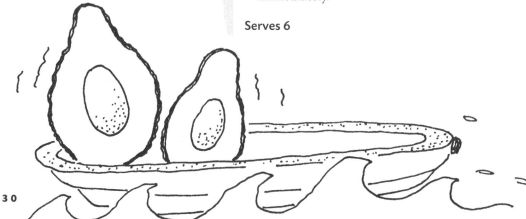

Zucchini Slaw

A colorful zucchini slaw can be a delicious change of pace
from the traditional all-cabbage salad. It makes a fine accompaniment
to burgers and barbecued meat.

2 medium-sized zucchini, julienned

2 carrots, julienned

2 celery ribs, diced

1 green bell pepper, diced

1 small head green or red cabbage, shredded

¼ cup fresh lemon juice

2 teaspoons Dijon mustard

⅔ cup extra virgin olive oil

Salt and freshly ground black pepper

1. In a large salad bowl, combine the zucchini, carrots, celery, bell pepper, and cabbage. Toss to mix.

2. In a small bowl, combine the lemon juice and mustard. Whisk in the oil until fully incorporated. Add salt and pepper to taste.

3. Pour the dressing over the vegetables and toss to mix. Taste and adjust the seasonings.

4. Let the salad sit for at least 30 minutes to allow the flavors to blend before serving.

NOTE: If you don't like raw zucchini, you can blanch it in boiling salted water for 30 seconds. Drain the zucchini, plunge it into cold water to stop the cooking, and drain again. Pat dry before combining it with the other vegetables.

Serves 4

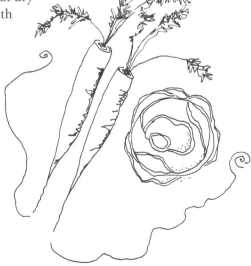

Creamy Mustard Zucchini Slaw

The sunflower seeds add the crunch the grated zucchini lacks.
This slaw is particularly good on sandwiches.

2 **medium-sized zucchini, grated**

2 **carrots, grated**

Salt

4 **tablespoons mayonnaise**

1 **tablespoon brine (liquid) from dill pickles**

1 **tablespoon mustard**

½ **cup toasted sunflower seeds**

Freshly ground black pepper

1. In a colander, combine the zucchini and carrots with 1 teaspoon salt. Mix well. Set aside to drain for about 30 minutes.

2. Squeeze out as much moisture as possible from the vegetables. Transfer to a medium-sized mixing bowl.

3. Combine the mayonnaise, brine, and mustard in a small bowl; blend well.

4. Add the mayonnaise mixture to the vegetables. Mix in the sunflower seeds. Taste and add plenty of pepper; it probably won't need additional salt.

5. Let stand for about 30 minutes before serving, or refrigerate for up to 4 hours and mix well before serving.

Serves 4

Toasted Sunflower Seeds

To toast sunflower seeds, which brings out their flavor, place them in a small skillet over medium heat. Toast, stirring frequently, for about 5 minutes, until the seeds begin to change color. Do not let the seeds scorch, or they will become bitter.

Zucchini Raita

Mouth-cooling raitas are meant to be served with spicy curries such as the
Thai-Style Coconut Curry with Chicken and Zucchini (see page 124).
This classic version can be made with zucchini or cucumbers.

3 cups grated zucchini

1 teaspoon salt

1 cup plain yogurt

1 tablespoon chopped fresh
cilantro

1 tablespoon chopped fresh
mint

1 tablespoon fresh lime juice

1. In a colander, combine the zucchini and salt. Set aside to drain for 30 minutes.

2. Squeeze any excess moisture from the zucchini. In a medium-sized bowl, combine the zucchini, yogurt, cilantro, mint, and lime juice. Mix well.

3. Taste and adjust the seasoning. Serve immediately or refrigerate for up to 8 hours and serve chilled. Stir well before serving.

Serves 4–6

Portrait of an Heirloom Squash

One of the most interesting heirloom squashes in current seed catalogs is the *tromboncino* (little trombone squash), which also goes by the Italian name of *zucchino rampicante* (climbing zucchini). This Italian squash should be planted so that it runs up a trellis or fence, making it a candidate for planting in a container on a patio. The tromboncino can be harvested young, when pale green, and enjoyed as a summer squash. Or it can be left to ripen on the vine and used in any Italian recipe calling for pumpkin, such as stuffed ravioli. If left longer on the vine, it becomes a gourd.

Cauliflower and Summer Squash à la Grecque

Vegetables cooked in a vinaigrette and served cold can wear the French title *à la Grecque*. In this preparation, golden zucchini, pattypans, or yellow squash will hold their color better in the acidic dressing than green zucchini. Serve as a first course, with crusty French bread for sopping up the delicious dressing, or as a refreshing side dish during hot weather, when cold dishes are most appealing.

1 cup fresh lemon juice

½ cup extra virgin olive oil

2 lemon slices

1 clove of garlic, crushed

1 tablespoon chopped fresh thyme, or 1 teaspoon dried

1 teaspoon salt

½ teaspoon freshly ground black pepper

¼ teaspoon crushed red pepper flakes

5–6 small yellow summer squash, pattypans, or golden zucchini, sliced

1 head cauliflower, broken into florets

1 green bell pepper, julienned

1. In a large nonreactive saucepan, combine the lemon juice, oil, lemon slices, garlic, thyme, salt, black pepper, and red pepper. Bring to a boil. Add the squash, cauliflower, and bell pepper. Reduce the heat and simmer until the vegetables are tender but not mushy, 20 to 30 minutes.

2. Let the vegetables cool to room temperature in the vinaigrette.

3. Serve at room temperature, or refrigerate and serve cold.

Serves 6

VARIATIONS: Other vegetables can be added to the mix, including green beans, carrots, pearl onions, mushrooms, artichoke hearts, and cherry tomatoes.

Dilled Zucchini

The scent of dill brings to mind pickles, and this zucchini dish can be served
as you would serve dill pickles: on an appetizer tray with olives and
other pickles or alongside sandwiches or burgers.

2 medium-sized or 4 small zucchini, halved lengthwise and cut into 3-inch spears

3 tablespoons extra virgin olive oil

2 tablespoons chopped fresh dill or 1 tablespoon dill seed

1. Bring a medium-sized saucepan of salted water to a boil. Add the zucchini and blanch for 1 to 2 minutes, until barely tender crisp. Drain well.

2. Transfer the zucchini to a serving dish and drizzle with the oil. Sprinkle with the dill.

3. Refrigerate for 1 to 4 hours. Serve cold.

Serves 6

Blanch Zucchini for Salads

Some people add raw zucchini to all kinds of salads, often as a cucumber substitute. I don't much care for raw zucchini — it is too bland, and squeaky against the teeth. I prefer to blanch the zucchini briefly, so that it stays tender crisp but its flavor and colors are enhanced. In most of the salad recipes, the zucchini is briefly boiled, plunged into a bath of cold water to arrest the cooking, and drained. After I drain the squash, I like to pat the pieces dry with paper towels or a clean kitchen towel so that they don't make the salad soggy. If the zucchini is grated, blanching is not necessary.

Born-Again Zucchini

"Zucchini can be, well, the word that comes up is 'insipid' or disappointing. Because it is mostly water. But if you salt it first and get the water out, the results are amazing. We call it 'born-again' zucchini."

Food writer and culinary instructor Molly Stevens has great enthusiasm for zucchini, now that she has incorporated this simple trick into her cooking repertoire. It is a trick that has been traveling through culinary circles lately. Stevens picked it up from a friend, then saw it confirmed in John Thorne's *Simple Cooking* newsletter.

Here's the trick, according to Stevens: Slice up 2 medium-sized zucchini into matchsticks or half-circles, depending on the recipe. Combine the zucchini with 1 tablespoon coarse salt in a bowl. Set it aside for 30 minutes, stirring it from time to time. Drain the zucchini and spread the slices out on a clean dish towel. Wrap them up in the cloth and wring it out as tightly as you can. The resulting zucchini is ready for quick cooking in a sauté pan. "It's amazing what it does for zucchini," says Stevens.

Stevens reflects more on zucchini, which she says has gotten a bad reputation since it has become a year-round staple in supermarkets. "But fresh from the garden, they are something special. That's the first thing. Then you have to salt it — it makes a huge difference when you are going to quick-cook zucchini by sautéing or stir-frying.

"I also like to make a zucchini gratinée, but there the trick is to bake it much longer than you'd think. I take a mix of zucchini and summer squash and layer it with seasonings and tomato. I bake for 1½ hours at 350°F. If you look at it at the halfway point, the baking dish is all bubbly and there's lots of juice. But then you continue to bake it for another 30 to 45 minutes and it almost dries out, and all the sugars in the vegetables caramelize. It's tremendous.

"Grilling is good. For one thing, squash is full of water, so it doesn't dry out on the grill. And the smoke adds flavor. That's good."

It is easy to coax more cooking tips from Stevens, who got her training as a chef in France and worked at La Varenne, the French cooking school founded by chef Anne Villan. When she returned to the United States, she worked as a chef instructor at the French Culinary Institute in New York, then at the New England Culinary Institute in Montpelier, Vermont. Lately she has focused on food writing as a contributing editor to *Fine Cooking* magazine, as the author of a book on New England cooking for Williams-Sonoma, and as the co-author, with Roy Finamore, of *One Potato, Two Potato,* a collection of 600 potato recipes.

As for winter squash, her most recent discovery is that butternut squash seeds are much better for eating than pumpkin seeds — they're more tender and flavorful. She prefers roasting winter squash for most recipes rather than steaming it. The roasting caramelizes the sugars, she explains, and brings out the flavor. She is also fond of combining winter squash, especially butternut, with mashed potatoes.

Stevens does a lot of traveling, keeping up a busy schedule of cooking classes at kitchenware stores throughout the United States. If she comes your way, you should try and take her class. You just might pick up a trick or two.

Zucchini Salad Bowl

Chopped salads were the rage in the 1950s, and this salad brings them to mind.
The original chopped salad — the Cobb salad — was created at the Brown Derby restaurant
in Los Angeles in 1926 by owner Bob Cobb as a way to use up leftovers in the kitchen.
No doubt if zucchini had been as popular then as it is now, the original
Cobb salad would have contained some.

2 cups peeled and diced potatoes

1 cup peas, fresh or frozen and defrosted

2 small zucchini, thinly sliced

1 cup diced carrots

½ cup diced red or sweet onion, such as Vidalia

¾ cup sour cream or mayonnaise

2 tablespoons distilled white vinegar

1 tablespoon diced sweet pickle

½ teaspoon salt

⅛ teaspoon freshly ground black pepper

Leaf lettuce, to serve (optional)

1. Bring a medium-sized saucepan of salted water to a boil. Add the potatoes to the boiling water and boil gently for 10 minutes, until the potatoes are tender. Drain, plunge into cold water to stop the cooking, and drain again.

2. Bring a second medium-sized saucepan of water to a boil. Add the fresh peas (do not add frozen peas) to the boiling water. Blanch for 1 minute. Add the zucchini and continue to blanch for 1 minute. Drain, plunge into cold water to stop the cooking, and drain again.

3. Combine the potatoes, zucchini, blanched fresh peas or defrosted frozen peas, carrots, and onion in a large bowl.

4. In a small bowl, combine the sour cream, vinegar, pickle, salt, and pepper. Pour the dressing over the vegetables; toss to mix.

5. Chill the salad for at least 1 hour or up to 8 hours.

6. Taste and adjust the seasonings. Serve chilled. If desired, arrange lettuce on a platter and spoon the vegetables on top.

Serves 4

Tomato-Zucchini Salad

Depending on which vegetable is overwhelming the storage capacity
of my refrigerator, I make this salad with either zucchini or cucumber.
It's terrific in a pita pocket along with a grilled burger.

2 medium-sized zucchini, quartered and sliced

4 large ripe tomatoes, seeded and diced

½ Vidalia or other sweet onion, diced

2 tablespoons chopped fresh dill or basil

3 tablespoons extra virgin olive oil

1 tablespoon red wine vinegar

Salt and freshly ground black pepper

1. Bring a medium-sized saucepan of salted water to a boil. Add the zucchini. Blanch for 1 to 2 minutes, until barely tender crisp. Drain well.

2. Combine the zucchini, tomatoes, onion, and dill in a salad bowl. Add the oil and vinegar; toss to coat. Season to taste with salt and pepper.

3. Allow the salad to stand for at least 30 minutes before serving, to develop the flavors.

Serves 4–6

Garnish with Flowers

Edible flowers make lovely garnishes for soups and salads. Squash blossoms are an obvious choice. Stack a few blossoms on a cutting board and slice into narrow ribbons. Scatter over the soup or salad.

Other edible flowers you may have in your garden:

- Johnny jump-ups
- nasturtiums
- violets
- any herb blossom, especially chive blossoms
- hollyhocks
- scented geraniums
- sweet woodruff

Mexican Zucchini Shrimp Salad

Here's a lovely, light south-of-the-border salad for lunch or dinner.

4 cups quartered and sliced zucchini or yellow summer squash

2 cups chopped cooked shrimp

¼ cup minced red bell pepper

¼ cup fresh lime juice

⅓ cup extra virgin olive oil

2 tablespoons minced fresh cilantro

2 tablespoons minced scallions, white and tender green parts

1 tablespoon minced fresh parsley

1 teaspoon Dijon mustard

Salt and freshly ground black pepper

1. Bring a medium-sized pot of salted water to a boil. Add the zucchini to the boiling water. Blanch for 1 to 2 minutes, until barely tender crisp. Drain, plunge into cold water to stop the cooking, drain again, and pat dry.

2. Combine the zucchini, shrimp, and bell pepper in a large salad bowl.

3. In a small bowl, whisk together the lime juice, oil, cilantro, scallions, parsley, and mustard. Add the dressing to the salad and toss to coat.

4. Season to taste with salt and pepper. Serve immediately or cover, chill in the refrigerator for up to 1 hour, and serve cold.

Serves 6–8

White Bean, Tuna, and Zucchini Salad

Cooked white beans and tuna canned in olive oil is a familiar Italian dish.
The addition of zucchini lightens the salad. For a wonderful hot-weather dinner,
serve with crusty French bread and chilled white wine.

3 cups quartered and sliced zucchini

3 cups canned cannellini beans, rinsed and drained

1 can (6–7 ounces) tuna packed in olive oil (preferably imported from Italy), drained

½ Vidalia or other sweet onion, thinly sliced

¼ cup chopped fresh parsley

3 tablespoons capers

5 tablespoons extra virgin olive oil

3 tablespoons red wine vinegar

1 clove of garlic, minced

Salt and freshly ground black pepper

Mixed greens, to serve

2 ripe tomatoes, cut into wedges

1. Bring a medium-sized pot of salted water to a boil. Add the zucchini to the boiling water. Blanch for 1 minute, until barely tender crisp. Drain, plunge into cold water to stop the cooking, drain again, and pat dry.

2. In a large bowl, combine the zucchini, beans, tuna, onion, parsley, and 2 tablespoons of the capers. Toss gently to mix.

3. Whisk together the oil, vinegar, and garlic in a small bowl. Pour over the bean mixture and toss to coat. Season very generously with salt and pepper.

4. Arrange a bed of greens on a large serving platter or individual serving plates. Mound the bean salad on top. Arrange the tomatoes around the beans. Garnish with the remaining 1 tablespoon of capers and serve.

Serves 4

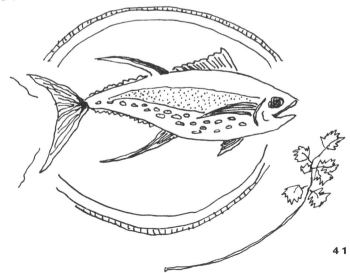

Salade Niçoise

One of the all-time great salads for satisfying summer dining. Canned or grilled fresh tuna works well in this recipe, but the traditional favorite is canned Italian-style tuna packed in olive oil; look for it in specialty food stores or some large supermarkets. The vegetables can be prepared in advance and left to marinate for a day or so before you assemble the salad.

¼ cup red wine vinegar

¼ teaspoon salt

⅛ teaspoon freshly ground black pepper

¾ cup extra virgin olive oil

4 medium-sized potatoes

½ pound green beans, cut into 2-inch lengths

4 cups thinly sliced zucchini

2 onions, thinly sliced

4 cups torn assorted lettuces or greens

1 can (6–7 ounces) tuna, drained if packed in water

2 tomatoes, cut into wedges

2 hard-cooked eggs, cut into wedges

1. In a small mixing bowl, combine the vinegar, salt, and pepper. Whisk in the olive oil until it is completely mixed in. Set aside.

2. Bring a medium-sized saucepan of salted water to a boil. Peel the potatoes, if desired, and cut into bite-size pieces. Add to the water and boil until tender but still firm, about 15 minutes. Drain well. Transfer to a medium-sized bowl and pour about one-quarter of the dressing over the still-warm potatoes. Cover and refrigerate.

3. Bring another medium-sized saucepan of salted water to a boil. Add the beans to the boiling water and blanch for 3 minutes. Add the zucchini and blanch for 1 minute longer, until the vegetables are barely tender crisp. Drain, plunge into cold water to stop the cooking, drain again, and pat dry. Combine the beans, zucchini, and onions in a bowl with the rest of the dressing. Toss to coat, cover, and refrigerate.

4. To assemble the salad, line a salad bowl or serving platter with the lettuce. Center the tuna over the lettuce. Arrange the potato pieces around the tuna. Remove the vegetables from the dressing with a slotted spoon and surround the tuna with mounds of the marinated vegetables. Drizzle the remaining dressing over the salad. Top with the tomatoes and eggs. Serve at once.

Serves 4

Mexican Rice, Zucchini, and Chicken Salad

When you tire of pasta salad, turn to rice salads to perk up faded summer appetites.

3 cups diced zucchini or yellow summer squash

1½ cups cooked white or brown rice

1½ cups diced or shredded cooked chicken

½ cup chopped scallions, white and tender green parts

2 tablespoons minced fresh parsley

⅓ cup canola or other light vegetable oil

3 tablespoons extra virgin olive oil

¼ cup fresh lemon juice

½ teaspoon chili powder

½ teaspoon salt

Freshly ground black pepper

½ cup crumbled queso blanco or farmer cheese

1. Bring a medium-sized pot of salted water to a boil. Add the zucchini to the boiling water. Blanch for 1 minute, until barely tender crisp. Drain, plunge into cold water to stop the cooking, drain again, and pat dry.

2. In a large bowl, combine the zucchini, rice, chicken, scallions, and parsley.

3. In a small bowl, whisk together the oils, lemon juice, chili powder, salt, and pepper to taste. Pour over the salad and toss to coat. Taste and adjust the seasoning.

4. Transfer the salad to a serving bowl, sprinkle with the cheese, and serve.

Serves 4

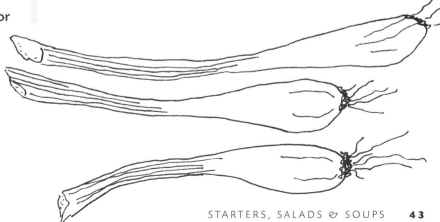

Chilled Zucchini-Mint Soup

The bright green color is part of what makes this soup so appealing and refreshing.
It must be eaten the day it is prepared, or the color will be lost.

1 tablespoon butter

1 cup diced onion

4 cups sliced zucchini

1 cup chicken broth, vegetable broth (see box below), or water

⅓ cup chopped fresh mint leaves, plus sprigs of mint to garnish

½ teaspoon salt

2½ cups buttermilk

1. In a medium-sized saucepan, melt the butter over medium-high heat. Add the onion and sauté until softened, 3 to 5 minutes.

2. Add the zucchini and broth. Cover and simmer for 10 to 15 minutes, until the zucchini is soft.

3. Remove from the heat and cool slightly. Process the soup in a blender or food processor until smooth. Add the chopped mint and salt; process just to mix.

4. Pour the soup into a large bowl; stir in the buttermilk. Chill the soup, covered, in the refrigerator for several hours.

5. Serve chilled, garnished with sprigs of mint.

Serves 6–8

Broth Recommendations

Broth is the foundation of a good soup, and home-made soup stock provides the best results. But much of the time, it is easier just to reach for canned or boxed stock. Several brands of very good chicken broth are available. Unfortunately, most vegetable broths have a very strong flavor. Taste before you use; if a recipe calls for a vegetable broth, reject those with strong carrot, tomato, or onion flavor. Vegetable broths that are labeled "un-chicken" or vegetarian are usually neutral-tasting and will work well in most soups.

Cold Curried Summer Squash Soup

Summer soups should be quick to make and light — like this one.
When the weather turns cold, you can also serve this soup hot.

6 small yellow summer squash, sliced

3 cups chicken or vegetable broth (see box, page 44)

1 large onion, thinly sliced

3 tablespoons rice

1 teaspoon curry powder

½ teaspoon dry mustard

1½ cups milk

Salt and freshly ground black pepper

Chopped fresh chives or cilantro, to garnish (optional)

1. In a large saucepan, combine the squash, broth, onion, rice, curry powder, and mustard. Bring to a boil. Reduce the heat and simmer, covered, for 40 minutes.

2. Transfer the soup to a blender or food processor and purée.

3. Return the soup to the pot and stir in the milk. Add salt and pepper to taste.

4. Chill for at least 2 hours before serving, garnished with chives, if using. You can also reheat the soup and serve hot; do not allow the soup to boil once the milk has been added, or it might curdle.

Serves 6

Summer Squash Math

- 1 pound summer squash yields about 4 cups sliced, diced, or julienned squash.
- 1 pound summer squash yields about 3½ cups grated squash

Creamy Yellow Summer Squash Soup

Made with a good homemade chicken broth, this soup is
outstanding — elegantly simple.

2 tablespoons butter

4 leeks, sliced

2 cups sliced yellow summer squash

4 cups homemade or canned chicken broth

1 cup milk or light cream

Salt and freshly ground black pepper

1. Melt the butter in a large saucepan over medium heat. Add the leeks and sauté until softened and translucent, about 5 minutes. Add the squash and sauté until softened, about 5 minutes. Stir in 1 cup of the broth.

2. Transfer the squash mixture to a blender or food processor and purée until smooth.

3. Return the mixture to the saucepan. Add the remaining 3 cups broth, the milk, and salt and pepper to taste.

4. Serve hot or cold.

Serves 4

Creamy Squash Blossom Soup

Before there are squash, there are blossoms. For the cook who can't wait,
here's a soup to start the harvest season.

3 tablespoons butter

1 small onion, diced

1 clove of garlic, minced

36 squash or pumpkin blossoms, chopped

3 cups chicken broth

1 cup half-and-half

Salt and freshly ground black pepper

1. Melt the butter in a large saucepan over medium heat. Add the onion and garlic and sauté until soft, 4 to 5 minutes. Add the blossoms and stir until softened, 1 to 2 minutes. Add the broth and bring to a boil. Reduce the heat; simmer for 10 minutes.

2. In batches, purée the soup in a blender or food processor until smooth.

3. Return the soup to the saucepan and stir in the half-and-half. Season to taste with salt and pepper. Reheat over low heat.

4. Serve hot.

Serves 4

Summer Squash and Blossom Soup

In this simplest of soups, everything depends on using a good stock,
preferably one that'shomemade.

2 **tablespoons butter**

2 **shallots, minced**

5 **cups chopped yellow summer squash**

6 **cups chicken broth, or more as needed**

Salt and freshly ground pepper

4–6 **squash blossoms, cut into ribbons**

1. Melt the butter over medium heat in a large saucepan. Add the shallots and sauté until tender and translucent, about 5 minutes. Add the squash and sauté until tender, about 5 minutes. Add the broth and bring to a boil. Reduce the heat and simmer until the squash is tender, about 10 minutes.

2. Let the soup cool slightly. In batches, purée the soup in a blender or food processor until smooth.

3. Return the soup to the pot. Add more broth if the soup is too thick. Season to taste with salt and pepper. Reheat gently.

4. Serve the soup hot, garnished with the blossom strips.

Serves 4

Tomato-Zucchini Soup

A light and easy soup made from garden vegetables, this can be served for lunch with bread or crackers or as a first course. You can make it even easier by using a food processor to mince the aromatic vegetables and to grate the zucchini. The tomatoes can be fresh or canned.

3 tablespoons extra virgin olive oil

1 onion, minced

1 small fennel bulb or 2 celery ribs, minced

1 carrot, minced

2 cloves of garlic, minced

1 ounce ham, minced (optional)

4 cups chicken broth or vegetable broth (see box, page 44)

2 cups diced and seeded tomatoes

2 cups grated zucchini

Salt and freshly ground black pepper

1. Heat the oil in a soup pot over medium heat. Add the onion, fennel, carrot, garlic, and ham, if using. Sauté until the vegetables are soft and fragrant, about 5 minutes.

2. Add the broth and tomatoes. Bring to a boil, then reduce the heat, and simmer for 30 minutes.

3. Add the zucchini and salt and pepper to taste. Simmer until the zucchini is cooked through, about 15 minutes.

4. Serve hot.

Serves 4

Grated Zucchini Improves Almost Any Soup

Consider adding grated zucchini to almost any soup. It is particularly good in tomato and vegetable soups, such as minestrone. Grate the zucchini by using a box grater and add to the soup during the last 15 minutes of cooking. You can also use thawed and drained frozen squash.

Cheddar Cheese Soup with Zucchini

When there's a chill in the air, a hearty soup like this one has strong appeal.
The grated zucchini provides a toothsome contrast to the smooth creamy soup.
Serve the soup as a main course, accompanied by a green salad
and a loaf of whole-wheat or hearty rye bread.

6 tablespoons butter

1 onion, diced

3 celery ribs, diced

1 carrot, diced

¼ cup all-purpose unbleached flour

5 cups chicken or vegetable broth (see box, page 44)

2 cups grated zucchini

12 ounces Cheddar cheese, grated

1 cup half-and-half or light cream

¼ cup dry sherry

Salt and freshly ground black pepper

1. Melt the butter in a large heavy saucepan over medium heat. Add the onion, celery, and carrot; sauté until softened but not browned, about 5 minutes.

2. Sprinkle the flour over the vegetables and stir until the mixture is coated with the flour. Slowly stir in the broth. Bring the soup to a boil, then reduce the heat to a simmer and cook for 20 minutes.

3. In two batches, purée the soup in a blender until smooth.

4. Return the soup to the pot. Bring to a simmer and stir in the zucchini. Bring to a boil. Reduce the heat and simmer for 10 minutes, until the zucchini is tender.

5. Whisk in the cheese and half-and-half. Over low heat, stir until the cheese is melted, about 5 minutes. (Do not let the soup boil once the cheese has been added.)

6. Stir in the sherry. Season to taste with salt and pepper.

7. Serve hot.

Serves 6

Mushroom-Barley Soup with Zucchini

Mushroom-barley is a comfort soup that's just right for cold winter days.
It's a great way to use the frozen grated zucchini or summer squash stashed away
in your freezer, and it brings a touch of summer to the cold-weather soup.
Serve with whole-wheat bread.

1 cup (1 ounce) dried sliced porcini mushrooms

2 cups boiling water

2 onions, quartered

2 carrots, chopped

2 cloves of garlic

1½ pounds white mushrooms

2 tablespoons olive or canola oil

8 cups chicken or mushroom broth, or water

⅔ cup uncooked pearled barley

1 teaspoon dried thyme

2 cups grated zucchini or summer squash (drained if frozen)

Salt and freshly ground black pepper

1. Combine the dried porcini and boiling water in a medium-sized bowl. Set aside to soak.

2. In a food processor, combine the onions, carrots, and garlic. Pulse until finely chopped. Add ½ pound of the mushrooms and pulse until finely chopped. Slice the remaining 1 pound of mushrooms and set aside.

3. Heat the oil in a large saucepan over medium heat. Add the chopped vegetables and sauté until the vegetables are well browned and the liquid has mostly evaporated, about 15 minutes. Add the broth, barley, thyme, and sliced mushrooms. Add the porcini and their soaking liquid, avoiding any grit that has settled to the bottom of the bowl.

4. Bring the soup to a boil. Reduce the heat and simmer until the barley is tender, 40 to 60 minutes.

5. Add the zucchini and salt and pepper to taste. Simmer the soup for 5 minutes, until the zucchini is tender.

6. Serve hot.

Serves 4–6

The Oakville, Washington, Zucchini Jubilee

THE PEOPLE OF OAKVILLE were worried. Summer had been cold, and the zucchini weren't growing. How can you have a zucchini festival without zucchini? This was in the summer of 2001, the fifth year of Oakville's zucchini festival.

Oakville is a small town (population 700) in a depressed timber-logging region. But it is a town with can-do spirit. In the hopes of scaring up a little tourist interest, the chamber of commerce looked for something to celebrate. No matter the state of the economy, there is always zucchini in the garden, so why not honor that underappreciated vegetable?

Needless to say, even in the cold summer of 2001 there were plenty of zucchini. According to Janice Howell, the head of the chamber of commerce and the festival chairman, it takes about 250 to 500 pounds of donated zucchini to run a zucchini festival, which attracts about 100 people each year.

The festival includes the ever-popular Zukie Boutique, where kids get a chance to dress up a zucchini with lace, fabric, and buttons. Then there is the Zuke-Rod Run, a zucchini race. For this event, people construct cars out of zucchini, using wheels and axles provided by the festival. The cars are released down a ramp, and the fastest zuke wins. And artistic types are drawn to the zucchini-carving contest, where pumpkin-carving tools are used to create zucchini monsters.

Still, nothing attracts more excited interest than the yearly zucchini bake-off. Nursery owner Beth Fern is a frequent winner. Her first win came in 1997, the first year of the festival.

For that contest, she found an old recipe in an agricultural Extension Service publication. If you take zucchini or yellow summer squash, peel it; discard the seeds; dice it; then cook it with sugar and cherry-flavored Kool-Aid, you end up with something very similar to cherry pie filling. "I slapped it in a piecrust, called it Nearly Cherry Pie, and it took first place," said Fern.

But what about the zucchini candies I had heard about? The ones that are like Gummi Bears? Fern explained, "Well, the next step is to put the Kool-Aid–flavored zucchini in a food dehydrator for 12 to 14 hours and dry it. Then you have candied fruit. Not really Gummi Bears. More like the candied fruit you use in fruitcakes. I've used dark cherry, tropical punch, orange, grape — really you can use any flavor. I don't even buy candied fruit anymore. And you can do it with any squash or cucumber, not just zucchini." In 2001, Beth Fern took first place with her Pineapple Zucchini Bread.

The one recipe that hasn't been shared but is always talked about is the Z Hot Dog, which is a hot dog heaped with breaded and fried zucchini slices. This festival food hasn't hit the mainstream yet, but could well be the next craze. Move over, designer pizza.

New England Harvest Bisque

It is a fall tradition in many apple-growing regions to pick apples — in your own backyard, if you are lucky, or at a pick-your-own orchard. Vermont even boasts a pick-your-own squash farm. And many CSA (community-supported agriculture) farms offer their members the chance to go out into the fields and harvest their own shares. This is a great soup to make on a fall evening after such a day in the field or orchard. Cooking the squash in apple cider gives the soup a strong apple presence that is balanced by the earthy flavors of leek and garlic.

4 tablespoons butter

3 pounds butternut squash, peeled, seeded, and cut into cubes

1 leek, white part only, sliced

4 cloves of garlic, peeled

2 cups apple cider

2 teaspoons minced fresh ginger

3 cups chicken or vegetable broth (see box, page 44) or water

Salt and freshly ground black pepper

Sour cream or crème fraîche (optional)

Freshly grated nutmeg

1. Melt the butter in a large Dutch oven over medium heat. Add the squash, leek, and garlic. Sauté until the leek is softened and fragrant, about 5 minutes.

2. Add the cider and ginger. Bring to a boil. Cover, reduce the heat, and simmer until the squash is tender, about 1 hour.

3. Divide the vegetables into three batches. Add 1 cup of the broth to each batch and purée in a blender or food processor. Combine the batches in a saucepan. Bring the soup to a simmer. Season to taste with salt and pepper.

4. Serve hot, topping each bowl of soup with a dollop of sour cream, if using, and a sprinkle of freshly grated nutmeg.

NOTE: Chicken broth greatly enhances the flavor of this soup, contributing a richness that makes the sour cream superfluous. Vegetable broth does the same, but it is hard to find a neutral-tasting one. If you use water alone to make the soup, which is just fine, do add the sour cream to give the soup a richer, more satisfying mouth feel.

Serves 4–6

Winter squash and Apple soup

The combination of winter squash and apples is a popular one.
Apple plays more of a background role in this version.

1 medium-sized buttercup, butternut, or red kuri, or 1 small Baby Blue Hubbard squash

4 tart green apples, peeled, cored, and chopped

4 cups chicken or vegetable broth (see box, page 44)

1 cup fresh bread crumbs

1 onion, chopped

1 teaspoon dried rosemary

½ teaspoon dried marjoram

Salt and freshly ground black pepper

Fresh parsley, minced, to garnish

1. Cut the squash into several pieces. Remove the seeds and fibers and discard. Boil the squash in water to cover until completely tender, about 1 hour. Drain and peel, or scrape away the flesh from the skins. Discard the skins.

2. Combine the squash, apples, broth, bread crumbs, onion, rosemary, and marjoram in a large saucepan. Bring to a boil, then reduce the heat and simmer until the squash is tender, about 20 minutes.

3. In batches, purée the soup in a blender or food processor until smooth.

4. Season the soup with salt and pepper to taste. Cover and refrigerate. (The soup can be frozen at this stage. Thaw overnight in the refrigerator.)

5. Reheat over medium heat, stirring frequently. Serve hot, garnished with parsley.

Serves 12

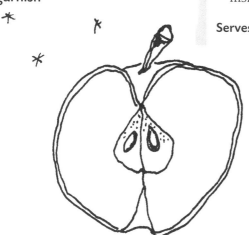

Coconut Curried Winter Squash Soup

The powerful fragrance of curry is a wonderful foil to the sweet flavors
of winter squash. Coconut milk counteracts the heat of the spices
while adding an exotic touch.

1 medium-sized buttercup, butternut, red kuri, or small Baby Blue Hubbard squash (3–4 pounds), halved and seeded

2 tablespoons peanut or canola oil

4 cloves of garlic, minced

1 jalapeño chile, seeded and finely minced

1 tablespoon curry powder

1 tablespoon finely minced fresh ginger

1½ cups chicken or vegetable broth (see box, page 44)

1½ cups coconut milk

Juice of 1 lime (about 2 tablespoons), or more as needed

Salt and freshly ground black pepper

¼ cup chopped fresh cilantro

1. Preheat the oven to 400°F.

2. Place the squash skin-side up in a baking dish. Add 1 inch of water to the baking pan.

3. Bake for about 1 hour, until the squash is completely tender when pierced with a fork. Let cool slightly.

4. While the squash cools, heat the oil in a small skillet over medium-low heat. Add the garlic, jalapeño, curry, and ginger. Simmer until the spices are fragrant and the garlic just begins to color, about 5 minutes more. Do not let the spices scorch or they will become bitter. Remove from the heat.

5. Scoop the flesh from the squash skin. Combine half of the squash in a blender or food processor with half the spices and half the broth. Purée until smooth. Transfer to a saucepan. Repeat with the remaining squash, broth, and spices.

6. Add the coconut milk and lime juice to the soup. Taste and adjust the seasoning, adding salt, pepper, and lime juice as needed.

7. Reheat over medium heat until hot, stirring frequently. Just before serving, stir in the cilantro. Serve hot.

Serves 6

Cream of Winter Squash Soup

A wonderful way to use up leftovers! Basically, you are diluting the winter squash with broth and smoothing out the texture with cream. You can use whatever winter squash you have on hand, seasoned or plain.

2 tablespoons butter

1 cup minced onion

2½ cups chicken or vegetable broth (see box, page 44)

1 cup cooked and mashed winter squash or pumpkin

1 teaspoon ground cinnamon

¼ teaspoon ground nutmeg

Salt and freshly ground black pepper

¾ cup light cream, half-and-half, or milk

Toasted croutons (optional)

1. Melt the butter in a large saucepan over medium heat. Add the onion and sauté until softened, about 5 minutes. Add 1 cup of the broth and simmer for 10 minutes.

2. Combine the broth mixture and squash in a blender or food processor and purée until smooth.

3. Return the soup to the pot and stir in the remaining 1½ cups broth, cinnamon, nutmeg, and salt and pepper to taste. Bring to a boil. Reduce the heat and stir until smooth. Cover and simmer for 10 minutes.

4. Add the cream. Heat gently, but do not allow the soup to boil again.

5. Serve hot, garnished with croutons, if using.

Serves 4

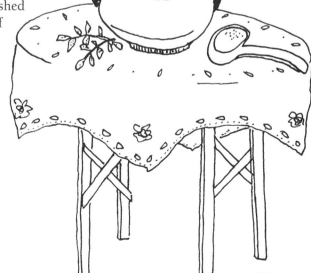

Pumpkin & Squash Seed Treats

Native Americans who met the Spanish invaders on the Rio Grande included pumpkin seeds among their gifts of peace. The conquistadors willingly incorporated pumpkin seeds into their cooking repertoire. A dish of chicken cooked in a sauce of blanched almonds, pumpkin seeds, cumin seeds, popped corn, chiles, and garlic is a legacy of that time.

To prepare seeds for snacking or garnishing, wash pumpkin or squash seeds and discard any fibers. Fill a medium saucepan with salted water and bring to a boil. Add the seeds, reduce the heat, and simmer gently for 1½ to 2 hours. Drain in a colander.

Spread out the seeds on a baking sheet. Using a pastry brush, coat the seeds with safflower or peanut oil. Salt generously. Preheat the oven to 250°F; bake seeds until they are browned and crunchy, about 45 minutes.

Crack open the shells and enjoy the seed kernels within.

If you are watching your fat intake, use this method to prepare seeds: Wash pumpkin or squash seeds and discard any fibers. Soak the seeds overnight in a mixture of 2 teaspoons salt per 1 cup water; be certain that the mixture covers the seeds.

Drain the seeds in a colander. Spread them out on paper towels to dry. Preheat the oven to 300°F.

Transfer the seeds to a baking sheet and spread out in a single layer. Bake for 30 to 45 minutes; do not allow the seeds to brown.

Crack open the shells and enjoy the seed kernels within.

Winter Squash and Shrimp Bisque

Shrimp and winter squash might seem like an unlikely combination, but it turns out to be a natural. The winter squash enhances the sweetness of the shrimp.

5 cups peeled and cubed butternut squash

½ cup (1 stick) butter

1 cup diced onion

½ cup unbleached all-purpose flour

5 cups chicken broth

1 cup dry white wine

1 cup half-and-half

Salt and freshly ground black pepper

1 pound shrimp, peeled and deveined

1. Steam the squash over boiling water until completely tender, about 15 minutes.

2. Melt the butter in a large saucepan over medium heat. Add the onion and sauté until softened, about 5 minutes. Stir in the flour until a thick paste forms. Gradually add the broth and bring to a boil, stirring constantly.

3. Add the squash and wine. Simmer the soup for 10 minutes.

4. In batches, transfer the soup to a food processor or blender. Process until smooth.

5. Return the soup to the pot and stir in the half-and-half. Season to taste with salt and pepper.

6. Add the shrimp and heat just until the shrimp are cooked through, 3 to 5 minutes.

7. Serve hot.

Serves 6

Serving Soup in Pumpkin Bowls

Serving soup in individual pumpkin bowls is fun for special occasions, and it doesn't involve a lot of extra work. Use mini pumpkins that are sold as table decorations. Carefully slice the tops off the pumpkins, reserving the tops for lids. Hollow out the pumpkins, wash them with warm water, and then let them thoroughly air-dry before using them. The extra preparation pays off in the end when you compost the bowls instead of washing and putting them away, as you would soup bowls.

Lock Your Doors!

IN LIGHT OF THE MYTH that New Englanders must lock their car doors every August to prevent stealth gardeners from filling unattended vehicles with zucchini, it was inevitable that someone would think to organize a zucchini festival. And that's just what the folks in Ludlow, Vermont, did.

According to legend of dubious origin, the Vermont State Zucchini Festival has its roots in the 1996 discovery of the ruins of the former Duchy of Zee, just south of Ludlow. The discovery resulted in the reconstruction of the "crown jewels" by a local artisan, Dusty Baron. Officials secured the approval of the Duchy's representatives to hold an annual festival and elect a Duchess of Zucchini to reign over each year's events, which usually take place on the third weekend of August.

Actually, this zucchini festival is less about zucchini and more about a small-town summer festival. For weeks in advance, area merchants give away "Z Bucks" with every purchase, which are then used as tender at an auction held at the festival. The festival hosts some zucchini-related events, such as competition for the largest zucchini; a "Green Baron" Model Airplane Race with models constructed from zucchini; zucchini carving; and a zucchini cook-off, with area restaurants competing on a single theme. In 2001 that theme was pizza. There is also classic country entertainment, including music, rides for the kids, crafts, horse racing, and the ever-popular cow chips roulette (a fenced area is divided into 1-foot squares; observers bid on the various squares, hoping to hit the jackpot when the cow deposits her "chip").

The highlight of the weekend, of course, is the crowning of the Duchess of Zucchini, who gets to wear the crown jewels and carry the jeweled zucchini scepter. In 2001, the duchess was duly announced, but she failed to make an appearance. That was the bad news. The good news was that no one put any zucchini in the unlocked cars.

Navy Bean and Squash Soup

Make this soup summer or winter, with yellow summer squash or winter squash. It is a rather versatile soup.

1 **pound dried navy beans, soaked overnight in water to cover**

8 **cups water, or more as needed**

1 **ham bone, with some meat**

1 **cup chopped celery**

1 **cup chopped carrots**

1 **cup chopped onion**

  Salt and freshly ground black pepper

6 **cups cooked winter squash (cubed or puréed) or uncooked cubed zucchini or yellow summer squash**

1. Drain the beans. Transfer to a large soup pot. Add the 8 cups of water. Add the ham bone, celery, carrots, onion, and salt and pepper to taste. Bring the mixture to a boil. Cover, reduce the heat, and simmer for 1 hour, or until the beans are completely tender.

2. Remove the ham bone and set aside. Transfer at least half of the soup to a blender or food processor and purée. Return the soup to the pot and add the squash. Cut the meat from the ham bone, dice, and add to the soup. Add water, if necessary, to give the soup a good consistency.

3. Simmer the soup, covered, for about 20 minutes.

4. Taste and adjust the seasonings. Serve hot.

Serves 8

Soup in a Pumpkin

When choosing a pumpkin for this soup, look for a well-shaped one
that will stand up level on the table. You will bake and serve the soup
in the pumpkin — a lovely touch that requires very little work.

1 **well-shaped 5-pound pie pumpkin**

1 **cup grated Gruyère or mozzarella cheese**

1 **cup chopped baked ham**

2 **cups toasted croutons**

2 **cups light cream, or more as needed**

Pinch nutmeg

Salt and freshly ground black pepper

1. Preheat the oven to 325°F. Remove the top from the pumpkin and reserve. Scoop out the seeds and fibers.

2. Fill the pumpkin with layers of cheese, ham, and croutons.

3. In a small mixing bowl, combine the cream, nutmeg, and salt and pepper to taste. Pour into the pumpkin, adding more cream if necessary to fill the shell. Cover with aluminum foil and place the pumpkin on a large baking pan.

4. Bake for 1½ to 2 hours, stirring several times, until the pumpkin is tender inside.

5. Remove the aluminum foil. Place the pumpkin on a large serving dish. Cover with the reserved pumpkin top. Serve the soup directly from the pumpkin.

Serves 4

3. Vegetarian Main Dishes

With vegetables at their peak throughout the summer, it is natural to eat all-vegetable dinners, and even meat-eaters enjoy more vegetarian meals. Pasta and pizza with vegetables are particular favorites. For the most part, these dishes can be made quickly and won't keep you away from the beautiful weather outdoors. When winter whets the appetite for warming foods, the winter squash recipes fit the bill and satisfy vegetarians and meat-eaters alike.

Fettuccine with Zucchini

I love the way the title of this recipe trips off my tongue but, in fact, both yellow summer squash and zucchini should be used to add to the visual appeal of this simple and delightful celebration of squash. For an uncomplicated dish like this one, it is best to use fresh pasta and real Parmigiano-Reggiano from Italy.

3 tablespoons extra virgin olive oil

3 tablespoons butter

4 medium-sized zucchini and yellow summer squash, quartered and thinly sliced

4 cloves of garlic, minced

2 ripe tomatoes, seeded and diced, or 1 cup halved cherry tomatoes

¼ cup chopped fresh basil or parsley

1 cup vegetable or chicken broth or ½ cup water and ½ cup white wine

Salt and freshly ground black pepper

1¼ pounds fresh spinach fettuccine, or half spinach fettuccine and half egg fettuccine, or 1 pound dried fettuccine

1 cup freshly grated Parmigiano-Reggiano, plus additional to serve

1. Begin heating a large pot of salted water for the pasta.

2. In a large skillet, heat the oil and butter over medium-high heat. Add the zucchini and garlic, cover, and "sweat" until tender crisp, 3 to 5 minutes. Stir in the tomatoes, basil, and broth. Season to taste with salt and pepper. Keep warm.

3. Cook the pasta in the boiling water until al dente. Drain briefly.

4. Transfer the pasta to a serving bowl. Add the squash mixture; toss to coat. Add the cheese and toss again. Taste and season generously with salt and pepper. Serve hot, with additional cheese at the table.

Serves 4–6

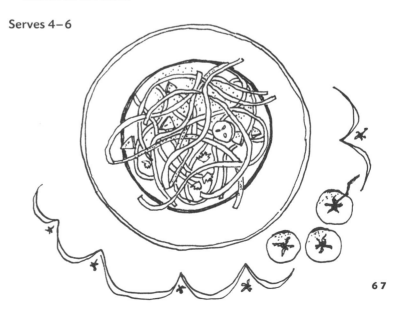

Fettuccine Alfredo with Summer Vegetables

Luxurious and rich are the only ways to describe fettuccine Alfredo.
You can justify this indulgence by adding heaps of vegetables.

2 small zucchini, julienned

2 small yellow summer squash, julienned

Salt

3–4 tablespoons extra virgin olive oil

1 leek, sliced

1 carrot, julienned

1 red bell pepper, julienned

1¼ pounds fresh fettuccine, or 1 pound dried

1 clove of garlic, minced

1½ cups half-and-half

Freshly ground black pepper

1 tablespoon butter

1 cup freshly grated Parmigiano-Reggiano cheese

5 fresh basil leaves, cut into ribbons, to garnish

1. If you have the time (see page 147), combine the zucchini, summer squash, and 2 teaspoons salt in a colander. Toss to mix and set aside for 30 minutes to drain. Transfer the squash to a clean dish towel and wring dry.

2. Begin heating a large pot of salted water for the pasta.

3. Heat 3 tablespoons of the oil in a large skillet over medium-high heat. Add the leek, carrot, and bell pepper; sauté until just barely tender crisp, 3 to 5 minutes. Transfer to a medium-sized saucepan with a slotted spoon.

4. If necessary, add the remaining 1 tablespoon oil to the skillet and heat over medium-high heat. Add the zucchini and summer squash and sauté until just barely tender crisp, 3 to 5 minutes. Transfer to the saucepan with a slotted spoon.

5. Warm the saucepan over low heat. Add the garlic and half-and-half. Season to taste with salt and pepper. Keep warm.

6. Cook the pasta in the boiling water until just al dente. Drain briefly.

7. Transfer the pasta to a large serving bowl and toss with the butter and cheese. Pour the vegetable sauce over the pasta and toss again. Taste and adjust the seasoning, adding more salt and pepper as needed. Garnish with the basil and serve at once.

Serves 6

Pesto Linguine with Summer Squash

Yellow summer squash or golden zucchini is the squash of choice here,
to allow the yellow color to play against the green of the pesto. For even
more color, use a mixture of spinach and regular linguine.

4 medium-sized yellow summer squash, quartered and thinly sliced

Salt

3 tablespoons extra virgin olive oil

1¼ pound fresh linguine, or 1 pound dried

⅔ cup pesto (page 27)

Freshly ground black pepper

Toasted pine nuts, to garnish

1. If you have the time (see page 147), combine the squash and 2 teaspoons salt in a colander. Toss to mix and set aside to drain for 30 minutes. Transfer the squash to a clean dish towel and wring dry.

2. Begin heating a large pot of salted water for the pasta.

3. Heat the oil in a large skillet over medium-high heat. Add the squash and sauté until tender crisp, 3 to 5 minutes. Keep warm.

4. Cook the pasta in the boiling water until just al dente. Reserve ½ cup of the pasta cooking water. Drain briefly.

5. Return the pasta to the pot. Add the pesto and reserved cooking water. Toss to coat. Add the squash and pepper to taste; toss to mix.

6. Transfer the pasta to individual serving bowls or a large serving bowl. Garnish with pine nuts, if using, and serve.

Serves 4–6

Toasting Pine Nuts

Toasting nuts intensifies their flavor and makes them crunchier. To toast pine nuts, pour a handful into a small skillet over medium heat. Toast, stirring frequently, until the nuts are fragrant and very lightly browned, about 5 minutes. Watch carefully and do not let the nuts scorch.

Baked Penne with Summer Squash and Mushrooms

A simple, kid-pleasing way to sneak vegetables into a favorite pasta meal. This dish is especially easy to make because the recipe calls for bottled pasta sauce.

3 tablespoons extra virgin olive oil

6 ounces mushrooms, sliced

Salt and freshly ground black pepper

1 medium-sized zucchini, quartered and sliced

1 medium-sized yellow squash, quartered and sliced

1 red or green bell pepper, diced

4 cloves of garlic, crushed

1 jar (26 ounces) well-seasoned pasta sauce

¼ cup torn fresh basil

1 pound penne

8 ounces mozzarella cheese, shredded

1 cup freshly grated Parmesan cheese

1. Begin heating a large pot of salted water for the pasta. Preheat the oven to 350°F. Lightly oil a 9- by 13-inch baking dish.

2. Heat the oil in a large skillet over medium-high heat. Add the mushrooms and season with salt and pepper to taste. Sauté until the mushrooms give up their juice, about 5 minutes. Add the zucchini, yellow squash, bell pepper, garlic, and salt and pepper to taste. Sauté until the vegetables are softened, about 4 minutes. Remove from heat and stir in the sauce and basil.

3. Cook the pasta in the boiling water until al dente. Drain briefly.

4. Transfer the pasta to the baking dish. Add the sauce, half of the mozzarella, and half of the Parmesan; mix well. Sprinkle the remaining cheese evenly over the top. (The dish can be covered and held in the refrigerator for up to 6 hours. Increase the baking time by 15 minutes if the casserole goes into the oven cold.)

5. Bake for 20 to 30 minutes, until heated through.

6. Serve hot.

Serves 4

Orzo with Summer Squash and Feta Cheese

Quick, light, refreshing, colorful, and easy to coordinate: By the time the pasta is cooked, the vegetables are ready. This is the perfect summer dish for busy people.

2 medium-sized zucchini, diced

2 medium-sized summer squash or golden zucchini, diced

Salt

4 tablespoons extra virgin olive oil

1 red bell pepper, diced

2 cloves of garlic, minced

Juice of 1 lemon

1 tomato, seeded and diced

¼ cup chopped fresh mint

¼ cup chopped fresh parsley

Freshly ground black pepper

1 pound orzo

4 ounces feta cheese, crumbled

1. If you have the time (see page 147), combine the zucchini, summer squash, and 2 teaspoons salt in a colander. Toss to mix and set aside to drain for 30 minutes. Transfer the squash to a clean dish towel and wring dry.

2. Begin heating a large pot of salted water for the pasta.

3. Heat 3 tablespoons of the oil in a large skillet over medium-high heat. Add the zucchini, summer squash, bell pepper, and garlic. Sauté until the vegetables are tender crisp, 3 to 5 minutes. Stir in the lemon juice, tomato, mint, and parsley. Season to taste with salt and pepper. Reduce the heat to low.

4. Cook the orzo in the boiling water until just al dente. Drain briefly and transfer to a large serving bowl.

5. Toss the orzo with the remaining 1 tablespoon oil. Add the vegetable mixture and crumbled cheese. Toss to thoroughly combine. Taste and add salt and pepper as necessary. Serve immediately.

Serves 4–6

Peeling Fresh Tomatoes

To peel tomatoes, dip them into boiling water for about 10 seconds. Then use a sharp paring knife to separate the skin from the flesh.

Vegetable Lasagne

The secret to making a rich-tasting vegetable lasagne lies in cooking the vegetables and combining them with the tomato sauce. This lasagne is a delicious improvement over the watery spinach lasagne that is a common alternative to meat lasagna.

¼ cup extra virgin olive oil

1 small eggplant (about 1 pound), peeled and diced

8 ounces mushrooms, sliced

1 medium-sized yellow summer squash, diced

1 medium-sized zucchini, diced

4 cups well-seasoned tomato sauce

4 cloves of garlic, minced

Salt and freshly ground black pepper

1 pound ricotta cheese

1 large egg, slightly beaten

2 tablespoons chopped fresh basil or ¼ cup pesto (page 27)

12 no-cook lasagna noodles

1 pound mozzarella cheese, grated

1 cup freshly grated Parmesan cheese

1. In a large skillet or Dutch oven, heat the oil over medium-high heat. Add the eggplant and sauté until juicy and tender, about 8 minutes. Add the mushrooms; sauté until they give up their juice, about 8 minutes. Add the summer squash and zucchini; sauté for 3 minutes, until almost tender. Pour in the tomato sauce. Add half of the garlic. Taste and add salt and pepper as needed. Keep over low heat while you assemble the lasagna.

2. Preheat the oven to 350°F.

3. Combine the ricotta, egg, and basil in a medium-sized bowl and mix well.

4. To assemble the lasagna, spread about 2 cups of the sauce in a 9- by 13-inch baking dish. Place three lasagna noodles over the sauce. The noodles should not touch or overlap. Spread a third of the ricotta mixture evenly over the noodles. Top with another 1½ cups sauce. Sprinkle a quarter of the mozzarella and one-quarter of the Parmesan cheese on top. Repeat the layers two more times, beginning each new layer with noodles. Top with the remaining three lasagna noodles. Spread the rest of the sauce on top. Sprinkle with the remaining cheese. Cover with aluminum foil.

5. Bake the lasagne for 30 minutes. Remove the foil and bake for another 10 to 15 minutes, until hot and bubbly.

6. Let the lasagne stand for at least 5 minutes before cutting into serving pieces. Serve warm or hot.

Serves 6–8

Make-Ahead Lasagne

The lasagne can be assembled and held for up to 8 hours in the refrigerator. Add 15 minutes to the baking time if it is cold when it is placed in the oven. The lasagne can also be baked in advance and frozen for up to 1 month. Reheat it still frozen and covered with foil, adding 30 minutes to the baking time. Uncover for the last 10 minutes.

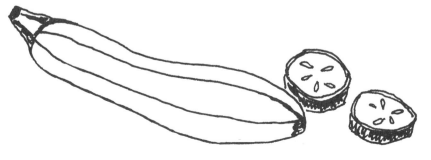

Black Bean and Summer Squash Stew

If you start with canned black beans, you can make this satisfying, hearty stew in less than an hour. I like the visual combination of black beans and yellow squash, so golden zucchini makes a fine substitute for the yellow squash. Like most stews, this one tastes even better on the second day. Leftovers make a delicious filling for burritos.

2 tablespoons extra virgin olive oil

1 onion, diced

1 red bell pepper, diced

2 green chiles, such as jalapeños or poblanos, diced

2 medium-sized yellow summer squash or golden zucchini, quartered and sliced

4 tomatoes, seeded and diced

2 cans (15 ounces each) black beans, rinsed and drained, or 3 cups cooked black beans

Salt and freshly ground black pepper

¼ cup chopped fresh cilantro

Hot pepper sauce (optional)

Hot cooked rice or tortilla chips, to serve

1. In a nonreactive Dutch oven or large saucepan, heat the oil over medium-high heat. Add the onion, bell pepper, and chiles. Sauté until the onion is softened and translucent, about 5 minutes. Add the squash. Sauté until the squash is softened, about 5 minutes.

2. Add the tomatoes and beans; season with salt and pepper. Bring to a boil. Reduce the heat to medium-low and simmer for 15 to 30 minutes, until the flavors blend.

3. Stir in the cilantro. Taste and add salt and pepper as necessary. Add the hot sauce if you want to give the stew more spice. Serve hot over rice. Or serve the stew without rice and pass a bowl of tortilla chips for crumbling on top.

Serves 4–6

Feed a Crowd

Add other garden vegetables, especially corn, to stretch out this stew.

Summer Vegetable Couscous

Cinnamon is the seductive surprise spice in this vegetable stew. Combined with cumin, the cinnamon evokes the flavors of the Middle East. This one-dish meal provides grains, beans, and vegetables for healthy, hearty eating.

3 tablespoons extra virgin olive oil

1 onion, slivered

1 green or red bell pepper, diced

2 medium-sized yellow summer squash or golden zucchini, quartered and sliced

2 medium-sized zucchini, quartered and sliced

2 cloves of garlic, minced

2 teaspoons ground cumin

½ teaspoon ground cinnamon

1½–2 cups (15- or 19-ounce can) cooked or canned chickpeas, drained

1½ cups seeded and diced tomatoes (fresh or canned)

1 cup water

1½ cups couscous

2¼ cups boiling water

Salt

¼ cup chopped fresh cilantro, plus sprigs to garnish

Freshly ground black pepper

1. Heat the oil in a large skillet over medium-high heat. Add the onion and bell pepper. Sauté until fragrant and softened, 3 to 5 minutes. Remove the skillet from the heat. With a slotted spoon, transfer the onion and pepper to a medium-sized saucepan.

2. Return the skillet to the heat and add the summer squash, zucchini, garlic, cumin, and cinnamon. Sauté until fragrant and softened, 4 to 5 minutes. Add the squash mixture to the saucepan, along with the chickpeas, tomatoes, and water. Bring the vegetables to a boil. Reduce the heat and simmer for about 30 minutes to allow the flavors to develop.

3. Meanwhile, in a large bowl, combine the couscous and boiling water. Add about ½ teaspoon salt, stir, cover, and set aside to steam until all of the water is absorbed and the grains are tender, 10 minutes. Uncover and fluff with a fork.

4. Stir the cilantro into the vegetable mixture. Taste. Add salt and pepper as needed.

5. To serve, make a bed of couscous on individual plates or one large platter. Spoon the vegetables over the couscous. Garnish with cilantro and serve hot.

NOTE: Any combination of summer squash, sliced or diced, can be used in this stew. If you happen to have mildly flavored chiles or peppers on hand, such as poblano chiles or Italian frying peppers, use those instead of the bell pepper. If you have the time and inclination, peel fresh tomatoes before dicing.

Serves 4–6

Double Squash Cornbread Supper

There is grated squash in the cornbread topping and sliced squash in the filling, which makes a double dose of our favorite vegetable in a rustic supper dish.

CORNBREAD TOPPING

- 2 **cups grated zucchini**
- ½ **teaspoon salt**
- 1 **cup stone-ground yellow cornmeal**
- ¾ **cup unbleached all-purpose flour**
- 2 **tablespoons sugar**
- 2 **teaspoons baking powder**
- ½ **teaspoon baking soda**
- 2 **large eggs, slightly beaten**
- ¾ **cup plain yogurt**
- ¼ **cup canola oil**

1. Start the cornbread topping by combining the grated zucchini and salt in a colander. Toss to mix well, and set aside to drain for 30 minutes.

2. Preheat the oven to 425°F.

3. To prepare the chili filling, combine the oil, cumin, and chili powder in a large ovenproof skillet over medium-high heat. Add the onion, bell pepper, and chiles. Sauté until the onion is softened, 3 to 5 minutes. Add the summer squash and sauté until softened, about 3 minutes. Add the tomatoes, beans, and cilantro. Add salt and pepper to taste. Let the chili simmer while you finish the topping.

4. To finish the cornbread topping, combine the cornmeal, flour, sugar, baking powder, and baking soda in a medium-sized bowl. Mix well. Combine the eggs, yogurt, and oil in a small bowl and mix well. Squeeze the zucchini to remove any excess moisture and add to the flour mixture. Mix well. Pour the egg mixture into the flour mixture and stir just until well combined. The batter will be lumpy.

CHILI FILLING

- 2 tablespoons olive oil
- 2 teaspoons ground cumin
- 1 tablespoon chili powder
- 1 onion, diced
- 1 red or green bell pepper, diced
- 2 fresh green chiles, such as poblano or jalapeño
- 1 medium-sized yellow summer squash, quartered and sliced
- 1½ cups seeded and diced tomatoes (fresh or canned)
- 1½ cups cooked black beans, red kidney beans, or pinto beans (home-cooked or canned)
- 2 tablespoons chopped fresh cilantro
- Salt and freshly ground black pepper

5. To assemble the dish, remove the skillet from the heat. Evenly spread the cornbread batter over the chili, spreading it to the edges of the pan.

6. Bake for 20 to 25 minutes, until the top is golden and firm. A tester inserted near the center should come out clean.

7. Let stand for about 5 minutes before serving with a pie server or large spoon.

Serves 6

Ode to Zucchini

The zucchini inspires more
than just recipes.

All hail the great and noble Zucchini!
A treat like music by Paganini.

Beats other veggies by a mile,
It is so good . . . and versatile.

Boiled or baked, or maybe steamed,
Coated and fried, or even creamed.

A drop of lemon or drop of lime
Will tease your taste buds every time.

Adjusts to spices in great variety,
Served well in low or high society.

Without it, no great meal is complete.
Try them any which way, and Bon Appétit!

— Bernard Bernhardt

Summer Squash Enchiladas

Summer squash in a chile-accented cheese sauce is folded into corn tortillas and baked to make a delicious vegetarian main dish. Serve with refried beans and a green salad.

4 tablespoons butter

¼ cup all-purpose unbleached flour

2 teaspoons chili powder

2 cups milk

2 cups grated Cheddar or Monterey Jack cheese

Salt and freshly ground black pepper

2 tablespoons extra virgin olive oil

1½ cups diced onions

3 cloves of garlic, minced

1½ teaspoons minced fresh chile, or to taste

6 cups diced summer squash

16 corn tortillas

3 cups seeded and diced fresh tomatoes

1. Melt the butter in a small saucepan over medium heat. Stir in the flour and chili powder to make a thick paste. Add the milk a little at a time, stirring well after each addition. Add the cheese. Heat gently until the cheese is melted, about 5 minutes. Season to taste with salt and pepper. Keep warm.

2. Preheat the oven to 400°F. Lightly grease a 9- by 13-inch baking dish.

3. In a large skillet, heat the oil over medium-high heat. Add the onions, garlic, and chile. Sauté until the onions are softened and fragrant, 3 to 5 minutes. Add the squash and sauté until tender crisp, about 5 minutes. Add two thirds of the sauce and toss to coat.

4. To assemble the enchiladas, spoon some of the filling onto each tortilla and roll. Place seam-side down on the baking dish. Spoon the remaining sauce on top. Sprinkle with the tomatoes.

5. Bake for 30 minutes, until the enchiladas are heated through.

6. Serve immediately.

Serves 8

Cheese and Squash Rellenos

Relleno is Spanish for "stuffed," but these chiles are actually "unstuffed." The dish is a layered casserole made of the ingredients that are often used for chiles rellenos. For convenience and to go easy on folks who might not like hot foods, this casserole is made with canned mild chiles. But feel free to substitute the chiles of your choice.

3 medium-sized yellow summer squash, sliced

1½ cups cooked rice

1 can (7 ounces) mild chiles, chopped

6½ cups grated Monterey Jack cheese

1 tomato, sliced

2 cups sour cream

⅓ cup diced green bell pepper

2 tablespoons chopped fresh cilantro or parsley

2 tablespoons chopped scallion, white and tender green parts

1 teaspoon dried oregano

Salt and freshly ground black pepper

1. Bring a medium-sized pot of salted water to a boil. Add the summer squash and blanch for 3 minutes, until just barely tender. Drain well.

2. Preheat the oven to 350°F. Lightly butter a 9- by 13-inch baking dish or a 2-quart casserole.

3. Spread the rice in the bottom of the baking dish. Layer the chiles, 5½ cups of the cheese, the squash, and the tomato on top of the rice.

4. Combine the sour cream, bell pepper, cilantro, scallion, and oregano in a small bowl. Add salt and pepper to taste. Spoon this mixture over the tomato. Sprinkle with the remaining 1 cup cheese.

5. Bake for 30 minutes, until the casserole is heated through and the cheese is melted.

6. Serve hot.

Serves 6

Goat Cheese Pizza with Zucchini and Roasted Pepper

I'm a big fan of the flavor of good goat cheese, and I'm a tremendous fan of this beautiful pizza. The combination of garlicky zucchini and tangy goat cheese is just perfect.

1 recipe Basic Pizza Dough (recipe follows)

2 red bell peppers

Extra virgin olive oil

4 cups quartered and sliced zucchini

4 cloves of garlic, minced

Salt and freshly ground black pepper

8 ounces soft mild goat cheese (chèvre)

1. Prepare the pizza dough and set it aside in a warm, draft-free place to rise until doubled in bulk, about 1 hour.

2. Meanwhile, roast the peppers over a gas flame or under a broiler until charred all over, about 10 minutes. Place the peppers in a bag and let them steam for 10 minutes to loosen the skins. Discard the skins and seeds and cut the flesh into strips.

3. Heat 3 tablespoons of the oil in a medium-sized skillet over medium-high heat. Add the zucchini and garlic. Sauté until almost tender, about 3 minutes. Season to taste with salt and pepper. Remove from the heat and set aside.

4. Preheat the oven to 500°F, with an oven rack on the lowest shelf.

5. Divide the dough into two balls. Lightly oil two 10-inch or 12-inch round pizza pans or two 12- by 15-inch baking sheets. Assemble and bake the pizzas one at a time. Stretch one ball of dough to fit a pan. Brush the top of the dough with olive oil. Scatter half the zucchini over the crust. Scatter half the red pepper strips over the zucchini. Crumble half the goat cheese over all. If you like black pepper, give the pizza a light dusting.

6. Bake the pizza for 10 to 12 minutes on the bottom oven rack, until the crust is golden. Meanwhile, assemble the second pizza. Bake the second pizza when the first pizza is done.

7. Serve both pizzas while still warm.

Serves 6

Basic Pizza Dough

This dough is very quick to make in a food processor and makes great-tasting crust.

    3¾–4 cups unbleached all-purpose flour
        1 tablespoon salt
    1½ cups warm (110°–115°F) water
        1 packet (¼ ounce) or 1 tablespoon
            active dry yeast
        3 tablespoons olive oil

1. In a food processor fitted with a dough hook or in a large bowl, combine the flour and salt. Measure the warm water into a glass measure, add the yeast, and stir until foamy. Stir in the olive oil. In the food processor with the motor running, pour in the water mixture and process until the dough forms into a ball. Continue processing for 1 minute to knead the dough. Alternatively, add the yeast mixture to the dough and stir until the dough forms a ball. Turn onto a lightly floured surface and knead until the dough is springy and elastic, about 5 minutes. The dough should be firm and just slightly sticky, not dry.

2. Lightly oil a large bowl. Place the dough ball in it, turning the dough to coat with the oil. Cover and let rise until doubled in bulk, about 1 hour. The dough is now ready for fitting into pans and topping with sauce, cheese, and vegetables.

Makes two 10-inch to 12-inch round or rectangular pizzas

Mushroom Zesto Pizza

Mushroom lovers will greet this pizza with pleasure. A pesto made of roasted mushrooms, grated zucchini, walnuts, and Parmesan provides the sauce. Fresh tomatoes and fresh mozzarella top it off.

1 recipe Basic Pizza Dough (page 81)

1 medium-sized zucchini, grated

Salt

2 large ripe tomatoes, thinly sliced

4 tablespoons extra virgin olive oil

1 pound white button mushrooms, halved

½ cup walnut pieces

4 cloves of garlic

½ cup fresh basil leaves

½ cup freshly grated Parmesan cheese

Salt and freshly ground black pepper

1 pound fresh mozzarella, thinly sliced

1. Prepare the pizza dough and set aside in a warm, draft-free place to rise until doubled in bulk, about 1 hour.

2. Meanwhile, combine the zucchini with 1 teaspoon salt in a colander. Toss to mix and set aside to drain for 30 minutes. Arrange the tomato slices on wire racks set over a baking sheet. Sprinkle with salt, flip over the tomatoes, and salt the second side; set aside to drain for about 30 minutes.

3. Preheat the oven to 425°F. Lightly oil a large shallow roasting pan or half sheet pan.

4. Toss the mushrooms with the olive oil in a large bowl. Transfer to the pan and arrange in a single layer.

5. Roast until the mushrooms are browned and juicy, about 15 minutes, stirring once or twice. Add the walnuts and continue to roast for another 7 minutes, until the mushrooms are well browned and still juicy and the walnuts are fragrant and beginning to brown.

6. Remove the mushrooms and walnuts from the oven. Increase the oven temperature to 500°F. Let the mushrooms cool briefly.

7. Combine the garlic, basil, and Parmesan in a food processor and pulse until finely chopped. Add the mushrooms and their juices and the walnuts and pulse until chopped and well mixed. Do not purée; there should still be some texture to the pesto. Squeeze the excess moisture from the zucchini and mix in. Season to taste with salt and plenty of pepper.

8. Divide the dough into two balls. Lightly oil two 10-inch or 12-inch round pizza pans or two 12- by 15-inch baking sheets. Assemble and bake the pizzas one at a time. Stretch one ball of dough to fit a pan. Spread half of the mushroom pesto over the dough. Pat the tomatoes dry with paper towels. Arrange half the tomatoes on top. Top the pizza with half the mozzarella.

9. Bake the pizza on the lowest rack of the oven for 10 to 12 minutes, until the crust is golden. Meanwhile, assemble the second pizza. Bake the second pizza when the first pizza is done.

10. Serve both pizzas warm.

Serves 6

Mushroom Tips

When buying mushrooms, look for ones that are firm and evenly colored, with tightly closed caps. If all the gills underneath are showing, the mushrooms are past their prime but still edible. Avoid mushrooms that are broken or have soft spots.

Store mushrooms, unwashed, in the refrigerator for up to 3 days. The best way to store them is on a tray, in a single layer, covered with a damp towel. The worst way to store mushrooms is in a sealed plastic bag.

Zesto Pizza

Fresh tomatoes, fresh pesto, and fresh mozzarella make a heavenly pizza.
Salting the tomatoes and patting them dry is the secret to making pizza
with fresh tomatoes. Otherwise, the tomatoes will release their excess juice on
the pizza as it bakes, making a soggy mess.

1 **recipe Basic Pizza Dough
(page 81)**

2 **cups grated zucchini
Salt**

2 **ripe large tomatoes, thinly
sliced**

2 **cups pesto (page 27)**

10 **ounces fresh mozzarella
cheese, sliced**

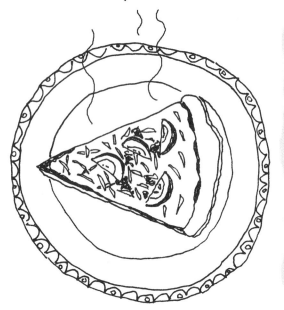

1. Prepare the pizza dough and set aside in a warm, draft-free place to rise until doubled in bulk, about 1 hour.

2. Meanwhile, in a colander combine the zucchini and 1 teaspoon salt. Toss to mix and set aside to drain for 30 minutes. Arrange the tomatoes on wire racks set over a baking sheet. Sprinkle with salt, flip over the tomatoes, and salt the second side; set aside to drain for about 30 minutes.

3. Preheat the oven to 500°F, with an oven rack on the lowest shelf.

4. Squeeze the zucchini to eliminate any excess moisture. In a medium-sized bowl, combine the zucchini and pesto. Mix well.

5. Divide the dough into two balls. Lightly oil two 10-inch or 12-inch round pizza pans or two 12- by 15-inch baking sheets. Assemble and bake the pizzas one at a time. Stretch one ball of dough to fit a pan. Spread half the pesto mixture over the dough. Pat dry half of the tomatoes on paper towels and arrange on top of the pesto. Top the pizza with half of the mozzarella.

6. Bake the pizza for 10 to 12 minutes on the bottom oven rack, until the crust is golden. Meanwhile, assemble the second pizza. Bake the second pizza when the first pizza is done.

7. Serve both pizzas warm.

Serves 6

Zucchini Tart Niçoise

Ratatouille baked in a pie shell holds up beautifully on a buffet table,
making a delicious contribution to a brunch or dinner. If you are serving it as the
main course, round out the meal with a green salad and crusty French bread.

4 tablespoons extra virgin
olive oil

2 onions, minced

2 cloves of garlic, minced

2 green bell peppers, sliced in
rings

2 medium-sized zucchini,
quartered and sliced

1 small eggplant, peeled and
diced

1 cup seeded and diced
tomatoes

Salt and freshly ground black
pepper

1 unbaked 9- or 10-inch pie
shell

¼ cup freshly grated Parmesan
cheese

1. Heat 3 tablespoons of the oil in a large skillet over medium-high heat. Add the onions and garlic. Sauté until the onions are soft, 3 to 5 minutes.

2. Stir in the bell peppers, zucchini, eggplant, tomatoes, and salt and pepper to taste. Reduce the heat to medium, cover, and simmer until the vegetables are tender, about 45 minutes, stirring occasionally.

3. Preheat the oven to 350°F.

4. Spoon the vegetables into the pie shell.

5. Bake for 10 minutes. Remove the pie from the oven and sprinkle the cheese on top. Drizzle the remaining 1 tablespoon oil over the pie. Return to the oven and bake for 5 minutes more, until the cheese is melted.

6. Let the tart rest on a wire rack for about 5 minutes. Serve hot or at room temperature.

Serves 4–6

My Brother Joe—
the Insect Warrior

WHEN MY BROTHER JOE moved to Alabama a few years back and described the greenhouse he was building, the fruit trees he was planting, and the garden plots he was digging, I felt envy.

We come from good Russian potato-peasant stock, but only Joe and I, out of five kids, have a strong urge to grub in the soil. But apparently my urges are less urgent than his. I think living in Zone 4, with a four-month growing season, is enough. Joe gardens in Zone 8B, where plants are started in a greenhouse in January and red peppers are still being harvested in mid-December. He probably has the greenest thumb in the family, and knowledge of this fact occasionally has tinted my vision green with jealousy.

To a recent family Thanksgiving, Joe brought bags of speckled wax beans, glossy red peppers, and some unusual winter squash that he called Seminole pumpkins. If I had known he was going to be showing off with a dozen of the sweetest, largest red peppers I've ever eaten, I would have brought a blue Hubbard squash, although I'm not sure I could have afforded the extra airplane seat for my 40-pounder.

As the Thanksgiving weekend progressed, I found out what gardening in the summer in Alabama is all about. It is a battle between man and insect, and the insects always win. "I'm always fighting the elements," my brother admitted. "I have a brief window of good growing conditions in the spring. Sugar snap peas go in February. I plant the rest of the garden around Easter, when we're through with the last frost. I have good conditions into June. But the warmer it gets, the worse the insects get. Fall isn't as bad, but I'm still sharing the harvest with the bugs. Then there is all the blight and fungus. They're worse in the heat, too."

Tell me about squash, I urged.

"Well, everybody grows zucchini, so I don't even try. That's a no-brainer," he said. "I grow three or four different kinds of summer squash. This past summer I grew zephyr squash, the two-color squash. And I tried a Lebanese round squash that was good. Pattypans do well."

And what about those Seminole pumpkins? "They are the strangest plants," he said. "The vines just keep growing. The older part of the vine dies back. But the ends of the vines put out new growth, and they keep going. I have some vines that are 35 feet long. They've grown through the fence and onto the lawn. The only thing stopping them right now is the neighbor's wood fence. The vines will put out little tendrils and will climb fences. I planted them Memorial Day weekend. Started harvesting in about 110 days — mid-September. It's almost three months later and they are still putting out blossoms and setting fruit. And they keep in storage for 10 to 11 months."

We cooked the Seminole pumpkins for our Thanksgiving dinner, easily cutting through the ridged beige skin to reveal the orange flesh and large cavities. We baked wedges with brown sugar and butter and ate them skin and all. Each Seminole pumpkin served two.

My brother reported that according to the Southern Exposure Seed Exchange, which sold him the seeds, there is documented proof that Seminole pumpkins were grown by Seminole Indians in the 1500s. I thought these pumpkins were fine, but not as rich tasting as my own butternuts. Well, I asked, can you grow other winter squash?

"The problem with winter squash," my brother admitted, "is that the insects do so much damage to the leaves. If the plant isn't determined to keep growing, the insect damage is going to overcome the plant."

I smiled. He may be able to harvest peas in February, while I'm still shoveling snow. He may be able to coax red peppers from his plants, whereas I don't even bother planting them. But he can't consistently harvest a decent crop of squash. My green thumb shines a little brighter now.

Zucchini Quiche

When you have refrigerated piecrust on hand, making quiche is a snap. Quiche makes a great brunch dish, without the last-minute cooking that omelettes and other egg dishes require. You can even make it a day in advance and reheat it. Quiche for dinner, with a green salad and good bakery bread, is always welcome. Serve it warm or at room temperature.

2 tablespoons extra virgin olive oil

2 cups thinly sliced zucchini

1 cup thinly sliced onion

1 clove of garlic, minced

1½ teaspoons salt

Freshly ground black pepper

1 unbaked 10-inch pie shell

½ cup grated mozzarella, Swiss, mild Cheddar, or Fontina cheese

4 eggs, beaten

1 cup heavy cream

1 cup milk

1. Preheat the oven to 375°F.

2. Heat the oil in a large skillet over medium-high heat. Add the zucchini, onion, and garlic. Sauté until tender crisp, 3 to 5 minutes. Season the vegetables with salt and pepper to taste and spoon into the pie shell. Sprinkle the cheese over the vegetables.

3. In a medium-sized mixing bowl, beat together the eggs, cream, and milk. Pour into the pie shell.

4. Bake for 30 to 40 minutes, until the quiche is set but still moist.

5. Cool on a rack and serve warm or at room temperature.

Serves 4–6

Crumb-Crusted Zucchini Quiche

If you don't have refrigerated pie pastry on hand and you don't want to make pastry for a quiche from scratch, consider this recipe, which replaces the pastry with a layer of crumbs. Crumbs made from good bakery or homemade bread will be superior to those of most store brands.

1 medium-sized zucchini, very thinly sliced

Salt

1 cup dry bread crumbs

2 tablespoons extra virgin olive oil

¼ cup butter

¼ cup unbleached all-purpose flour

⅔ cup milk

1 egg

½ cup grated Romano cheese

⅛ teaspoon ground nutmeg

⅛ teaspoon freshly ground black pepper

1. If you have the time (see page 147), combine the zucchini and 1 teaspoon salt in a colander. Toss to mix and set aside to drain for 30 minutes.

2. Preheat the oven to 350°F.

3. Butter a 9-inch quiche dish or pie pan. Coat with the bread crumbs, distributing them as evenly as possible.

4. Wrap the zucchini in a clean kitchen towel and wring dry.

5. Heat the oil in a medium-sized skillet over medium-high heat. Add the zucchini and sauté until tender crisp, 3 to 5 minutes. Transfer to paper towels and blot dry.

6. In a large saucepan, melt the butter over medium heat. Whisk in the flour to form a thick paste. Stir in the milk and cook until thickened and smooth, about 5 minutes.

7. Beat the egg in a small bowl. Add about ½ cup of the sauce to warm the eggs, and then pour the mixture back into the saucepan. Stir in the cheese, pepper, and nutmeg. Stir in the zucchini.

8. Carefully ladle the zucchini mixture into the prepared pie pan.

9. Bake for 35 minutes, until just set.

10. Cool on a wire rack. Serve warm or at room temperature.

Serves 4–6

Zucchini Feta Squares

If you like spanakopita, the spinach pie made with phyllo dough,
you'll probably enjoy this version made with zucchini.

6 cups grated zucchini

Salt

1 tablespoon extra virgin
olive oil

⅔ cup diced onion

2 cloves of garlic, minced

1 cup crumbled feta cheese

½ cup small-curd cottage cheese

1 teaspoon minced fresh dill

Freshly ground black pepper

⅓ cup butter, melted

10 sheets phyllo dough

1. In a large colander, combine the zucchini with 1 teaspoon salt. Toss to mix and set aside to drain for 30 minutes.

2. Preheat the oven to 400°F.

3. Heat the oil in a large skillet over medium-high heat. Add the onion and garlic. Sauté until the onion is softened and fragrant, about 3 minutes.

4. Squeeze the zucchini to remove any excess water. In a large bowl, combine the zucchini, onion mixture, feta cheese, cottage cheese, and dill. Season to taste with salt and pepper.

5. To assemble the dish, brush a 7- by 12-inch baking dish with the butter. Place a folded sheet of phyllo into the dish to cover the bottom. Brush the phyllo with butter. Repeat with four more pieces of folded phyllo. Spread the zucchini mixture evenly over the dough. Layer the remaining folded phyllo sheets, brushing butter on the top of each sheet.

6. Bake for 30 minutes, until the top is browned.

7. Let the pastry sit for at least 10 minutes before cutting into squares. Serve warm.

Serves 4–6

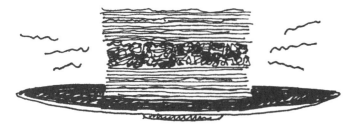

Zucchini Omelette

When the cupboard is almost bare but the garden overflows with zucchini, you can usually muster up a few eggs to make an omelette. This recipe serves two. If you are serving four, make two omelettes, one after the other, instead of making an eight-egg omelette.

1 medium-sized zucchini, quartered and sliced

Salt

2 tablespoons extra virgin olive oil

1 clove of garlic, minced (optional)

Freshly ground black pepper

1 tablespoon chopped fresh basil, or 1 teaspoon dried

¾ cup grated mild cheese, such as mild Cheddar or Swiss

4 eggs

2 tablespoons milk or cream

2 tablespoons butter

Quick Meal

Omelette making is simple to master and lets you whip up a decent meal with few ingredients and little time. Serve with fresh bakery bread and a green salad, and you have a quick and lovely meal.

1. If you have the time (see page 147), combine the zucchini and salt in a colander. Toss to mix and set aside to drain for 30 minutes. Transfer the zucchini to a clean dish towel and wring dry.

2. Heat the oil in a medium-sized skillet over medium-high heat. Add the zucchini; garlic, if using; and pepper to taste. Sauté until the zucchini is tender crisp, 3 to 5 minutes.

3. Remove the zucchini from the heat. Stir in the basil and the cheese.

4. Beat the eggs and milk in a small bowl until just blended. Season with salt and pepper.

5. In a large, preferably nonstick, skillet over medium-high heat, melt the butter. Once the butter melts, swirl it around in the pan until the foam subsides. Pour in the egg mixture and let it cook undisturbed for about 30 seconds, until the bottom is partially set. Using a fork or thin-bladed spatula, push the edge of the egg toward the middle, allowing the uncooked egg to flow out toward the edges. Repeat until the egg is still moist but no longer runny, about 3 minutes.

6. Carefully spoon the zucchini onto one side of the omelette. Fold the other side over the filling.

7. Serve immediately.

Serves 2

Spanish Omelette with Zucchini

There's no end of ways to dress up an omelette. Here, the basic omelette is adorned with a tomato sauce made with zucchini, peppers, and onions. If you are serving four people, make two omelettes rather than one big one.

1 medium-sized zucchini, quartered and thinly sliced

Salt

1 tablespoon extra virgin olive oil

2 tablespoons diced green bell pepper

1 tablespoon diced onion

1 tomato, seeded and diced

Dash Tabasco sauce

Salt and freshly ground black pepper

½ cup tomato sauce

4 eggs

2 tablespoons milk or light cream

2 tablespoons butter

1. If you have the time (see page 147), combine the zucchini and 1 teaspoon salt in a colander. Toss to mix and set aside to drain for 30 minutes. Transfer the zucchini to a clean dish towel and wring dry.

2. Heat the oil in a medium-sized skillet over medium-high heat. Add the zucchini, bell pepper, and onion. Sauté until the zucchini is tender crisp, 3 to 5 minutes. Stir in the tomato, Tabasco, pepper to taste, and ¼ cup of the tomato sauce. Simmer for 10 minutes.

3. Beat the eggs and milk in a small bowl until just blended. Season with salt and pepper.

4. In a large, preferably nonstick, skillet over medium-high heat, melt the butter. When the butter melts, swirl it around in the pan until the foam subsides. Pour in the egg mixture and let it cook undisturbed for about 30 seconds, until the bottom is partially set. Using a fork or thin-bladed spatula, push the edge of the egg toward the middle, allowing the uncooked egg to flow out toward the edges. Repeat until the egg is still moist but no longer runny, about 3 minutes.

5. Carefully spoon the tomato and zucchini sauce onto one side of the omelette. Fold the other side over the filling.

6. Serve immediately, passing the remaining ¼ cup tomato sauce at the table.

Serves 2

Corn and Squash Frittata

The dictionary defines *frittata* as "an open-faced omelette of Spanish-Italian origin." Whereas the omelette creates a shell for a filling, in a frittata the filling is mixed into the eggs. The frittata is finished in the oven, eliminating the difficult task of flipping it.

2 eggs

2 tablespoons unbleached all-purpose flour

½ teaspoon salt

¼ teaspoon baking powder

¼ teaspoon freshly ground black pepper

1 medium-sized summer squash, grated

Kernels cut from 3 ears fresh corn

2 tablespoons butter

Chopped fresh parsley, to garnish

1. Preheat the oven to 350°F.

2. In a medium-sized mixing bowl, combine the eggs, flour, salt, baking powder, and pepper. Mix well, then fold in the squash and corn.

3. Spray a large ovenproof skillet with nonstick cooking spray. In the skillet, melt the butter over medium heat. Swirl the butter around; when the foam subsides, add the egg mixture and cover. Cook the frittata slowly until the bottom is set, about 10 minutes.

4. Transfer the skillet to the oven and bake for 10 to 20 minutes, checking every 5 minutes or so, until the top of the frittata is no longer runny.

5. Garnish with the parsley and serve hot, warm, or at room temperature.

Serves 4

Feeding a City:
The Poughkeepsie Farm Project

FARMER DAN is a man with a mission. As head grower for the Poughkeepsie Farm Project, his job is not just to grow vegetables, herbs, and flowers. He also helps teach city dwellers about where their food comes from; how food can be grown in a chemical-free, sustainable way; and how to provide food for a socially and economically diverse community.

The Poughkeepsie Farm Project, located in the Hudson Valley region of New York State, about 2 hours north of New York City, is a community-supported agriculture (CSA) farm. These types of farm are springing up all around the United States and Canada in response to growing concerns about the practices of corporate farming. At a CSA farm, individuals or families pay the growers in the spring for a share of the future harvest, which is delivered weekly in brown bags filled to bursting with farm-fresh, usually organic, produce.

The Poughkeepsie Farm Project is considered a moderate-size CSA. It has just under 200 family and individual members, all of whom call Dan Guenther "Farmer Dan." His nickname reflects his intense desire to educate people about how foods are grown — by people, who work hard by the sweat of their brows. Food doesn't magically appear in the supermarket; it takes the work of people like Farmer Dan, who figures he is responsible for "filling 800 to 1,000 mouths each week." The farm also helps to support a soup kitchen and shelter for homeless people.

The farm is located on 6½ acres in Poughkeepsie, on a defunct 500-acre dairy farm owned by Vassar College. Members pay $300 per year for a small share (6 to 8 pounds of produce weekly) or $500 dollars for a large share (10 to 12 pounds of produce weekly). They are also required to work on the farm for about 12 hours each season, doing chores that involve harvesting, washing produce, or preparing it for distribution on Saturday mornings.

The first harvest is usually around May 15. It includes lots of different greens and other early-spring vegetables, thanks to the use of greenhouses and row covers. The harvest continues until the first week in November, when winter squash and pumpkins make up the bulk of the share. At the height of the summer, up to 23 different types of produce may be available. Zucchini and other summer squash are available for most of the summer.

The advantages of being a member of a CSA farm are numerous, according to Farmer Dan. "Our food is significantly cheaper than what you could buy at a health food store. There's such a diversity of product that sometimes people are walking away with a lot more than their so-called share. I mean, you can't give someone a few stems of chard; you have to give them a good-sized bunch so they can do something with it. You multiply that times 23 different items, and you're bound to be walking away with more than 12 pounds of vegetables."

Farmer Dan is happy to expound on the advantages of CSA agriculture, which he says "defies capitalism." The consumer, he says, "takes a risk by putting the money up front. But in a good season, it can be an excellent deal, and we have been having a lot of good seasons."

Of course, every good season has its share of bumper crops, and squash is always one of them. Lately, Farmer Dan has been growing a variety of zucchini known as zephyr. "All summer squash," he explains, "is picked immature. With most varieties, you have a day or so of being the perfect immature vegetable before it turns into an overgrown squash with tough skin and big seeds. Zephyr seems to last longer on the vine. You have a longer time for harvesting. I also like patty-pans — the sunburst variety. I tell people when they get large to slice them and cook them on the grill like a steak. They are good if you brush them with a vinaigrette, even better if you can marinate them in the vinaigrette for a while."

As for winter squash, his favorite varieties are delicata, "the ugliest and the tastiest," and sweet dumpling, which "doesn't need any butter or brown sugar or anything on it."

Low-Fat Zucchini Frittata

There's room in every diet for a vegetable-rich egg dish.
Here most of the fat is eliminated, but not the flavor.

1 egg

5 egg whites

2 tablespoons grated Parmesan cheese

1 tablespoon chopped fresh parsley

1 teaspoon chopped fresh basil, or ¼ teaspoon dried

⅛ teaspoon freshly ground black pepper

   Salt

   Olive oil cooking spray

1 cup diced zucchini

½ cup diced mushrooms

¼ cup sliced scallions, white and tender green parts

1 clove of garlic, minced

½ cup grated skim-milk mozzarella

1. Preheat the oven to 350°F. Coat a 1-quart baking dish with nonstick cooking spray.

2. In a small mixing bowl, beat the whole egg and the egg whites until blended. Beat in the Parmesan cheese, parsley, basil, black pepper, and salt to taste.

3. Coat a large nonstick skillet with olive oil cooking spray and heat over medium-high heat. Add the zucchini, mushrooms, scallions, and garlic. Sauté until the mushrooms have given up their juice, 5 to 8 minutes.

4. Remove the skillet from the heat and pour in the eggs. Transfer the mixture to the baking dish.

5. Bake, uncovered, for about 10 minutes, until the eggs are set.

6. Sprinkle the mozzarella on top. Bake for about 5 minutes, until the cheese is melted.

7. Slice the frittata into wedges or squares and serve hot.

Serves 3

Zucchini Strata

Stratas are great for brunch. They consist of layers of bread and vegetables (and sometimes meat) held together with eggs and cheese. Strata are much like frittatas, although frittatas often contain potatoes rather than bread.

4 slices cracked wheat bread

2 cups sliced zucchini

8 ounces sharp Cheddar cheese, grated

2 tablespoons butter, melted

1½ cups milk

3 eggs

¼ cup minced onion

½ teaspoon salt

½ teaspoon dry mustard

Cayenne pepper

1. Butter a 9-inch baking dish. Line the dish with the bread.

2. Bring a large pot of salted water to a boil. Add the zucchini to the boiling water and boil for 3 to 5 minutes, until tender. Drain, plunge the zucchini into cold water to stop the cooking, and drain again. Pat dry.

3. Combine the zucchini, cheese, and butter in a large mixing bowl. Toss to mix. Layer the zucchini mixture on top of the bread.

4. In a medium-sized mixing bowl, beat together the milk, eggs, onion, salt, dry mustard, and cayenne to taste. Pour over the casserole.

5. Refrigerate the strata for at least 1 hour, up to overnight.

6. Preheat the oven to 350°F.

7. Bake the strata for 40 to 50 minutes, until it is puffed, set, and browned.

8. Let the strata sit for about 5 minutes before serving.

Serves 4

zucchini soufflé

"Delicate" is the best way to describe this soufflé. The flavor is quite subtle, allowing the mildly herbal flavor of zucchini to express itself, and the green slices of zucchini are lovely against the white background of the soufflé.

4 medium-sized zucchini, very thinly sliced

Salt

2 tablespoons butter

2 tablespoons unbleached all-purpose flour

1 cup milk

1 cup grated Gruyère cheese

4 egg yolks, beaten

2 teaspoons fresh lemon juice

8 egg whites

1. Combine the zucchini and salt in a colander. Toss to mix and set aside to drain for 30 minutes. Transfer to a clean kitchen towel and wring dry.

2. Preheat the oven to 350°F. Butter and flour a 2-quart soufflé dish or four 1½- or 2-cup ramekins.

3. Melt the butter in a small saucepan over medium heat. Whisk in the flour to make a smooth paste. Add the milk and bring to a boil, stirring until the sauce thickens.

4. In a large mixing bowl, combine the zucchini, white sauce, cheese, egg yolks, and lemon juice. Mix well.

5. In another bowl, beat the egg whites until stiff. Gently fold the egg whites into the zucchini mixture. Pour the soufflé mixture into the prepared soufflé dish or ramekins. Place the dish(es) in a larger pan and place in oven. Fill the larger pan with water until it reaches halfway up the sides of the soufflé dish(es).

6. Bake for 15 to 45 minutes, depending on the size of the soufflé dish(es). The soufflé is done when the top is golden brown and puffed and a skewer inserted in the center reveals that the soufflé is dry, not wet.

7. Serve immediately.

Serves 4

Soufflé Tips

The French verb *souffler* means "to blow," and the thought of attempting a soufflé is enough to blow the mind of some cooks. This is unfortunate, for a delicious soufflé is not that difficult to prepare. Granted, it has some pitfalls, but this is true with many dishes.

A good recipe, steady heat, and a well-prepared soufflé dish are the only requirements. The soufflé dish should be well greased and floured and of an appropriate size. The height of a soufflé dish may be extended by encircling it with a strip of waxed paper. A long double thickness of the paper tied around the dish so that it extends 2 inches above the rim will give your soufflé the chance to puff up or "blow up" beautifully without fear that it will overflow the limits of the dish.

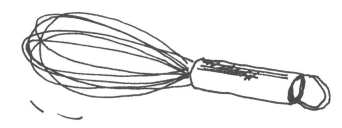

Corn and Summer Squash Soufflé

The color of sunshine predominates in this summery combination.

3 medium-sized yellow summer squash, grated

2¼ teaspoons salt

6 tablespoons butter

3 scallions, white and tender green parts, chopped

Kernels from 2 ears fresh corn

6 tablespoons unbleached all-purpose flour

1¼ cups milk

¼ teaspoon freshly ground black pepper

6 eggs, separated

½ cup grated Swiss cheese

1. Combine the squash and 1 teaspoon of the salt in a colander. Toss to mix and set aside to drain for 30 minutes.

2. Preheat the oven to 350°F and butter and flour a 2-quart soufflé dish.

3. Squeeze the squash to remove any excess moisture. Melt 1 tablespoon of the butter in a large skillet over medium heat. Add the squash and sauté until tender, about 5 minutes. Stir in the scallions and corn.

4. In a small saucepan over medium heat, melt the remaining 5 tablespoons butter. Whisk in the flour to form a smooth paste. Gradually add the milk. Cook until the mixture thickens, about 5 minutes. Season with the remaining 1¼ teaspoons salt and the pepper.

5. Beat the egg yolks in a large mixing bowl. Gradually add the white sauce, stirring constantly to incorporate. Mix in the cheese and vegetables.

6. Beat the egg whites until stiff. Gradually mix in the yolk mixture. Pour into the prepared soufflé dish.

7. Bake for about 55 minutes, until the top is puffed and golden. A skewer inserted in the center should reveal that the soufflé is dry, not wet.

8. Serve immediately.

Serves 6

Zucchini Pancakes

According to some, a pancake is the vehicle for consumption of butter and maple syrup. The zucchini in these pancakes will not interfere with that pleasure. Surprise your guests at brunch with these. Sunday mornings in August will never be the same.

2 medium-sized zucchini, grated

½ teaspoon salt

2 eggs, lightly beaten

1½ cups milk, or more as needed

2 tablespoons canola oil

2 cups pancake mix

1–2 teaspoons butter

Maple syrup, for serving (optional)

1. Combine the zucchini and salt in a colander. Toss to mix and set aside to drain for 30 minutes.

2. In a medium-sized mixing bowl, combine the eggs, milk, and oil. Beat well. Stir in the pancake mix and set aside to rest for 30 minutes.

3. Squeeze the zucchini to eliminate any excess moisture. Fold the zucchini into the pancake mixture. If necessary, add a little more milk to thin the batter.

4. Preheat a griddle or large skillet over medium-low heat. Preheat the oven to 200°F.

5. On the griddle, melt a teaspoon or two of butter. When the foam subsides, ladle the batter onto the griddle. Adjust the heat as needed so that the pancakes brown on the bottoms in 2 to 4 minutes. Flip the cakes and cook on the second side for 1 to 2 minutes. Place on an ovenproof plate and keep warm in the oven while you use the remaining batter to make more pancakes. Continue until all the batter is used.

6. Serve hot with maple syrup, if using.

Serves 4–6

VARIATION: To make savory zucchini pancakes, add ¼ cup freshly grated Parmesan cheese to the batter and proceed as above.

Potato-Carrot-Zucchini Pancakes

It is debatable whether these savory pancakes are best served as
a light main course or a hearty side dish. They get my vote as
a light vegetarian main dish, served with a salad.

1 **medium-sized zucchini,
   grated**

2 **eggs, lightly beaten**

2 **large potatoes, grated (peel-
   ing is optional)**

1 **large carrot, grated**

1 **onion, finely chopped**

¼ **cup oat bran flour or
   unbleached all-purpose flour**

1 **teaspoon salt**

1 **teaspoon chopped fresh basil,
   or ¼ teaspoon dried**

⅓ **teaspoon freshly ground black
   pepper**

   Canola oil

1. Preheat the oven to 250°F.

2. Squeeze excess water from the zucchini. In a large mixing
bowl, combine with the eggs, potatoes, carrot, onion, flour,
salt, basil, and pepper. Mix well.

3. In a large skillet, pour in the oil to a depth of ⅛ inch. Heat over
medium heat. When the oil is hot, drop the batter into it with a
large spoon to form several pancakes; slightly flatten each cake
with the back of the spoon. Cook until brown on both sides,
turning once, about 5 minutes per side.

4. Remove the cakes from the frying pan and keep warm on a
towel-lined baking sheet in the oven. Continue to make the
pancakes until all the batter is used.

5. Serve hot.

Serves 6–8

Risotto with Butternut Squash

There is no meat in this risotto, but it is best when made with chicken broth. To make an all-vegetarian version, substitute water. The sweet flavor of the butternut is outstanding in risotto — for me, it redefines comfort food.

½ cup white wine

3½ cups chicken broth or water

2 tablespoons extra virgin olive oil

4 shallots, finely diced

2 cloves of garlic, minced

1 tablespoon chopped fresh sage, or 1 teaspoon dried

1 cup uncooked arborio rice

1 teaspoon salt, or more

½ small (about 1 pound) butternut squash, peeled and diced

⅓ cup freshly grated Parmigiano-Reggiano cheese

Freshly ground black pepper

1. In a medium-sized saucepan, heat the wine and broth to a simmer.

2. Heat the oil in a large nonstick skillet over medium heat. Add the shallots, garlic, and sage. Sauté until the shallots appear transparent, 3 to 5 minutes. Add the rice and salt and toss to coat with the oil. Sauté for 3 to 5 minutes, until the rice appears toasted. Stir in the squash.

3. Add ½ cup of the simmering broth mixture to the rice. Reduce the heat to medium. Stir until the liquid is mostly absorbed. While cooking, continue to add broth, ½ cup at a time; stir frequently as the liquid is absorbed. It will take 18 to 35 minutes for all of the liquid to be absorbed and the rice and squash to become tender.

4. Stir in the Parmesan. Season to taste with pepper and additional salt, if needed.

5. Serve hot.

Serves 2–4

Caramelized Onion and Butternut Tart

Onions cooked very slowly develop an irresistible sweetness and flavor.
In this tart, the rosemary-scented onions form a flavor bridge between
the sweet winter squash and the tangy goat cheese.

3 tablespoons butter

6 onions, thinly sliced

Salt

½ cup white wine or water (optional)

1 teaspoon chopped fresh rosemary

Freshly ground black pepper

1 medium-sized butternut squash, peeled, seeded, and diced into ½-inch cubes

Pastry for two 9- or 10-inch piecrusts, unbaked

1 pound soft mild goat cheese

1. Melt the butter in a large skillet over low heat. Add the onions and sprinkle with 1 teaspoon salt. Cook very slowly, stirring occasionally, until the onions are golden brown and sweet, about 1 to 1¼ hours. If the mixture becomes dry and the onions start to stick, add wine as needed. Season to taste with the rosemary, salt, and pepper. (This step can be done up to 3 days in advance. Store in the refrigerator and bring to room temperature before continuing.)

2. Fill a pan with 2 inches of water. Bring to a boil. Steam the squash over the boiling water for 12 to 15 minutes, until easily pierced with a fork. Remove from the heat and set aside.

3. Preheat the oven to 375°F. Line two baking sheets with foil.

4. Place one piece of the pie pastry on each baking sheet. If you are using store-bought pastry, unfold it and pinch together any tears.

5. Spread half of the goat cheese over each pastry, leaving a 2-inch border around the edges. Spoon the onions over the goat cheese. Sprinkle the squash on top of the onions. Fold up the dough to partially cover the filling; crimp to seal the edges.

6. Bake for about 25 minutes, or until golden.

7. Cut into wedges and serve warm or at room temperature.

Serves 6

Delicata, Roquefort, and Leek Pizza

The interplay of flavors among the sweet squash, the earthy Roquefort, and the delicately oniony leeks is surprisingly harmonious.

1 recipe Basic Pizza Dough (page 81)

2 medium-sized delicata squash

Olive oil

2 leeks

Salt and freshly ground black pepper

6 ounces Roquefort cheese

A Few Pizza Tricks

Pizza stones are best for producing great pizza. If you don't have a stone, you can still make great pizza at home by baking the pizza on the bottom rack, where the heat is most intense. Preheat the oven to 500°F, allowing a little more time than normal. Commercial pizza ovens are set at around 800°F.

1. Prepare the pizza dough and set it aside in a warm, draft-free place to rise until doubled in bulk, about 1 hour.

2. Meanwhile, preheat the oven to 325°F. Lightly oil a baking sheet.

3. Slice the squash in half lengthwise. Remove the seeds and fibers and discard. Cut into ½-inch crescent-shaped slices. Combine in a bowl with 1 tablespoon olive oil. Toss to coat. Arrange on the baking sheet.

4. Roast the squash, turning once, for about 15 minutes, until the squash is tender and lightly browned.

5. Heat 3 tablespoons of oil in a medium-sized skillet over medium-high heat. Add the leeks and sauté until tender, about 5 minutes. Season to taste with salt and pepper. Remove from the heat.

6. Increase the oven temperature to 500°F. Place an oven rack on the lowest shelf.

7. Divide the dough into two balls. Lightly oil two 10-inch or 12-inch round pizza pans or two 12-inch by 15-inch baking sheets. Assemble and bake the pizzas one at a time. Stretch one ball of dough to fit a pan. Brush the dough with olive oil. Scatter half the leeks over the crust. Arrange half of the squash over the leeks in concentric circles. Crumble half of the Roquefort over all.

8. Bake the pizza for 10 to 12 minutes on the bottom oven rack, until the crust is golden. Meanwhile, assemble the second pizza. Bake the second pizza when the first pizza is done.

9. Serve both pizzas warm.

Serves 6

Farming in Vermont's Banana Belt

CECILIA ELWERT-BISSELL knows her squash. When she says that delicata and sweet dumplings are her favorite squash because there is no waste, she is speaking with the bred-in-the-bone practicality of a farmer.

"Delicata and sweet dumplings are standard now, but even five years ago they were exotic. Now you have to grow them, even though people are still finding out that you can eat the skin. Chefs particularly like them because they look pretty on a plate."

Since 1981, Cecilia Elwert-Bissell with her husband, Hank Bissell, have farmed 150 acres on Lewis Creek in Starksboro, Vermont. Their farm is located in what is known as "the banana belt" of Vermont. Because of the moderating influence of nearby Lake Champlain, the snows leave earlier and the frosts come later than in the rest of the state.

Lewis Creek Farm is a typical diversified New England family farm. The farm has about 30 acres in vegetables and another 50 acres in cover crops. They raise lambs for meat and chickens for eggs. The farm products are sold through their farm stand, at the Burlington Farmers' Market, to area stores and restaurants, and to a few statewide distributors. Their growing season ends around Thanksgiving. Ten to 15 full-time employees keep the farm running smoothly. Recently they have relied on seasonal Jamaican farm workers to help with the work load.

Summer squash, Cecilia Elwert-Bissell announces, "is a boring crop." She explains: "We used to do two plantings but we don't bother anymore. And we used to mulch with black plastic to get a jump on the growing season, but there's too many environmental problems with the plastic. And I think people have enough of zucchini after a while. Though we did find ourselves in a situation where one of our regular customers was in dire need of summer squash and our plants were done. Fortunately, one of our farm workers, who lives way up in the hills, had a bumper crop in his home garden. So he supplied the squash."

During the summer growing season, zucchini and yellow summer squash are harvested daily, when they are 7 to 8 inches long. Lewis Creek Farm raises about 3 tons of summer squash and 6 tons of winter squash every year. According to Hank Bissell, he can count on harvesting about 20 tons to the acre for most vegetables, including carrots, cabbage, and winter squash. Summer squashes yield about 10 tons per acre.

"I can't get into selling squash blossoms either," says Cecilia. "There's all that labor in harvesting. And you have to reprogram how you time your crops. Besides, I just have a philosophical problem with growing vegetables just for the flowers. Sometimes things get too precious. Distributors are asking for flowers, for microvegetables." There is clear disapproval in her voice.

Her tone warms up, though, as we move to the topic of winter squash. Apparently, winter squash aren't boring. "For one thing, you never know what kind of crosses you are going to get. Of course, you can't sell the weird hybrids, but they make good decorations."

On the subject of decoration, Cecilia has one regret. Each year she intends to carve the name of the farm into a few of the zucchini and winter squash, and every year she gets swamped with work and forgets. She assures me that the skins will heal over, leaving a scar that can be read. "Next year," she vows.

Hank has no such regrets. He somehow always finds the time for his favorite decorations. One year, the centerpiece of their Thanksgiving table was a ship carved out of a blue Hubbard squash, complete with sails and riggings. Another year, Hank carved a huge blue Hubbard so that the sides of the squash rested on his shoulders; his head fit inside, with holes for the eyes and mouth. That's how he greeted the children who came to the door on Halloween.

Trick or treat, anyone?

Winter Squash Soufflé

You can prepare the winter squash by baking, boiling, or steaming it. Pumpkin can be substituted for winter squash. Because this soufflé has only a hint of sweetness, it can be served as a main dish; it is especially good for brunch. You can also increase the amount of sugar to 1 cup, omit the pepper, and prepare this dish as a dessert soufflé.

4 **cups cooked and mashed winter squash or canned pumpkin purée**

5 **eggs, separated**

4 **tablespoons butter**

3 **tablespoons brown sugar**

½ **teaspoon salt**

1 **tablespoon grated orange or lemon zest**

¼ **teaspoon ground nutmeg**
  Freshly ground black pepper

1. Preheat the oven to 350°F. Butter and flour a 6-cup soufflé dish.

2. In a large mixing bowl, combine the squash with the egg yolks, butter, sugar, salt, orange zest, nutmeg, and pepper to taste. Beat well to combine.

3. In another bowl, beat the egg whites until stiff. Fold into the squash mixture. Transfer to the prepared soufflé dish.

4. Bake for about 40 minutes, until the top is golden brown. A skewer inserted in the center should reveal that the soufflé is dry, not wet.

5. Serve immediately.

Serves 6

4. Seafood, Chicken & Meat Main Dishes

This chapter offers a selection of main dishes that include squash combined with seafood, chicken, or meat. For the most part, they are quick-to-make one-dish meals. The squash isn't disguised, but neither does it form the centerpiece of the meal. The exception to this is the pumpkin in which stew is served (see page 133). The stew isn't dominated by the flavor of the pumpkin, but the pumpkin does hold center stage.

Pasta with Shrimp, Summer Squash, and Tomatoes

Zucchini and summer squash prove once again how amicably they can be combined with more assertive flavors — in this case, a whiff of smoke from the bacon, a glimmer of sea from the shrimp, a blessing of sunshine from the basil, and a lick of fruit from the wine. Enjoy the rest of the bottle of wine with the dinner, and make a toast to summer.

2 medium-sized yellow summer squash, quartered and sliced

2 medium-sized zucchini, quartered and sliced

2 teaspoons salt

3 thick-cut strips (about 1½ ounces) smoked bacon, diced

2 cloves of garlic, minced

2 shallots, minced

Salt and freshly ground black pepper

3 large ripe tomatoes, seeded and diced

½ cup dry white wine

1¼ pounds shrimp, peeled and deveined

¼ cup chopped fresh basil

¼ cup chopped fresh parsley

1 pound linguine

1. Combine the summer squash, zucchini, and salt in a colander. Toss to mix and set aside to drain for 30 minutes. Transfer to a clean dish towel and wring dry.

2. Fill a large pot with salted water for the pasta. Bring to a boil.

3. In a large skillet over medium heat, fry the bacon until crisp, 8 to 10 minutes. Remove the bacon with a slotted spoon and drain on paper towels. Set aside.

4. Add the garlic and shallots to the bacon fat remaining in the skillet. Sauté for 1 minute. Increase the heat to medium-high, add the zucchini and summer squash, and season with pepper. Continue to sauté until the squash begin to soften, 3 to 4 minutes. Stir in the tomatoes and wine. Simmer for 5 minutes. Add the shrimp and continue to simmer until the shrimp are pink and cooked through, about 5 minutes. Remove from the heat and stir in the basil and parsley.

5. Cook the pasta in the boiling water until just al dente. Drain briefly.

6. Transfer the pasta to a large serving bowl. Add the shrimp mixture and toss together until the pasta is well coated with the sauce. Serve immediately.

Serves 5–6

Seafood Stew with Summer Vegetables

For many, summer means a trip to the seacoast and time in the garden. Here's a dish to celebrate both. Nothing more than a loaf or two of crusty French bread, a green salad, and a crisp white wine is needed to accompany the stew.

4 tablespoons extra virgin olive oil

4 cloves of garlic, minced

2 leeks, sliced

2 shallots, minced

4 cups chicken or fish broth

3 tomatoes, seeded and chopped

  2-inch piece orange zest

1 teaspoon fennel seeds

24 hard-shell clams or mussels

1 pound white fish, such as halibut, cod, snapper, or sea bass, cut into chunks

1½ pounds shrimp, peeled and deveined

1 medium-sized yellow squash, quartered and sliced

1 medium-sized zucchini, quartered and sliced

¼ cup pesto (page 27), or ⅓ cup chopped fresh basil

  Salt and freshly ground black pepper

1. In a large saucepan or Dutch oven, heat the oil over medium-high heat. Add the garlic, leeks, and shallots. Sauté until tender crisp, 3 to 5 minutes.

2. Add the broth, tomatoes, orange zest, and fennel seeds. Bring to a boil. Reduce the heat and simmer for 10 minutes.

3. Add the clams to the broth, cover, and simmer for 5 minutes. Add the fish and simmer for 5 minutes. Add the shrimp, yellow squash, and zucchini. Cover and cook until the shrimp are cooked through, about 5 minutes.

4. Stir in the pesto. Taste and adjust the seasoning. Discard any clams that have not opened and the orange zest. Serve at once.

Serves 6–8

Baked Sole with Zucchini

Fish fillets are an ideal convenience food when you want to get supper on the table quickly. By calling for canned cream of mushroom soup and baking the vegetables with the fish, this 1950s-style recipe was designed to be easy and delicious. It still is. Serve with rice or boiled new potatoes.

1¼–1½ pounds fillets of sole or other thin white-fleshed fish

1 tablespoon fresh lemon juice

Salt

1 tablespoon butter

2 medium-sized zucchini, sliced ¼-inch thick

½ cup diced green bell pepper

½ cup diced onion

1 can (10¾ ounces) condensed cream of mushroom soup

2 tablespoons white wine

1 teaspoon chopped fresh dill

1 tablespoon chopped fresh parsley

1. Preheat the oven to 350°F. Lightly butter a shallow baking dish.

2. Sprinkle the fish with the lemon juice and salt. Slice the fillets into serving-size portions and roll up. Place in the baking dish seam-side down.

3. In a large saucepan over medium heat, melt the butter. Add the zucchini, green pepper, and onion. Sauté until tender crisp, 3 to 5 minutes. Stir in the soup, wine, dill, and parsley. Heat just to boiling. Pour the sauce over the fish.

4. Bake the fish for 15 to 20 minutes, until the fish just flakes. Do not overcook.

5. Serve hot.

Serves 4

Chicken and Shrimp Gumbo

The word *gumbo* is said to derive from the Bantu word for the okra that is commonly found in this stew. So it may seem sacrilegious to substitute summer squash for the okra. But the substitution works just fine, especially for northern gardeners whose growing season is too short for okra.

1 cup unbleached all-purpose flour

2 teaspoons dried thyme

1½ teaspoons salt, plus more to taste

1 teaspoon black pepper, plus more to taste

1 teaspoon cayenne pepper, plus more to taste

1 pound skinless bone-in chicken thighs

3 tablespoons plus ½ cup canola oil

1 green bell pepper, diced

1 onion, diced

1 cup diced celery

4 cloves of garlic, minced

1. In a medium-sized bowl, mix together ½ cup of the flour, the dried thyme, salt, black pepper, and cayenne. Add the chicken and toss until the chicken is well coated.

2. Heat the 3 tablespoons oil in a large Dutch oven over medium heat. Add the chicken pieces and brown on all sides, turning as needed, for 5 to 10 minutes. Remove the chicken and set aside.

3. Reduce the heat to medium-low and add the remaining ½ cup oil to the Dutch oven. Whisk in the remaining ½ cup flour to make a roux. Cook, whisking constantly, until the roux turns a reddish brown, 10 to 20 minutes. Once the roux begins to turn color, it goes quickly from light brown to dark brown, so watch carefully and do not let it burn. (If the roux becomes scorched, discard it and make another batch.) Remove the pan from the heat and stir in the bell pepper, onion, celery, and garlic.

- 5 cups chicken broth
- 2 bay leaves
- 2 tablespoons chopped fresh thyme
- 1 tablespoon fresh parsley
- 12 ounces andouille or chorizo sausage, thinly sliced
- 1 pound shrimp, peeled and deveined
- 1 medium-sized yellow summer squash, quartered and sliced
- 1 medium-sized zucchini, quartered and sliced
- Hot pepper sauce
- 1 tablespoon filé powder
- Hot cooked rice

4. Return the pot to high heat. Whisk in the broth and bring to a boil, still whisking. Reduce the heat and return the chicken to the pot. Add the bay leaves, fresh thyme, and parsley. Simmer until the chicken is cooked through, about 45 minutes. Remove the chicken from the pot. Discard the bones and shred the meat. Add the andouille to the pot. Simmer for 10 minutes.

5. Return the chicken to the pot, along with the shrimp, summer squash, and zucchini. Add additional salt, pepper, and cayenne to taste. Simmer until the shrimp is cooked through, about 10 minutes.

6. Remove from heat. Stir in the filé powder and serve over hot cooked rice.

Serves 8

Filé and Gumbo

Legend has it that it was the Choctaw Indians from the Louisiana bayou country who first used filé.

Today, filé powder is available in the spice or gourmet section of many large supermarkets and by mail order.

The seasoning is made from the ground, dried leaves of the sassafras tree and is a key part of Creole cooking, particularly gumbos. Filé must be stirred into a dish after it's removed from the heat, because cooking filé makes it tough and stringy.

Grilled Marinated Chicken and Summer Squash

The height of zucchini season is also the height of grilling season. Serve this flame-kissed combination in pita pockets or over rice or couscous.

MARINADE
- 3 cloves of garlic, minced
- ¼ cup chopped fresh parsley
- 1 teaspoon sugar
- ½ teaspoon Dijon mustard
- ½ teaspoon minced lemon zest
  Juice of 1 lemon
- ¼ cup dry white wine
- ½ cup extra virgin olive oil
  Salt and freshly ground black pepper

CHICKEN AND VEGETABLES
- 1 pound boneless skinless chicken breasts or thighs, cut into 2-inch by ½-inch strips
- 2 medium-sized zucchini or summer squash, sliced
- 2 onions, halved and sliced
- 1 red bell pepper, julienned

1. To make the marinade, in a small nonreactive bowl, combine the garlic, parsley, sugar, mustard, lemon zest, lemon juice, and wine. Whisk in the oil and season to taste with salt and pepper.

2. Place the chicken in a medium-sized bowl and add about half of the marinade. Toss to coat. Place the onions, red pepper, and zucchini in another bowl. Add the remaining marinade and toss to coat. Allow both to marinate at room temperature while you prepare the grill.

3. Prepare a medium-hot fire in a charcoal or gas grill with a vegetable grilling rack in place.

4. Grill the chicken until cooked through and grill-marked, turning occasionally, 5 to 10 minutes. Transfer the chicken to a serving bowl and keep warm.

5. Grill the vegetables in two batches to prevent them from steaming in a mound on the grill. Arrange half the zucchini, onions, and bell pepper on the grill rack in a single layer. Grill, turning occasionally until tender and grill-marked, 5 to 10 minutes. Repeat with the second batch.

6. Toss together the chicken and vegetables. Adjust the seasoning, adding more salt and pepper as needed. Serve at once.

NOTE: If you don't have a vegetable grill rack, you can grill the chicken pieces whole and the vegetables in large pieces (halves or quarters) and serve it straight off the grill, or slice in the kitchen before serving. Adjust the grilling times accordingly.

Serves 4

Chicken and Zucchini Provençale

Rich with the flavors of the Mediterranean, this chicken stew makes a fine one-dish meal. A Côtes de Provence is a good choice of wine; it can be used in the stew and for drinking with the meal.

1 whole chicken or 3½ pounds chicken parts

½ cup unbleached all-purpose flour

Salt and freshly ground black pepper

Pinch of dried thyme

3 tablespoons extra virgin olive oil

1 green bell pepper, halved and sliced

1 onion, halved and thinly sliced

4 ounces mushrooms, sliced

2 cups seeded and diced tomatoes (canned or fresh)

½ cup red wine or chicken stock

2 cloves of garlic, minced

1 tablespoon fresh thyme leaves

3-inch strip orange zest

2 bay leaves

1 medium-sized zucchini, quartered lengthwise and sliced

Chopped fresh parsley, to serve

1. Cut the breast of the chicken into quarters and the thighs into halves. Remove any fat, rinse, and pat dry. Place the flour in a shallow bowl. Season with salt and pepper and thyme. Dredge the chicken in the flour, shaking off any excess.

2. Heat the oil in a Dutch oven over medium-high heat. Add a single layer of the chicken and brown, turning as needed, for about 10 minutes per batch. Adjust the temperature as needed to allow the chicken to brown but not scorch. (Make sure the chicken is well browned, or the dish will look anemic.) Remove the browned chicken to a bowl or plate and keep warm. Repeat until all of the chicken pieces are browned.

3. In the oil remaining in the Dutch oven, sauté the bell pepper, onion, and mushrooms, over medium-high heat, until the mushrooms have given up their juice, about 5 minutes.

4. Return the chicken to the Dutch oven. Add the tomatoes, wine, garlic, fresh thyme, orange zest, and bay leaves, submerging the chicken in the liquid.

5. Cover and simmer until the chicken is cooked through, about 45 minutes, turning the chicken every 15 minutes or so.

6. Remove the chicken from the sauce with a slotted spoon; set aside. Add the zucchini. Bring to a boil. Boil until the sauce is thickened and reduced and the zucchini is tender, about 5 minutes.

7. Remove the orange zest and bay leaves. Return the chicken to the pan. Taste; adjust the seasonings. Serve hot; garnish with parsley.

Serves 4–6

Tex-Mex Chicken Skillet Supper

The *chipotles en adobo* — smoked-dried jalapeños in a vinegar sauce — add smoke
and heat to give this dish its character. A squirt of fresh lime juice applied
by each diner at the table brings all the flavors together;
it's a touch of magic that should not be omitted.

2 small yellow summer squash, halved and sliced

2 small zucchini, halved and sliced

Salt

2 tablespoons extra virgin olive oil

1 chipotle en adobo, minced (optional)

1 tablespoon chili powder

2 teaspoons ground cumin

1 pound skinless, boneless chicken breasts, cut into 2-inch-long strips

Salt and freshly ground black pepper

2 fresh poblano chiles or 1 green bell pepper, julienned

2 cloves of garlic, minced

1. If you have the time (see page 147), combine the summer squash and zucchini and 2 teaspoons salt in a colander. Toss to mix and set aside to drain for 30 minutes. Transfer the squash and zucchini to a clean dish towel and wring dry.

2. Heat 1 tablespoon of the oil in a large skillet over medium-high heat. Add the chipotle, if using, chili powder, cumin, and chicken. Sauté until the chicken is coated with spices and cooked through, about 8 minutes. Season to taste with salt and pepper. Remove the chicken from the skillet with a slotted spoon, set aside, and keep warm.

3. Return the skillet to the stove, add 1 tablespoon of the oil, and heat over medium-high heat. Add the poblanos, summer squash, zucchini, and garlic. Sauté until crisp tender, 3 to 5 minutes. Season to taste with salt and pepper.

4 scallions, white and tender green parts only, sliced

2 ripe tomatoes, seeded and diced

¼ cup chopped fresh cilantro

Warmed flour or corn tortillas or hot cooked rice, to serve

Sour cream, to serve

2–3 limes, cut into wedges, to serve

4. Return the chicken to the skillet. Add the scallions, tomatoes, and cilantro. Cook until the tomatoes are heated through, about 5 minutes. Taste and adjust the seasonings.

5. Serve hot. Pass the warm tortillas, sour cream, and lime at the table. Or spoon the rice onto a serving platter or individual plates. Spoon the chicken on top of the rice. Pass the sour cream and lime at the table.

Serves 4–6

About Chiles

Two chiles make this Tex-Mex dish sing with flavor. Chipotles en adobo (pronounced chih-POHT-lays en ah-DOH-boh) is a magical ingredient in many Mexican and Tex-Mex dishes. The magic comes from the smoke flavor — chipotles are smoke-dried jalapeños. You can find them in dried form, or conveniently rehydrated and puréed in adobo, which is a tomato-vinegar sauce. Find chipotles en adobo wherever Mexican foods are sold.

Most supermarkets have a good selection of fresh chiles. Poblanos are a thick-walled chile pepper with mild, almost fruity flavor. If you can't find poblanos, you can always substitute a green bell pepper or a jalapeño, depending on whether you want less or more heat.

Heirloom Seeds

TOM STEARNS farms in Holland, Vermont, which is right on the Canadian border in an area that is wide open and feels like the top of the world, "where winters are long and summers are short" (zone 3 in agricultural parlance). The vegetables that thrive there will grow in just about any adverse environment in the Northeast, which is a good thing. Stearns is a seed grower.

When it started, High Mowing Organic Seed Farm was the only seed company in the Northeast that grew all its own seeds. Today, Stearns contracts out some of the seed growing, but all the seeds are still grown organically, and about two thirds are grown according to the principles of biodynamic growing. Stearns's specialty is growing heirloom vegetables for their seeds, which he harvests and sells through the mail. For years, his handwritten catalog was a stark contrast to the colorful and glossy pages of most seed catalogs, and the descriptions of each plant were terse. Lately, Stearns has gotten his catalog information into a computer, so the catalog is no longer handwritten, but it still has a spare and lean look to it.

Stearns likes to find the oldest person in town to talk with about gardening, which is how he learned about Calais Flint Corn, a corn meant for grinding into cornmeal that was developed in Calais, Vermont. It's also where he located Aunt Mary's Paste Tomato, a sweet, meaty tomato good for cooking and preserving. True Red Cranberry Pole Bean is a bean he found in Lyndonville that was brought to Vermont by Shaker farmers from Pennsylvania.

Stearns explains: "Heirloom vegetables are older vegetable varieties that have been passed down through families. They haven't received a great deal of modern breeding work. So the vegetables tend to have more variety in terms of the size of the fruit and when they all mature. They also retain their genetic diversity, so they have great tolerance to disease and insect pests and to drought or shade or damp.

"Also, modern breeders are looking for vegetables that are of uniform size and all ripen at the same time, so the large-scale farmers can machine-harvest them. For a home gardener, that's exactly what you don't want! Who wants to have a bushel of beans to deal with for 1 week, then no beans for the rest of the summer? One of my favorite snap beans is Sequoia Purple Podded. It's a high-yielding flat bean with incredible flavor. It will produce over a 1½-month period. If you make two plantings 2 to 3 weeks apart, you can have fresh beans all summer!"

When asked about his 50 different tomato varieties, Stearns almost trips over his words: "I have black ones, green ones, striped, purple, orange, yellow, red, pink. Some are as small as pencil erasers and some average about 2½ pounds each. My Peacevine cherry tomatoes are so sweet, they taste more like a peach than a typical tomato."

Stearns disciplines his garden with hand labor and lots of manure. He works on a small scale, half an acre, which yields millions of seeds. "If I could sell every seed I harvest," he quips, "I'd be a millionaire."

What drives Stearns, however, is not a longing for riches but a genuine desire to make a living off a farm that uses sound environmental practices. There is no black plastic for warming the soil at High Mowing Farm, no Reemay cloth covers for warding off frost. So when he plants melon, eggplant, or pepper, he looks for varieties that are suited to a cloudy, cool New England summer.

Recently, his offerings have included Long Pie Pumpkin, a very prolific and early pumpkin that looks like an overgrown zucchini. Its green skin turns brilliant orange in storage. According to Stearns, "Many old Mainers claim to have never seen a round pumpkin until they were grown up and left the farm." The Long Pie Pumpkin makes a very tasty pie.

Among the heirloom squash varieties Stearns offers is *Costata Romanesca* zucchini, an Italian variety that is light green with stripes and ridges running lengthwise. Many regard this variety as having "a flavor unsurpassed among zucchinis."

Thai-Style Coconut Curry with Chicken and Zucchini

To perk up jaded appetites, try this exotic curry with a coconut-milk base.
The stew is rather soupy, so serve it in pasta bowls on a bed of
white rice or Thai rice noodles.

2 tablespoons peanut or canola oil

3 tablespoons yellow Thai curry paste or 2 tablespoons curry powder

1 large onion, halved and thinly sliced

1¼ pounds boneless, skinless chicken breasts or thighs, cut into ¼-inch strips

2 cloves of garlic, minced

1 jalapeño, sliced (seeding is optional; the dish will be hotter with the seeds)

1 red bell pepper, julienned

1 teaspoon minced fresh ginger

Salt and freshly ground black pepper

3 small zucchini, quartered and sliced

1½ cups coconut milk

¼ cup chopped fresh cilantro

2 tablespoons fresh lime juice

Hot cooked rice or rice noodles

½ cup chopped roasted peanuts

1. In a Dutch oven or large saucepan, heat the oil over medium heat. Add the curry paste and onion. Sauté until the onion is translucent, about 5 minutes.

2. Add the chicken, garlic, jalapeño, bell pepper, and ginger. Sauté until the chicken is cooked through, about 5 minutes. Add salt and pepper to taste.

3. Stir in the zucchini and mix until combined with the spices. Stir in the coconut milk, cilantro, and lime juice. Bring to a simmer. Simmer until the zucchini is tender, about 10 minutes. Taste and add salt and pepper, if needed.

4. To serve, spoon a bed of rice or noodles into individual pasta bowls. Top with the chicken, vegetables, and sauce. Garnish with the peanuts.

Serves 4

Baked Barbecued Chicken with Zucchini

Barbecue sauce provides the smoke and flavor in this easily assembled dish.
Pop the casserole in the oven, then go and relax.

2 medium-sized zucchini, sliced

2 boneless, skinless chicken breasts, halved

Salt and freshly ground black pepper

1 cup barbecue sauce

¼ cup chopped onion

1 tablespoon dry sherry

1 teaspoon chopped fresh basil, or ½ teaspoon dried

1 teaspoon chopped fresh oregano, or ½ teaspoon dried

1. Preheat the oven to 375°F. Grease a 1½-quart baking dish.

2. Layer the zucchini in the baking dish. Arrange the chicken over the zucchini. Sprinkle with salt and pepper. In a small bowl, combine the barbecue sauce, onion, sherry, basil, and oregano and mix together. Pour over the chicken. Cover the baking dish.

3. Bake for 1 hour, basting the chicken with the sauce every 15 minutes or so.

4. Serve hot.

Serves 4

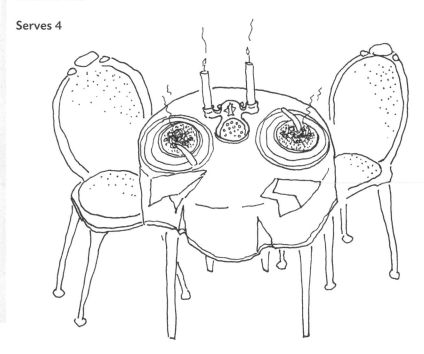

Chicken Pot Pie with Butternut Squash

Pot pies are a favorite in my household, and I like to vary them with the seasons. A spring version may feature snow peas or fresh peas in lieu of the frozen vegetables, with chopped fresh scallions or chives replacing the leeks. The summer version will have fresh green beans and zucchini as the vegetables. A winter version, after the winter squash are just a memory, may have carrots or rutabagas in place of the butternut.

FILLING

- 3 medium-sized (1 pound) potatoes, peeled and diced
- 1 small (1 pound) butternut squash, peeled and diced
- Salt
- 6 tablespoons butter
- 2 leeks, halved and thinly sliced
- 6 tablespoons unbleached all-purpose flour
- 3 cups chicken or turkey broth
- 3–4 cups cooked shredded or chopped chicken or turkey, cut into bite-size pieces
- 1 cup frozen peas or French-cut green beans
- 2 teaspoons chopped fresh thyme, or 1 teaspoon dried
- Freshly ground black pepper

1. In a medium-sized saucepan, combine the potatoes and squash (you should have about 4 cups). Add just enough water to cover. Add about ½ teaspoon salt. Cover and bring to a boil. Boil just until tender, about 8 minutes. Drain.

2. Melt the butter in a large saucepan over medium heat. Add the leeks and sauté until tender crisp, about 5 minutes. Stir in the flour to make a paste. Stir in the broth and bring to a boil, stirring frequently.

3. Stir in the chicken, potatoes and squash, peas, and thyme. Add salt and black pepper to taste. Bring to a boil. Keep hot while you prepare the biscuits.

4. Preheat the oven to 450°F.

5. For the topping, combine the flour, baking powder, and salt in a large bowl or food processor. If you are using a bowl, cut in the butter with a pastry blender or two knives until the mixture resembles soft crumbs and stir in the milk to make a soft dough. If you are using a food processor, add the butter. Process until the mixture resembles soft crumbs. Pour in the milk with the motor running, and process just long enough to form a soft dough. Turn out the dough onto a lightly floured board and knead a few times. Lightly roll out or pat out to a thickness of 1 inch. Cut into 3-inch rounds.

BISCUIT TOPPING

3 cups unbleached all-purpose flour

2 tablespoons baking powder

1½ teaspoons salt

⅔ cup butter

    About 1 cup milk

6. Pour the hot chicken mixture into a 9- by 13-inch baking pan. Place the biscuit rounds on top.

7. Bake for 15 to 18 minutes, until the biscuits are golden and the chicken mixture is bubbling.

8. Serve hot.

NOTE: The chicken mixture must be hot when you place the biscuits on top. This prevents the bottom of the biscuits from becoming gummy.

Serves 6–8

The Best of Fall-Foliage Season

Fall-foliage season in Vermont is ushered in by church suppers featuring chicken pot pies. "Is it simply the favorite dish of tourists?" I asked one old-timer as I snooped around in a church kitchen, trying to catch the masters at their work. "Oh, no," she told me. "Fall is when you kill off the chickens that aren't worth feeding through the winter. We had chicken pot pie church suppers long before we had leaf peepers."

If you are traveling through Vermont in the fall and you want a good old-fashioned meal, then stop in at one of the church suppers (call ahead to see if reservations are required). But don't expect the pot pie to be loaded with vegetables like the recipe on this page. Most are seriously heavy with chicken and cream sauce. A few will have the occasional pea or carrot slice. Some will be served with a side of slaw or three-bean salad. Or they will pass a bowl of overcooked peas or green beans.

But don't get me wrong: I love church suppers. One goes to a church supper for the experience, the atmosphere, and the friendly chats with strangers. So what if my homemade version is better than most? It's nice to be served by someone else — and be excused from washing the dishes.

Spaghetti Squash with Chicken

Here, a chicken and bell pepper mixture that would taste fine on pasta tops spaghetti squash instead. My children called the dish "interesting" and asked for seconds. This is truly a feast of vegetables. Serve with Italian bread for sopping up the delicious sauce.

3 tablespoons extra virgin olive oil

1 pound boneless, skinless chicken breasts or thighs, cut into ½-inch cubes

1 green bell pepper, diced

1 red bell pepper, diced

1 onion, halved and slivered

Salt and freshly ground black pepper

2 cups seeded and diced fresh tomatoes

⅓ cup dry white wine

¼ cup chopped fresh basil

6 cloves of garlic, minced

1 large spaghetti squash, cooked

4 tablespoons butter, melted

Freshly grated Parmesan cheese

1. In a large skillet or heavy saucepan, heat the oil over medium-high heat. Add the chicken, bell pepper, and onion. Season with salt and pepper. Sauté until the chicken is cooked through, about 10 minutes.

2. Stir in the tomatoes, wine, basil, and half the garlic. Taste and adjust the seasonings. Bring to a boil. Reduce the heat and simmer while you prepare the squash.

3. Use a large fork or spoon to scrape out all of the spaghetti squash in long strands into a large shallow serving bowl. Discard the skin. Add the butter, remaining garlic, and salt and pepper to taste to the squash. Toss to mix.

4. To serve, toss the spaghetti squash with the chicken mixture. Taste and adjust the seasoning (the squash requires a lot of salt). Serve hot, passing the Parmesan at the table.

Serves 5–6

Cooking Tips

To cook spaghetti squash, pierce in several places, place in a large pot with water to cover, and boil until the squash begins to yield to pressure from the back of a wooden spoon, about 1 hour. Alternatively, cut in half, remove the seeds and fibers, and place in a baking dish, skin-side up. Add 1 inch of water and bake at 350°F until the skin begins to give, about 1 hour. To cook it in a microwave, puncture the squash, place on a paper towel, and microwave on high for 6 minutes. Turn the squash over and microwave for another 6 minutes, or until the skin is easily pierced with a fork.

Ground Beef and Zucchini Italian Casserole

This dish is nutritious and easy and makes good use of inexpensive ground beef.
It can be served over rice or stuffed into pita pockets.

2 tablespoons extra virgin olive oil

1 cup diced onions

1 green bell pepper, diced

2 cloves of garlic, minced

1 pound ground beef

2 cups tomatoes, peeled, seeded, and diced (fresh or canned)

2 cups thinly sliced zucchini

1 tablespoon chopped fresh basil, or 1 teaspoon dried

1 tablespoon chopped fresh oregano, or 1 teaspoon dried

Dash hot pepper sauce

Salt and freshly ground black pepper

1. Preheat the oven to 350°F.

2. In a large skillet, heat the olive oil over medium-high heat. Add the onion, bell pepper, and garlic. Sauté for 2 minutes. Stir in the ground beef. Continue to sauté until the beef is browned, about 8 minutes.

3. Stir in the tomatoes, zucchini, basil, oregano, and hot pepper sauce. Add salt and pepper to taste. Transfer the mixture to a 9- by 13-inch baking dish.

4. Cover and bake for 30 minutes.

5. Serve hot.

Serves 4

Beef and Zucchini Stovetop Casserole

Slow-cooking tenderizes the relatively tough cut of meat used in this dish.
Although the cooking time is about 2 hours, it leaves you free
to be elsewhere — in the garden, perhaps — while supper simmers.
The meat and sauce can be served over noodles.

2 tablespoons canola or olive oil

1½ pounds shoulder steak, cut into bite-size strips

1 onion, diced

8 ounces mushrooms, sliced

1 can (8 ounces) tomato sauce or purée

1 cup water

Salt and freshly ground black pepper

5 cups cubed zucchini

8 ounces Monterey Jack or Swiss cheese, sliced

1. Heat the oil in a large skillet or Dutch oven over medium-high heat. Add the beef in a single layer and brown well on both sides, about 10 minutes. You may have to do this in batches. As each batch is browned, remove it from the skillet with a slotted spoon. Keep warm.

2. Add the onion to the skillet and sauté until softened, about 3 minutes. Add the mushrooms and continue to sauté until they give up their juice, about 5 minutes.

3. Add the tomato sauce, water, and salt and pepper to taste. Simmer, uncovered, until the meat is tender, about 1½ hours.

4. Add the zucchini and continue to simmer for 15 minutes.

5. Add the cheese, cover, and simmer until the cheese is melted, about 5 minutes.

6. Serve hot.

Serves 6–8

Campground Beef Stew

Just the kind of stew the Girl Scouts were likely to make on their annual camping trip.
It's amazing how many different ways cream of mushroom soup can come in handy.
The stew is cooked and served in individual serving-sized packets of aluminum foil,
so there are no pots and no dinner dishes to clean afterward.

2 **pounds beef stew meat, cubed**

2 **medium-sized potatoes, peeled and cubed**

2 **medium-sized zucchini, sliced**

4 **carrots, sliced**

2 **small onions, sliced**

2 **cans (each 10¾ ounces) cream of mushroom soup**

Salt and freshly ground black pepper

1. Prepare a medium-hot fire, letting the coals burn down until they are covered with gray ash.

2. In a large bowl, combine the beef, potatoes, zucchini, carrots, onions, and cream of mushroom soup. Season to taste with salt and pepper.

3. Prepare six 18-inch squares of heavy-duty aluminum foil. Divide the stew into six equal portions. Spoon onto the foil squares. Join the four corners of each square and twist the top to seal.

4. Grill for 50 to 60 minutes. Do not allow the fire to flame at any point.

5. Serve hot, directly from the foil packages.

Serves 6

Beef Stew with Winter Squash

A hearty stew with potatoes, carrots, and winter squash is a dish to look forward to on a cold wintry night. Like all stews, this one tastes even better on the second day.

3 pounds beef stew meat, cubed

½ cup unbleached all-purpose flour

Salt and freshly ground black pepper

2 tablespoons canola oil

4 onions, sliced

2½ cups water

1 teaspoon chopped fresh basil, or ½ teaspoon dried

1 teaspoon chopped fresh thyme, or ½ teaspoon dried

3 medium-sized potatoes, peeled and cubed

2½ cups sliced carrots

2 cups cubed and peeled winter squash, such as butternut

1½ cups peas

½ can (3 ounces) tomato paste

1. In a medium-sized bowl, combine the beef, flour, and salt and pepper. Toss to coat.

2. Heat the oil in a large Dutch oven over medium-high heat. In batches, add the meat and brown well, about 5 minutes. As each batch is browned, remove to a bowl and keep warm. Sauté the onions until softened, 3 to 5 minutes.

3. Return all the browned meat to the Dutch oven and add the water, basil, and thyme. Reduce the heat and simmer for 50 minutes.

4. Add the potatoes, carrots, and squash. Cook for 30 minutes longer.

5. Add the peas and tomato paste. Cook for 10 minutes, until all the vegetables are tender.

6. Serve hot.

Serves 6

Stew in a Pumpkin

Serving dinner from a pumpkin shell is a festive touch that can easily become a fall tradition. Be sure to choose a well-shaped pumpkin that will sit level; save the funny-shaped ones for pie.

2 pounds beef stew meat, cubed

¼ cup unbleached all-purpose flour

Salt and freshly ground black pepper

2 tablespoons canola or olive oil

2 cloves of garlic, minced

1 large onion, sliced

2 cups beef broth

1 cup red wine

1 teaspoon chopped fresh thyme, or ½ teaspoon dried

1 bay leaf

1 well-shaped 5- to 6-pound pie pumpkin

Butter

1 can (15 ounces) chickpeas, rinsed and drained

1 cup seeded and chopped tomatoes

2 carrots, sliced

2 medium-sized potatoes, peeled and cubed

2 medium-sized zucchini, sliced

1. Combine the meat, flour, and salt and pepper in a medium-sized bowl. Toss to coat.

2. In a large skillet, heat the oil over medium-high heat. Add the meat in batches and brown well, about 5 minutes per batch. Remove the meat with a slotted spoon and keep warm in a bowl. After the meat is browned, sauté the garlic and onion until the onion is softened, 3 to 5 minutes. Return the meat to the skillet and stir in the broth, wine, thyme, and bay leaf. Reduce the heat and simmer until the meat is tender, about 1 hour.

3. While the stew simmers, prepare the pumpkin. Preheat the oven to 350°F.

4. Remove the top of the pumpkin and set aside. Scoop out the seeds and fibers and discard. Score the inside several times. Rub the insides with salt and pepper. Place the pumpkin upside down in a large shallow baking pan. Reserve the pumpkin lid. Add about ½ inch of water to the pan.

5. Bake for 1 hour, or until the flesh is tender.

6. Drain the water from the baking pan. Stand the pumpkin upright in the pan. Rub the inside surfaces with butter. Keep warm.

7. Add the chickpeas, tomatoes, carrots, potatoes, and zucchini to the stew. Simmer for 45 minutes.

8. To serve, spoon the stew into the warm pumpkin and replace the lid. Bring it to the table and serve out of the pumpkin, taking up some of the pumpkin flesh with each spoonful.

Serves 4

Spaghetti with Zucchini-Meat Sauce

Choose sweet or hot sausage, add more or less jalapeño and red pepper flakes, and jazz up this pasta dish with just the right amount of spice. The zucchini plays a background role, adding a touch of coolness to the sauce.

2 tablespoons extra virgin olive oil

1½ pounds sweet or hot Italian sausage, removed from its casing

2 green bell peppers, minced

1 cup minced onion

1 clove of garlic, minced

3 medium-sized zucchini, grated

2 cups seeded and chopped tomatoes

¼–½ cup chopped jalapeños

1 teaspoon fresh lemon juice, or to taste

½ teaspoon crushed red pepper flakes, or to taste

Salt

1 pound spaghetti

½ cup freshly grated Parmesan cheese

1. Begin heating a large pot of salted water for the pasta.

2. In a Dutch oven or large saucepan, heat the oil over medium-high heat. Add the sausage, bell peppers, onion, and garlic. Sauté until the meat is well browned, about 10 minutes. Drain the mixture to remove the excess fat.

3. Add the zucchini, tomatoes, and jalapeños. Taste and add the lemon juice, crushed red pepper flakes, and salt. Simmer for 30 minutes.

4. While the sauce simmers, cook the spaghetti in the boiling water until just al dente. Drain briefly.

5. Transfer the pasta to a large serving bowl. Add the sauce and toss. Add the cheese and toss again. Serve hot.

Serves 6

Quick Zucchini and Meat Sauce

When dinner has to be on the table in less than an hour, I often make pasta with meat sauce. I just brown ground meat — could be beef, could be turkey, could be Italian sausage removed from its casing — then add a jar of commercial pasta sauce (there are a few good ones; you just have to taste to find out which ones you like).

When zucchini is overabundant, I sometimes grate one or two medium-sized zucchini and add them right to the sauce as it simmers. Or I quarter and slice zucchini or summer squash and sauté it with the meat before adding the sauce. Both are easy, fast ways to add a vegetable to a meal that everyone enjoys.

Summer Vegetable Sauté with Sausage

The balsamic vinegar added at the end brings all the flavors together in this dish, but if you are drinking wine with dinner, you might trying adding a few tablespoons of the wine instead. Serve with good crusty bread to soak up all the vegetable juices.

2 small yellow summer squash, halved and sliced

2 small zucchini, halved and sliced

Salt

3 tablespoons extra virgin olive oil

1 pound fresh (not breakfast-style) sausage (pork, chicken, or turkey), removed from its casing

1 onion, halved and slivered

1 green bell pepper, julienned

1 red bell pepper, julienned

2 cloves of garlic, minced

Freshly ground black pepper

Kernels cut from 2 ears of corn (about 1 cup)

2 ripe tomatoes, seeded and diced

¼ cup chopped fresh basil

¼ teaspoon crushed red pepper flakes (optional)

1 tablespoon balsamic vinegar

1. If you have the time (see page 147), combine the summer squash, zucchini, and 2 teaspoons salt in a colander. Toss to mix and set aside to drain for 30 minutes. Transfer the squash to a clean kitchen towel and wring dry.

2. Heat 1 tablespoon of the oil in a large skillet over medium-high heat. Add the sausage and sauté, stirring and breaking up the meat with your spoon, until the meat is thoroughly cooked and no pink shows, about 8 minutes. Remove the skillet from the heat. Remove the sausage from the skillet with a slotted spoon, set aside, and keep warm.

3. Return the skillet to the stove, add 1 tablespoon of the oil, and heat over medium-high heat. Add the onion and bell peppers. Sauté until the vegetables are tender crisp, 3 to 5 minutes. Remove the skillet from the stove. Remove the vegetables with a slotted spoon and add to the sausage. Keep warm.

4. Return the skillet to the stove, add 1 tablespoon of the oil, and heat over medium-high heat. Add the summer squash and zucchini. Sauté for about 3 minutes. Add the garlic and pepper to taste. Continue to sauté until the squash are tender crisp, 2 minutes longer.

5. Return the sausage and vegetables to the skillet. Add the corn and tomatoes. Cook until the tomatoes are heated through, about 5 minutes.

6. Add salt and pepper to taste, the basil, red pepper flakes, if using, and vinegar.

7. Taste and adjust the seasonings. Serve hot.

Serves 4

Sausage-Stuffed Squash Blossoms

Italian sausage in tomato sauce is a fairly rustic dish.
But stuff it into squash blossoms and you have a dinner-party dish.
A bed of rice provides a tasty background for the squash blossoms.

1 pound sweet or hot Italian sausage, removed from its casing

1 cup diced onion

1 cup diced green bell pepper

1 cup well-seasoned tomato sauce

½ cup freshly grated Parmesan cheese

Salt and freshly ground black pepper

16–20 squash blossoms

1. Preheat the oven to 325°F and lightly oil a 9- by 13-inch baking dish.

2. Crumble the sausage into a large skillet over medium-high heat. Add the onion and green pepper. Sauté until the sausage is cooked through, about 8 minutes. Drain off the excess fat.

3. Add the tomato sauce to the sausage. Stir in the cheese. Taste and adjust the seasonings, adding salt and pepper as needed.

4. Stuff the blossoms with the sausage mixture. Place in the baking dish.

5. Bake for 10 minutes, or until the blossoms are heated through.

6. Serve at once.

Serves 4

Sausage Savvy

Sausages now come in a variety of styles and flavors at the supermarket. For the summer vegetable sauté and stuffed squash blossoms, almost any well-seasoned fresh sausage will do. The traditional Italian-style sausages, sweet or hot, made with pork or turkey, will work fine, but you can also experiment with chicken sausage seasoned with Cajun spices, or perhaps sun-dried tomatoes and basil.

Lamb Stew with Summer Vegetables

Lamb shoulder is an inexpensive cut that is great for stewing.
This is best made the day before, so that the gravy can be defatted once the stew
has been refrigerated. Serve the stew on a bed of hot buttered rice.

½ cup unbleached all-purpose flour

1 tablespoon chopped fresh thyme, or 2 teaspoons dried

1 teaspoon chopped fresh or dried rosemary

Salt and freshly ground black pepper

2 pounds lamb shoulder, trimmed and cut into 1-inch cubes

3 tablespoons extra virgin olive oil

1 cup diced onion

1 cup beef broth or water

2 teaspoons tomato paste

1½ cups diced carrots

3 cups diced zucchini

1 cup diced yellow summer squash

1 can (15 ounces) chickpeas, rinsed and drained

1. In a medium-sized bowl, combine the flour, thyme, rosemary, salt, and pepper. Add the lamb and toss to coat.

2. Heat the oil in a large skillet or Dutch oven over medium-high heat. Using a slotted spoon, lift the lamb out of the flour, shaking off the excess flour. Add to the skillet in a single layer and brown on all sides. Do not crowd the pan while browning the meat; you may have to brown the meat in batches.

3. Add the onion to the skillet. Sauté until softened and fragrant, about 3 minutes. Add the broth and tomato paste. Reduce the heat and simmer for about 45 minutes, until the meat is tender.

(The stew may be prepared up to this point, then cooled and refrigerated overnight. Remove the fat that hardens on top and reheat before continuing.)

4. Add the carrots and simmer for 15 minutes.

5. Add the zucchini, summer squash, and chickpeas. Continue to simmer until the vegetables are tender, about 15 minutes.

6. Serve hot.

Serves 6

Lamb

Lamb is a meat that people either love or hate. We happen to love it in my household. Much of the lamb sold today is naturally raised on foraged grasses, so it is a relatively healthful product.

The gamy flavor that many people object to is strongest in the fat. When preparing lamb for cooking, trim away all the hard white fat you can see. Also, when using lamb in stews or pot roasts, it is a good idea to make it a day ahead. After a night in the refrigerator, all of the fat in the sauce will have risen and hardened at the top, where it is easily removed. The stew or pot roast then can be reheated and served with the delicious pan juices.

Don't worry about overcooking the meat; stews and pot roasts should be cooked until the meat is falling-apart tender. Add zucchini and other quick-cooking vegetables after you have defatted the gravy.

Pot-Roasted Lamb Shanks with Zucchini

Slow-cooked lamb shanks on a bed of mashed potatoes is a wonderful comfort dish. If you are in the mood for wine with this dish, use the same wine you cooked with, such as a cabernet sauvignon or a merlot. This is another dish that is improved if you cook the meat the day before so that the fat can be removed from the gravy.

2 cloves of garlic, slivered

6 lamb shanks

Salt and freshly ground black pepper

3 tablespoons extra virgin olive oil

2 onions, diced

2 cups seeded, diced, and drained tomatoes

½ cup dry red wine or water, or more as needed

1 bay leaf

3 medium-sized zucchini, quartered and sliced

1. With the tip of a sharp knife, insert the garlic slivers into the lamb shanks. Season with salt and pepper.

2. Preheat the oven to 350°F.

3. In a large Dutch oven, heat the oil over medium-high heat. Add as many shanks as will fit in a single layer, season with salt and pepper, and brown on all sides, about 12 minutes. Continue until all the shanks are browned. Transfer the shanks to a plate and keep warm.

4. Drain the excess fat from the Dutch oven, leaving about 1 tablespoon. Add the onions and sauté until soft, about 3 minutes. Add the tomatoes, wine, bay leaf, and salt and pepper to taste.

5. Braise in the oven for about 1½ hours, until the meat is completely tender. (The shanks can be prepared up to this point, then cooled, covered, and refrigerated overnight. Remove the hardened fat from the gravy and reheat in the oven or on top of the stove.)

6. Add the zucchini and mix well. Add more water if needed. Return to the oven for about 30 minutes, until the zucchini is cooked through.

7. Remove the bay leaf. Serve hot.

Serves 6

Lamb Burgers with Zucchini Tzatziki

Tzatziki is a Greek salad, traditionally consisting of chopped cucumbers dressed with yogurt and mint. Zucchini makes a fine stand-in for the cucumber. My favorite versions contain enough garlic to blunt the taste of the mint. The burgers are great grilled, but broiling is always an option. I like this best when made with lamb, but turkey also works well.

TZATZIKI

- 2 medium-sized zucchini, quartered and thinly sliced
- 1½ cups plain yogurt
- 2 tablespoons chopped fresh mint, or to taste
- 4 cloves of garlic, minced
- 3 tablespoons extra virgin olive oil
- 1½ tablespoons white or red wine vinegar
- Salt and freshly ground black pepper

LAMB BURGERS

- 1 pound ground lamb, formed into 8 small patties
- 4 pita pockets
- 3–4 tomatoes, sliced

1. To make the tzatziki, bring a medium pot of salted water to a boil. Add the zucchini and blanch for 1 minute. Drain, plunge into cold water to stop the cooking, drain again, and pat dry.

2. In a medium-sized bowl, combine the zucchini, yogurt, mint, garlic, oil, vinegar, and salt and pepper to taste. Set aside to allow the flavors to develop.

3. Prepare a medium-hot fire in a gas or charcoal grill.

4. Grill the burgers about 4 inches from the heat until cooked through, 3 to 5 minutes per side, turning once.

5. To serve, cut the pitas in half and place a lamb patty in each. At the table, pass the tzatziki and tomatoes; the diners can add them to the pitas as desired.

Serves 4

Moussaka

Zucchini replaces eggplant in this Greek lamb classic. Beef could replace the lamb. The warmly spiced tomato sauce, redolent with cinnamon, defines the dish.

2 pounds lean ground lamb

1 large onion, chopped

3 cloves of garlic, minced

4 large ripe tomatoes, seeded and coarsely chopped

½ cup tomato sauce

¼ teaspoon chili powder

2 tablespoons chopped fresh mint

2 teaspoons minced fresh lemon thyme or regular thyme

½ teaspoon ground cinnamon

Salt and freshly ground black pepper

½ pound Monterey Jack cheese, grated

¼ cup extra virgin olive oil

8 cups thickly sliced zucchini

1. Preheat the oven to 350°F. Lightly oil a deep baking dish.

2. In a large skillet over medium-high heat, combine the lamb, onion, and garlic. Cook, stirring frequently, until the meat is browned and the onion is soft, 10 to 12 minutes.

3. Drain off the fat and add the tomatoes, tomato sauce, chili powder, mint, lemon thyme, cinnamon, and salt and pepper to taste. Mix well and bring to a boil. Reduce the heat and simmer for about 40 minutes.

4. Remove the skillet from the heat, stir in half of the cheese, and set aside.

5. In another large skillet, heat the oil. Sauté half the zucchini slices until tender crisp, about 5 minutes. With a slotted spoon, transfer the first batch of sautéed zucchini to the baking pan. Sauté the remaining zucchini.

6. Top the first layer of zucchini with half the meat. Top with half of the remaining cheese. Spoon half of the remaining zucchini on top, followed by the remaining meat and half of the remaining cheese. Top with the remaining zucchini. Sprinkle the remaining cheese on top.

7. Bake for 30 minutes, until heated through.

8. Serve hot.

Serves 6–8

5. Summer Squash Side Dishes

In an ideal summer, the garden will produce a few zucchini or summer squash every couple of days — not enough to have you wringing your hands, but enough to make a summer squash side dish practical and economical. The recipes in this chapter range from the simple to the slightly more complex and from the mild to the bold. They are recipes in which the vegetable plays the starring role. Though they are called "side dishes," they are likely to be the star on the dinner plate.

Basic Sautéed Zucchini

Simply sautéed is one of the best ways to enjoy fresh zucchini and summer squash. As the season moves along, you may want to add a light topping of Parmesan cheese to bring extra flavor. For a basic dish like this one, it is best to use the very best Parmesan, which is the real stuff from Italy: Parmigiano-Reggiano.

- 2 **medium-sized zucchini or yellow summer squash, or 8 small pattypans, sliced ¼-inch thick**
- 2 **teaspoons salt**
- 3 **tablespoons extra virgin olive oil or butter**
- 2 **cloves of garlic, minced**
  Freshly ground black pepper
- 2 **tablespoons chopped fresh parsley**
- 2 **tablespoons freshly grated Parmigiano-Reggiano cheese (optional)**

1. If you have the time (see box below), combine the zucchini and salt in a colander. Toss to mix and set aside to drain for 30 minutes. Transfer the zucchini to a clean kitchen towel and wring dry.

2. In a large skillet, heat the oil over medium-high heat. Add the zucchini and garlic. Sauté until the zucchini is lightly colored and tender, 4 to 5 minutes.

3. Transfer to a serving dish and season to taste with pepper. Sprinkle the parsley and Parmesan, if using, over the zucchini. Serve immediately.

Serves 4

If You Have the Time, Salt First

Several recipes contain an optional first step of salting the zucchini, allowing it to drain for about 30 minutes, and wringing dry in a clean towel. This rids squash of excess moisture and produces a startling improvement in texture. Try it and see for yourself whether you think it is worth the extra time and effort. I think it is.

Pan-Fried Zucchini with Herbs

The flour coating gives the zucchini a lovely crisped exterior.

½ cup unbleached all-purpose flour

2 teaspoons minced fresh parsley

2 teaspoons minced fresh rosemary

1 teaspoon minced fresh thyme

Salt and freshly ground black pepper

2 tablespoons extra virgin olive oil, or more as needed

1 tablespoon butter, or more as needed

2 shallots, minced

1 clove of garlic, minced

6 small zucchini, sliced into ¼-inch rounds

1. In a shallow bowl, combine the flour, parsley, rosemary, thyme, and salt and pepper to taste.

2. Combine the 2 tablespoons oil and 1 tablespoon butter in a large skillet. Heat over low heat, just until the butter is melted. Add the shallots and garlic. Sauté for 2 minutes.

3. Dredge the zucchini slices in the flour mixture, shaking off any excess, and place in a single layer in the skillet. Turn up the heat slightly and brown on both sides, about 2 minutes per side, taking care not to let the zucchini stick (you may need to add more oil or butter). Remove to a paper towel–lined plate; keep warm. Continue until all the zucchini is cooked.

4. Serve hot.

Serves 4

Sautéed Shredded Zucchini

One technique for quick-cooking zucchini is to grate it to create a large surface area, then sauté it very rapidly. The zucchini can be placed on top of the main course — meat, fish, chicken, pasta with sauce — as a garnish that doubles as a side dish.

2 **medium-sized zucchini, grated**

2 **tablespoons extra virgin olive oil**

2 **cloves of garlic, minced**

2 **tablespoons chopped fresh herbs, such as basil, thyme, parsley, tarragon, and mint (optional)**

Salt and freshly ground black pepper

1. Wrap the zucchini in a clean kitchen towel and wring dry.

2. In a large skillet, heat the oil over medium-high heat. Add the zucchini and garlic. Sauté until tender, about 3 minutes. Stir in the herbs, if using, and salt and pepper to taste.

3. Serve immediately.

Serves 3–4

Zucchini "Noodles"

If you have a mandoline, you can make beautiful long, spaghetti-like strands of zucchini in no time at all. Making long, thin strips with a knife is more work and it is harder to get perfectly uniform results, but these "noodles" are worth it. Not only are they delicious, but you can use them to make attractive "nests" on your dinner plates.

6 medium-sized zucchini
  Salt
3 tablespoons butter
  Freshly ground black pepper
  Freshly grated Parmigiano-Reggiano cheese (optional)

1. To cut the noodles by hand, trim the ends off the zucchini and cut into ⅛-inch slices lengthwise. Stack the slices and cut into ⅛-inch strips, cutting just to the pulpy inner core, which should be discarded. Or, using a mandoline, shred the zucchini into long, ⅛-inch strips, cutting just to the pulpy inner core, which should be discarded.

2. In a colander, combine the zucchini and 1 teaspoon salt. Toss to mix and set aside to drain for 30 minutes.

3. Bring a medium-sized pot of water to a boil. Add the zucchini to the boiling water and blanch for 1 minute. Drain, immediately plunge into cold water to stop the cooking, and drain again. Pat dry with a clean kitchen towel.

4. Melt the butter in a large skillet over medium heat. Add the zucchini and toss to coat with the butter. Season the zucchini with salt and pepper to taste.

5. Transfer to a serving bowl and serve. Sprinkle with the cheese, if using.

Serves 6

Use Overgrown Zucchini

You can use somewhat overgrown zucchini to make noodles. Use just the outside layers of the zucchini and discard the pulpy, seedy core. As you slice or shred, work from the outside in, rotating the zucchini as you go. When you get close to the core, stop.

Buttered Baby Zucchini

The rewards of baby zucchini are many. First is their delicate flavor, as well as their charming appearance on the plate. Best of all, by harvesting squash when they are tiny, you guarantee yourself a generous abundance throughout the summer.

8 small zucchini or other summer squash, halved lengthwise

3 tablespoons butter

1 onion, cut into rings

1 clove of garlic, minced

Salt and freshly ground black pepper

1. Bring a medium-sized saucepan of lightly salted water to a boil. Add the zucchini and cook until tender, about 3 minutes. Drain.

2. Over medium-high heat, melt the butter in a small skillet. Add the onion and sauté until softened, 3 to 5 minutes. Add the garlic and salt and pepper to taste.

3. To serve, place the squash on individual plates. Top with the sautéed onion rings and garlic butter.

Serves 4

From a Cook's Garden

ELLEN AND SHEP OGDEN are a perfectly matched couple. He loves to grow; she loves to cook. Together they founded The Cook's Garden, a seed company dedicated to providing top-quality seeds to gardeners with an interest in cooking.

The Cook's Garden began as an organic market garden in 1983, supplying unusual and flavorful vegetables to chefs and cooks in southern Vermont. That market garden is long since gone, though the Ogdens still live and garden in Londonderry, Vermont. The Cook's Garden evolved into a seed company with a public trial and display garden in Burlington, Vermont, which is open to visitors from May through September. As a mail-order seed company, The Cook's Garden specializes in vegetables that taste good and perform well for cooks. Many of the seeds they offer are organically raised, and many are heirloom varieties.

Currently, Ellen is hard at work testing recipes for a cookbook that focuses on garden vegetables. She has no trouble getting enough vegetables. What she doesn't grow in her kitchen garden, Shep brings home from the trial gardens in Burlington, which is how she found herself, one recent afternoon, steaming eight different varieties of pattypan squash to see which tasted best. Starship, she said, proved to be "fabulously good." This is a dark green pattypan type that is ideal when it is harvested quite small. "Pattypans are fun," says Ellen. "They have good flavor, and when they get too big, they make great decorations."

As for yellow summer squash, Ellen doesn't grow it or eat it. When she wants a yellow squash, she'll use a golden zucchini. She finds yellow summer squash "too bitter. And the seeds get too big too quickly."

Ellen is a fan of Ronde de Nice, an heirloom zucchini variety that is round. "They make a nice one-person serving if you pick them small enough. I like them when they are about as big as softballs. I cut off the top, scoop out most of the insides, then I fill it and bake it in a pan with a little water. It is awkward on a plate, though. It's best to serve it on its own plate."

Another heirloom variety that Ellen recommends is tromboncino, which is long, thin, and curved to a bell at the end. It is a vigorously vining plant that should be grown on a trellis. For best eating, the vegetables should be harvested when they are 8 to 18 inches long. "The necks are the best part, with few seeds. I just cut off the bulbous end and use the neck, which is juicy and sweet." Tromboncino can be left on the vine; after 90 days, it will ripen into a gourd.

Asked about winter squash, Ellen named delicata as her favorite variety. "You can just slice it and bake it. Red kuri is good for soup — just bake it and scoop out the flesh. I think it might have the highest nutritional value of all the winter squash because of its deep orange color. It is the typical macrobiotic squash, very beautiful looking. An Italian variety, *marina di Chioggia,* is the classic winter squash for gnocchi and ravioli fillings. It looks a lot like a Hubbard squash, but it is pumpkin-shaped, so it is easier to whack off slices. And for pumpkin pie, nothing beats small sugar, which is always the perfect size for a pie."

Ellen admits that being both a cook and gardener can be a conflict. "You don't want to spend a whole day in the garden, then have to spend hours cooking. That's where the simplicity of a well-prepared vegetable dish comes in." She recommends keeping olive oil, onions, garlic, half-and-half, butter, and mustard on hand. She also recommends growing fresh herbs. "Then you can do just about anything you want with whatever the garden has to offer."

Herbed Pattypans

The technique here is to "sweat" the squash in its own juices, and the result is intensified flavor. This dish is particularly attractive when made with pattypan squash, but you could also use zucchini or summer squash, sliced about ¼-inch thick.

2 tablespoons extra virgin olive oil

4 small pattypan squash (about 1 pound), halved vertically and sliced ¼-inch thick

Salt and freshly ground black pepper

1 clove of garlic, minced

2 tablespoons chopped fresh herbs (mint, oregano, basil, cilantro, sage, summer savory, thyme, or a combination)

1. In a large skillet, heat the oil over medium heat. Add the squash and toss to coat in the oil. Season to taste with salt and pepper. Cover and cook for 5 minutes over medium heat.

2. Add the garlic and herbs. Cover and cook for 1 to 2 minutes more, until the squash is completely tender but not mushy. Taste and adjust the seasonings.

3. Serve at once.

Serves 4

Basic Roasted Zucchini Spears

Roasting vegetables at a high temperature brings out their sweetness and flavor.
If you want to enjoy zucchini as simply as possible, this is a wonderful way to do so.

2 medium-sized zucchini, halved and cut into 3-inch-long spears

1 clove of garlic, minced (optional)

2 tablespoons extra virgin olive oil or any herb-flavored oil

Salt and freshly ground black pepper

Balsamic vinegar

1. Preheat the oven to 450°F. Lightly oil a baking sheet.

2. If you are using the garlic, combine it with the oil in a small bowl. Arrange the zucchini skin-side down on the roasting pan. Lightly brush the cut sides with the oil and sprinkle generously with salt and pepper.

3. Roast for about 15 minutes, until the squash are tender and lightly browned.

4. Transfer the squash to a serving plate. Drizzle with the balsamic vinegar. Serve hot.

Serves 4

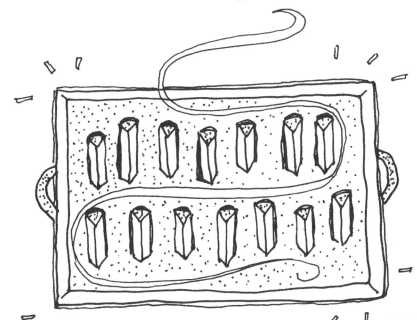

Roasted Baby Summer Squash

This is one of the most appealing ways to serve summer squash.
Choose small, straight squash for the best appearance on the plate.

8 baby summer squash (zucchini, yellow summer squash, or pattypan squash, or any combination of the three)

2 tablespoons extra virgin olive oil, plus additional oil for brushing

Salt and freshly ground black pepper

1 cup packed mixed herb leaves (basil, parsley, sage, oregano, rosemary, thyme, mint)

4 cloves of garlic

1. Preheat the oven to 450°F. Lightly oil a baking sheet.

2. Slice zucchini and yellow summer squash in half lengthwise. Slice pattypan squash in half horizontally. The squash should sit flat in the pan, cut-side up; take a small slice off the bottoms as needed to make the squash sit level. Score the cut side of the flesh in a diamond pattern, slicing almost to the skin. Lightly brush the cut sides with oil and sprinkle generously with salt and pepper.

3. Combine the 2 tablespoons of oil, herbs, and garlic in a food processor. Process to make a paste. Season to taste with salt and pepper. Spread the paste over the cut sides of the squash.

4. Roast for about 15 minutes, until the squash are tender and lightly browned.

5. Serve hot.

Serves 4

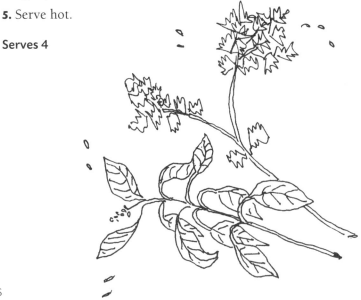

Sweet-and-sour Zucchini

Zucchini's willingness to adapt to any flavor combination is evident
in this simple sweet-and-sour side dish.

3 **medium-sized zucchini, cut into ½-inch slices or strips**

   Salt

¼ **cup canola oil**

2 **tablespoons white vinegar**

2 **tablespoons sugar**

3 **tablespoons chopped fresh basil**

   Freshly ground black pepper

1. If you have the time (see page 147), combine the zucchini and 2 teaspoons of salt in a colander. Toss to mix and set aside to drain for 30 minutes. Transfer the zucchini to a clean dish towel and wring dry.

2. In a large skillet, heat the oil over medium-high heat. Add the zucchini and sauté until lightly colored and softened, about 5 minutes. Using a slotted spoon, transfer the zucchini to a serving bowl.

3. Add the vinegar, sugar, basil, and salt and pepper to taste to the oil in the skillet. Simmer for 3 minutes.

4. Pour the sweet-and-sour sauce over the zucchini and serve.

Serves 4

Grilling Tips

Zucchini and summer squash are perfect candidates for the grill. Their high water content and relatively low sugar content guarantee that they won't dry out or burn too readily over the intense fire of the grill. Over the years I have grilled hundreds of pounds of vegetables, and here is what I know.

■ A vegetable grill rack is invaluable if you plan to grill vegetables frequently. It is a flat metal plate with a grid of holes that is designed to let the smoke and heat through but prevent vegetables from slipping through the grate into the fire. It also works well for grilling fish. You can take a mixture of vegetables, all diced or julienned to the same size, toss them with olive oil and herbs, and sauté on the vegetable grill rack.

■ There is no need to marinate vegetables before grilling. With the exception of mushrooms and eggplant, they don't absorb the marinade.

■ Vegetables should be lightly coated with oil before they are grilled. This helps to seal in flavors. Butter doesn't work well because the vegetables usually cool down on their trip from grill to table, and congealed butter looks and feels unpleasant.

■ Slicing summer squash about ⅜-inch thick is ideal. This sounds a little persnickety, but it is the optimum thickness for producing a grilled vegetable that doesn't char or become leathery.

■ I prefer to grill vegetables with the grill lid up. This prevents the vegetables from acquiring a sooty patina deposited from previously grilled meats.

■ Kabobs are my least favorite form of grilled vegetables. It is very difficult to create a vegetable kabob in which all the vegetables are cooked to the same degree. Also, the vegetables have a wicked habit of turning on the skewer once they start to cook, so it is hard to get all the vegetables done on the same side at the same time. One remedy is to use two skewers at a time, which stabilizes the vegetables. Squash slices should be speared through the skin, rather than through the middle, for the greatest stability.

Dilled and Grilled summer squash Chips

Slicing squash about ⅜-inch thick allows it to cook through when grilled but remain tender and juicy. If you slice them thinner, they will char; if you slice them thicker, they will develop a tough outer skin, and the centers may or may not cook through.

2 pounds zucchini, yellow summer squash, or pattypan squash, sliced ⅜-inch thick

3 tablespoons extra virgin olive oil

1 tablespoon fresh lemon juice, plus more as needed

2 cloves of garlic, minced

3 tablespoons chopped fresh dill

Salt and freshly ground black pepper

Coarse sea salt or kosher salt or fresh lemon juice (optional)

1. Prepare a medium-hot fire in the grill.

2. In a large bowl, combine the squash, oil, lemon juice, garlic, dill, and salt and pepper to taste. Toss gently to coat.

3. Grill the squash slices until they are grill-marked and tender, turning once, about 5 minutes for the first side and 4 minutes for the second side.

4. Transfer to a serving plate and sprinkle with the coarse salt or drizzle with fresh lemon juice, if using. Serve hot.

Serves 4

Rack 'em Up

If you have a vegetable grill rack (a flat metal plate that is drilled with holes to allow the heat and smoke of a fire to penetrate), you can grill any size vegetable without worrying that the vegetable slices will fall into the fire. If you don't have a grill rack, slice the squash lengthwise, or choose large squash or pattypans.

Breaded Squash Fans

The trick here is to slice baby squash so that the slices remain connected at the top, but can be fanned out along the bottom. This provides maximum surface area for the breading and transforms a simple side dish into something quite elegant.

6–8 baby yellow summer squash

½ cup all-purpose unbleached flour

Salt and freshly ground black pepper

2 large eggs

⅔ cup dried bread crumbs

¼ cup freshly grated Parmesan cheese

1 teaspoon chopped fresh thyme, or ½ teaspoon dried

¼ cup extra virgin olive oil

1. Bring a medium-sized saucepan of salted water to a boil. Slice each squash lengthwise every ¼ inch, leaving all the slices connected at the neck of the squash.

2. Blanch the squash for 3 minutes. Drain well. Spread out each squash in a fan pattern. Pat dry.

3. Preheat the oven to 200°F and place a wire rack on top of a baking sheet.

4. In a shallow bowl, combine the flour and salt and pepper to taste. In a second shallow bowl, beat the eggs. In a third shallow bowl, combine the bread crumbs, Parmesan, and thyme.

5. Heat the oil in a large skillet over medium-high heat. Dredge the squash in the flour, dust off any excess, dip in the eggs, and coat with the bread crumbs. Add to the skillet in a single layer and fry on both sides until golden, 4 to 5 minutes per side. Do not crowd the skillet. Transfer the cooked squash to the prepared baking sheet and keep warm in the oven while you finish cooking the remaining squash.

6. Serve hot.

Serves 6–8

Pattypan Fritters

Sliced pattypans, coated in batter and fried, make a delicious side dish, served plain or dressed up with a marinara sauce or a fresh tomato relish. Any summer squash will work here, but the scalloped slices of pattypans are particularly attractive.

1 cup unbleached all-purpose flour

2 teaspoons chopped fresh oregano, or 1 teaspoon dried

1 teaspoon salt

¼ teaspoon freshly ground black pepper

4 cloves of garlic, minced

2 eggs, lightly beaten

About ½ cup water

Canola oil, for frying

4 medium-sized pattypan squash, or 2 medium-sized zucchini or yellow summer squash, thinly sliced

1. Preheat the oven to 200°F and place a wire rack on top of a baking sheet.

2. In a medium-sized mixing bowl, combine the flour, oregano, salt, pepper, and garlic. Add the eggs and enough water to make a batter the consistency of pancake batter. Mix well to smooth out any lumps.

3. Pour oil into a skillet to a depth of about ½ inch and turn the heat to high. When the oil is hot, drop the squash slices, a few at a time, into the batter. One slice at a time, lift up the slices and slide into the pan. The oil should be hot enough to sizzle on contact. Add just enough slices to fill the pan without crowding. Cook until a fine golden crust forms on the bottom, about 2 minutes. Turn and cook on the second side until golden, another 1 to 2 minutes. Remove the squash from the oil with tongs or a slotted spatula and transfer to the wire rack to drain. Keep warm in the oven while you continue to fry all the squash.

4. Serve immediately.

Serves 4

Batter-Fried Zucchini

Serve these delectable morsels plain or with a well-seasoned tomato sauce.
They will disappear almost as soon as they are made.

2 cups unbleached all-purpose flour

2½ teaspoons salt

¼ teaspoon freshly ground black pepper

4 egg yolks, beaten

¾ cup beer

2 tablespoons butter, melted

4 cups sliced zucchini or other summer squash (½-inch thickness)

Oil, for deep-frying

2 egg whites

1. To make the batter, in a medium-sized bowl, combine the flour, 1½ teaspoons of the salt, pepper, egg yolks, and beer. Stir until no lumps remain. Stir in the butter. Let the batter rest for 1 hour at room temperature.

2. Combine the zucchini and the remaining 1 teaspoon salt in a colander. Toss to mix and set aside to drain for 30 minutes. Transfer the slices to a clean kitchen towel and wring dry.

3. In a large, deep saucepan over medium-high heat, begin heating 3 to 4 inches of oil.

4. Beat the eggs whites until stiff. Fold into the batter.

5. When the oil reaches a temperature of 365°F on a deep-fat thermometer, begin frying. One piece at a time, dip the zucchini into the batter. Slip the slices into the hot oil. Fry just a few pieces at a time. Fry until the pieces are golden, 3 to 4 minutes.

6. Drain on paper towels. Serve immediately.

Serves 4

Zucchini with Pesto

If you thought pesto was just for pasta, try this magical combination. The pesto goes beautifully with the zucchini.

4 medium-sized zucchini or yellow summer squash, julienned

2 teaspoons salt

¼ cup extra virgin olive oil

⅔ cup pesto (page 27)

1. If you have the time (see page 147), combine the zucchini and salt in a colander. Toss to mix and set aside to drain for 30 minutes. Transfer the zucchini to a clean kitchen towel and wring dry.

2. In a large skillet, heat the oil over medium-high heat. Add the zucchini and sauté until tender crisp, about 3 minutes.

3. Add the pesto and toss to mix well. Serve at once.

Serves 4

Green and Yellow Squash in Cream

Cream adds a touch of luxury to everyday garden vegetables.
Here, green and yellow squash are presented in a dilled cream sauce.

1 medium-sized golden zucchini or yellow summer squash, thinly sliced

1 medium-sized green zucchini, thinly sliced

Salt

2 tablespoons butter

1 cup light cream

Freshly ground black pepper

1 tablespoon chopped fresh dill

1. If you have the time (see page 147), combine the squash and 1 teaspoon salt in a colander. Toss to mix and set aside to drain for 30 minutes. Transfer the squash slices to a clean dish towel and wring dry.

2. In a large skillet over medium heat, melt the butter. Add the squash and sauté until just tender crisp, 3 to 5 minutes.

3. Add the cream and salt and pepper to taste. Simmer over low heat for 15 minutes.

4. Add the dill, mix well, and serve immediately.

Serves 4

Green and Yellow Squash in Yogurt Sauce

If the previous recipe is too rich for you, consider this alternative
healthful version, in which the squash is sautéed in olive oil instead of butter
and is dressed with a low-fat yogurt sauce instead of cream.

1 medium-sized golden zucchini or yellow summer squash, thinly sliced

1 medium-sized green zucchini, thinly sliced

Salt

3 tablespoons extra virgin olive oil

1 clove of garlic, minced

Freshly ground black pepper

1 cup plain low-fat yogurt

¼ cup minced scallions or chives

1. If you have the time (see page 147), combine the zucchini and 2 teaspoons salt in a colander. Toss to mix and set aside to drain for 30 minutes. Transfer the zucchini to a clean kitchen towel and wring dry.

2. Heat the oil in a large skillet over medium-high heat. Add the zucchini and garlic. Sauté until the zucchini is tender crisp, about 5 minutes. Season with salt and pepper. Remove from the skillet with a slotted spoon and arrange on plates.

3. In a small bowl, combine the yogurt, scallions, and salt and pepper to taste.

4. Spoon the yogurt sauce over the zucchini and serve.

Serves 4

Italian Relish

Summer squash in a tomato sauce can be served hot as a side dish or chilled and served as a relish. It makes a fine accompaniment to grilled chicken, pork, and beef.

2 tablespoons extra virgin olive oil

½ cup chopped onion

1 clove of garlic, minced

2 medium-sized summer squash, chopped

1 can (8 ounces) pizza sauce

1 can (8 ounces) stewed tomatoes

1 teaspoon chopped fresh oregano, or ¼ teaspoon dried

½ teaspoon chopped fresh or dried rosemary

1 teaspoon chopped fresh thyme, or ¼ teaspoon dried

Salt and freshly ground black pepper

1. In a large skillet, heat the oil over medium-high heat. Add the onion and garlic and sauté until softened, 3 to 5 minutes. Stir in the squash, pizza sauce, tomatoes and their liquid, oregano, rosemary, and thyme. Add salt and pepper to taste. Bring to a boil. Reduce the heat, cover, and simmer for 10 to 12 minutes.

2. Uncover and continue to cook until the relish is tender but not mushy, about 10 minutes.

3. Serve hot, at room temperature, or chilled.

Serves 4–6

Summer Squash Paprikash

For the best flavor, use sweet Hungarian paprika, preferably fresh.
Fresh paprika has a rich, pungent flavor that adds much more to a dish than color.
This is a deliciously rich-tasting way to prepare summer squash. If you use
nonfat sour cream, it is also a reasonably healthful preparation.

2 tablespoons butter or extra virgin olive oil

1 cup diced onion

1½ teaspoons paprika

1 teaspoon poppy seeds

1 teaspoon sugar

4 cups diced yellow summer squash

½ teaspoon salt

⅓ cup water

2 tablespoons all-purpose unbleached flour

¾ cup sour cream (nonfat sour cream is acceptable)

1 teaspoon fresh lemon juice

1. In a large skillet over medium heat, melt the butter. Add the onion and sauté until the onion is softened and fragrant, 3 to 5 minutes.

2. Stir in the paprika, poppy seeds, and sugar. Add the squash, salt, and water. Cook, uncovered, until the water evaporates and the squash is softened, 3 to 5 minutes.

3. Sprinkle the flour over the squash. Stir to mix. Stir in the sour cream and lemon juice. Cook for 1 to 2 minutes more, until the sauce thickens.

4. Serve immediately.

Serves 4–6

scalloped squash

Slow baking reveals hidden flavors in the squash that the onion and cheese sauce complement perfectly. If you like scalloped potatoes, you will love this dish. I have seen people who claim not to like vegetables eat huge quantities of this simple dish.

3 tablespoons butter

3 tablespoons unbleached all-purpose flour

1½ cups milk

1½ cups grated sharp Cheddar cheese

2 medium-sized summer squash, sliced at an angle

2 medium-sized zucchini, sliced at an angle

1 onion, halved and sliced

Salt and freshly ground black pepper

¼ cup dried bread crumbs

1. Preheat the oven to 350°F. Butter a 9- by 13-inch baking dish.

2. In a medium-sized saucepan over medium heat, melt the butter. Whisk in the flour to make a smooth paste. Whisk in the milk and bring to a boil. Reduce the heat and stir in the cheese. Cook, stirring constantly, until the cheese is melted and the sauce is smooth.

3. Layer the squash and onion in the baking dish, sprinkling with salt and pepper as you layer. Cover with the cheese sauce. Sprinkle the bread crumbs over the dish.

4. Bake for 60 minutes.

5. Serve hot.

Serves 4–6

Make Your Own Bread Crumbs

You can easily make your own bread crumbs, which will be better than any you can buy, if you start with bakery or homemade bread. Lay bread slices on a baking sheet and bake at 200°F until the bread is dry, golden, and crisp, 30 to 45 minutes. Cool completely, then break into pieces and process until fine in a blender or food processor fitted with a metal blade.

You might as well make extra, since bread crumbs will keep in an airtight container for several weeks. Two large slices of bread will yield ½ cup. To season the bread crumbs, mix in salt, freshly ground black pepper, and a teaspoon or so of dried herbs, such as basil, oregano, or thyme.

Zucchini au Gratin

If you have fond memories of green beans baked in cream of mushroom soup and topped with canned onion rings, try this retro version of zucchini au gratin.

6 tablespoons butter

1 cup dried bread crumbs

4 medium-sized zucchini, cut lengthwise into ¼-inch slices

1 can (10¾ ounces) cream of mushroom soup

⅔ cup shredded Cheddar or American cheese

2 tablespoons minced onion

Salt and freshly ground black pepper

1. Melt 2 tablespoons of the butter in a large skillet. Place ½ cup of the bread crumbs in a small bowl. Add the melted butter; toss to mix. Set aside.

2. In the skillet over medium-high heat, melt the remaining 4 tablespoons butter. Add the zucchini and sauté for 3 to 5 minutes, until just tender. Add the bread crumb mixture, the cream of mushroom soup, cheese, onion, and salt and pepper to taste. Reduce the heat and cook just until the cheese is melted, about 5 minutes.

3. Leave in the skillet or transfer to a serving dish. Top with the remaining ½ cup bread crumbs and serve hot.

Serves 6

Zucchini-Tomato Gratinée

Here's a simple preparation: a layer of zucchini baked
under tomatoes and bread crumbs.

2 medium-sized zucchini, thinly sliced

2 tomatoes, seeded and chopped or sliced

2 onions, thinly sliced

Salt and freshly ground black pepper

¼ cup butter

1 cup dry bread crumbs

1. Preheat the oven to 350°F. Butter a 9- by 13-inch baking dish.

2. Cover the bottom of the pan with a layer of zucchini, followed by tomatoes, then onions. Season with salt and pepper and dot with butter. Continue to layer in the baking dish until all ingredients are used. Sprinkle the crumbs on top.

3. Bake the gratinée, uncovered, until the vegetables are tender, about 20 minutes.

4. Serve hot.

Serves 4–6

VARIATIONS: Add chopped fresh herbs, particularly basil, oregano, and summer savory, to the layers. Add minced garlic to the layers. Grate 12 ounces of Cheddar, Fontina, mozzarella, or Parmesan cheese and layer it with the vegetables.

Greek Baked Zucchini

In this gratinée, the zucchini is further dressed with herbs and feta cheese.

5 large tomatoes, seeded and chopped

1 clove of garlic, minced

½ cup extra virgin olive oil

1 teaspoon sugar

1½ teaspoons chopped fresh mint, or ¾ teaspoon dried

1 teaspoon chopped fresh oregano, or ½ teaspoon dried

6 cups sliced zucchini

2 onions, halved and sliced

4 ounces feta cheese, crumbled

½ cup dried bread crumbs

1 tablespoon butter

1. Preheat the oven to 350°F. Butter a 9- by 13-inch baking dish.

2. In a medium-sized mixing bowl, combine the tomatoes, garlic, oil, sugar, mint, and oregano.

3. Arrange a layer of zucchini in the bottom of the baking dish. Cover with a layer of the tomato mixture and a layer of onions. Repeat the layers until all the vegetables are in the baking dish. Sprinkle the feta cheese, then the bread crumbs, on top. Dot with small pieces of butter.

4. Bake for 45 minutes, until the squash is tender.

5. Serve hot.

Serves 6

Sauté of Summer Vegetables

Restaurant plates are often garnished with this sort of simple vegetable combination. The vegetables can be varied; the point is to choose a colorful mixture.

1 medium-sized zucchini or yellow summer squash, julienned

Salt

2 tablespoons butter

1 clove of garlic, minced

1 carrot, julienned

1 red bell pepper, julienned

Freshly ground black pepper

1. If you have the time (see page 147), combine the zucchini and 1 teaspoon salt in a colander. Toss to mix and set aside to drain for 30 minutes. Transfer the zucchini to a clean kitchen towel and wring dry.

2. In a large skillet over medium-high heat, melt the butter. Add the garlic and carrot. Sauté, stirring constantly, until the carrot is slightly softened, about 3 minutes. If necessary, adjust the heat to keep the butter from browning.

3. Add the squash and bell pepper. Continue to sauté, stirring constantly, until the vegetables are tender crisp, about 3 minutes.

4. Season to taste with salt and pepper. Serve hot.

Serves 3–4

Medley of Roasted Summer Vegetables

Roasted vegetables have a nutty, sweet flavor that sautéed and steamed vegetables lack. If it isn't too hot to turn on the oven, consider roasting your vegetables. This preparation is one that restaurants might use as a garnish. However, these vegetables are too delicious to relegate to the role of garnish. Make these the centerpiece of a meal.

2 cloves of garlic

⅓ cup lightly packed mixed fresh herb leaves, such as basil, mint, parsley, chives, sage, and thyme

Juice of 1 lemon (about 3 tablespoons)

3 tablespoons extra virgin olive oil

Salt and freshly ground black pepper

2 small yellow summer squash, julienned

2 small zucchini, julienned

1 carrot, julienned

1 leek, thinly sliced

1 red bell pepper, julienned

1. Preheat the oven to 425°F. Lightly oil a large shallow roasting pan or half sheet pan.

2. In a food processor, combine the garlic and herbs. Mince finely. Add the lemon juice and process until well blended. With the motor running, slowly add the oil and process until the mixture is completely blended. Season to taste with salt and pepper.

3. Combine the summer squash, zucchini, carrot, leek, and bell pepper in the roasting pan. Pour the marinade over the vegetables and toss to coat. Spread out the vegetables so that they form a single layer in the pan.

4. Roast for 15 to 20 minutes, until the vegetables are lightly browned and tender. Stir or shake the pan occasionally for even cooking.

5. Transfer the vegetables to a serving bowl or platter. Taste and adjust the seasoning. Serve at once.

Serves 4–6

South-of-the-Border Squash

Enhance any Tex-Mex main course with this side dish. Or drain off the cooking liquid and use the squash along with refried beans as a filling for burritos or tacos.

3 tablespoons extra virgin olive oil

2 cups sliced yellow summer squash or golden zucchini

2 cups sliced green zucchini

2 green bell peppers, minced

1 onion, minced

2 cups corn kernels

1 ripe tomato, seeded and chopped

½ cup water

Salt and freshly ground black pepper

Chopped fresh cilantro, for garnish (optional)

1. In a large skillet, heat the oil over medium-high heat. Add the summer squash, zucchini, bell peppers, and onion. Sauté until softened, about 5 minutes.

2. Add the corn, tomato, and water. Cover and simmer until the corn is cooked through, 10 to 12 minutes.

3. Season to taste with salt and pepper. With a slotted spoon, transfer the vegetables to a serving bowl. Garnish with a sprinkling of cilantro, if using, and serve.

Serves 4–6

Zucchini Succotash

Succotash is an American dish consisting of lima beans and corn. It is no stretch of the imagination to add summer squash, thereby combining the "three sisters" of Native American food — squash, beans, and corn.

3 tablespoons butter or canola oil

1 clove of garlic, minced

1 green bell pepper, minced

1 red bell pepper, minced

2 tablespoons minced onion

2 cups corn kernels

2 cups cooked lima beans

2 cups diced zucchini

Salt and freshly ground black pepper

1. In a large skillet, heat the oil over medium-high heat. Add the garlic, bell peppers, and onion. Sauté until softened, about 5 minutes.

2. Add the corn, lima beans, and zucchini. Simmer, covered, over medium heat for about 20 minutes, until the vegetables are cooked through.

3. Season to taste with salt and pepper and serve hot.

Serves 6

Summer Squash Sauté with Bacon and Tomatoes

Some might call squash a bland and boring vegetable, especially after a month of zucchini dishes. So brighten up dinner with bold flavors, as in this dish, which includes bacon, garlic, wine, and basil.

¼ pound bacon, chopped

1 cup diced onion

3 cloves of garlic, minced

½ cup minced fresh parsley

6 cups diced summer squash

1½ cups seeded and diced tomatoes

½ cup dry white wine

¼ cup water

2 tablespoons minced fresh basil

Salt and freshly ground black pepper

1. In a large skillet over medium-high heat, fry the bacon until almost done, turning frequently, 8 to 10 minutes.

2. Drain off all but 2 tablespoons of the bacon fat. Add the onion, garlic, and parsley and sauté until the onion is softened and fragrant, about 5 minutes. Add the squash, tomato, wine, water, and basil. Simmer until the squash is tender, 5 to 10 minutes.

3. Season to taste with salt and pepper. Serve at once.

Serves 8

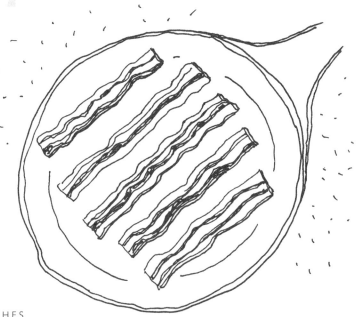

Ragout of summer squash

Summer squash stewed with tomatoes makes a delightful side dish
with any grilled or broiled meat.

2 tablespoons extra virgin
olive oil

2 tablespoons butter

2 cups sliced yellow summer
squash, pattypan squash,
or zucchini

3 large onions, sliced

2 large green bell peppers,
diced

2 celery stalks, diced

2 tomatoes, seeded and
quartered

2 tablespoons chopped fresh
basil

2 tablespoons chopped fresh
tarragon

1 tablespoon chopped fresh
parsley

1 clove of garlic, minced

Salt and freshly ground black
pepper

Grated Parmesan cheese

1. In a large saucepan over medium-high heat, heat the oil and
melt the butter. Add the squash and sauté until softened, about
5 minutes. Remove from the pan with a slotted spoon; set aside.

2. Add the onions, bell peppers, and celery to the saucepan. Sauté
until softened, 3 to 5 minutes. Add the tomatoes, basil, tarragon, parsley, garlic, and salt and pepper to taste. Simmer for
25 minutes.

3. Return the squash to the pan and heat through for 5 minutes.

4. Taste and adjust the seasonings. Sprinkle with the cheese and
serve hot.

Serves 4–6

Summer Vegetable Kabobs

The trick to making good vegetable kabobs is to select vegetables that have relatively similar cooking times or to precook longer-cooking ones. The combination here is good for ease of grilling, flavor, and color.

1 medium-sized golden zucchini or yellow summer squash, cut into 2-inch chunks

1 medium-sized green zucchini, cut into 2-inch chunks

8 cherry tomatoes

1 green bell pepper, cut into 2-inch squares

4 onions, quartered

1 cup vinaigrette or Italian salad dressing

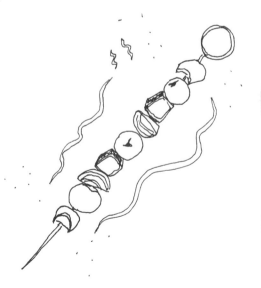

1. In a large bowl, combine the vegetables with the vinaigrette. Toss to coat and set aside.

2. Soak bamboo skewers in water for 30 minutes.

3. Prepare the grill for medium-hot heat.

4. Thread the vegetables onto the skewers, making sure that the zucchini and summer squash are threaded through their skins, not through their centers. (The vegetables will be held more securely if you use two bamboo skewers for each kabob rather than one; it reduces the tendency for the vegetables to spin on the skewer.)

5. Grill the kabobs, basting with the dressing remaining in the bowl and turning occasionally, until the vegetables are tender and grill-marked, about 10 minutes.

6. Serve hot.

Serves 4

Grilled Vegetable Packets

Anyone who has ever cooked outdoors over a campfire knows that the simplest way to grill vegetables is to wrap them in aluminum foil and bake them over the coals. Just butter the foil and wrap up the vegetables, selecting ones with similar cooking times. Sliced zucchini or summer squash, tomatoes, bell peppers, and onions can be combined in a packet with excellent results. Grill the packets for about 20 minutes, turning each package once or twice during the grilling process. Potatoes are also delicious cooked this way, but they should be cooked in their own packets and given an extra 20 minutes for cooking.

Zucchini Cheese Squares

Here's a thrifty-gardener recipe. You can use fresh zucchini that is a little oversized, or you can make use of the zucchini you so frugally grated and froze last summer. If you are using frozen zucchini, you can skip the salting step, but be sure to drain the zucchini.

1 cup grated zucchini
  Salt
1 cup grated carrot
1 cup diced onion
¼ cup chopped fresh dill
¼ cup chopped fresh mint
¼ cup chopped fresh parsley
1 cup grated Cheddar, Fontina, or Muenster cheese
½ cup crumbled feta cheese
1½ cups unbleached all-purpose flour
  Freshly ground black pepper
3 eggs, lightly beaten

1. Combine the zucchini and 1 teaspoon salt in a colander. Toss to mix and set aside to drain for 30 minutes. Rinse under running water to remove the salt, and squeeze by the handful to remove excess water. Pat dry with paper towels.

2. Preheat the oven to 350°F. Butter a 9-inch baking dish.

3. In a large bowl, combine the zucchini, carrot, onion, dill, mint, parsley, cheeses, and flour. Toss to combine. Add the eggs and salt and pepper and combine thoroughly.

4. Transfer to the baking dish.

5. Bake for 50 minutes, until browned.

6. Let cool for about 5 minutes. Cut into squares and serve.

Serves 6

ratatouille

In the perfect ratatouille, the flavors are blended, yet each vegetable remains distinct. The vegetables are neither mushy nor undercooked. To do this properly, sauté each vegetable separately in a large skillet, and then combine them in a saucepan just long enough to blend the flavors.

7 tablespoons extra virgin olive oil

1 medium-sized eggplant, peeled and diced

Salt and freshly ground black pepper

1 onion, diced

1 small green bell pepper, diced

1 small red bell pepper, diced

2 small yellow summer squash, diced

2 small zucchini, diced

2 ripe tomatoes, seeded and diced

4 cloves of garlic, minced

1 can (8 ounces) unseasoned tomato sauce or tomato purée

1. In a large skillet, heat 3 tablespoons of the oil over medium-high heat. Add the eggplant and season with salt and pepper. Sauté until browned, juicy, and cooked through, 10 to 12 minutes. Using a slotted spoon, transfer to a medium-sized saucepan.

2. Return the skillet to medium-high heat and add 2 more tablespoons of the oil. Add the onion and bell peppers. Sauté until tender crisp, 3 to 5 minutes. Transfer to the saucepan with a slotted spoon.

3. Return the skillet to medium-high heat and add the remaining 2 tablespoons oil. Add the summer squash and zucchini and season with salt and pepper. Sauté until tender crisp, 3 to 5 minutes. Transfer to the saucepan and add the tomatoes, garlic, and tomato sauce.

4. Simmer for 15 minutes over medium heat.

5. Taste and adjust the seasoning. You can serve immediately, but the flavor will improve if the ratatouille sits at room temperature for 1 to 2 hours. Serve at room temperature, or reheat and serve warm.

Serves 6–8

Flavor Extras

Sometimes I add herbs, capers, and other flavors to ratatouille. But if you start with garden-fresh vegetables, this dish needs no embellishment beyond salt and pepper.

The Perfect Summer Dish

Ratatouille is the perfect summer vegetable dish. Its possibilities are endless. You can serve it as a side dish, alongside any simply prepared meat, fowl, or fish. Vegetarians will be content with ratatouille served as a main course, with perhaps some bread and cheese to accompany it. It makes a delicious topping for pasta or pizza. Or, you can make a ratatouille lasagne by layering lasagna noodles, ratatouille, white sauce, and cheese.

Consider packing ratatouille into a pita pocket or a long roll, with a shaving of Parmesan cheese or a couple of slices of fresh mozzarella. Because ratatouille improves with age, you won't mind having it as leftovers. If refrigerator space is limited, freeze the leftovers and enjoy them when convenient.

Baked Zucchini and Eggplant Casserole

The vegetables are the same as those for ratatouille, but here they are baked in a cheesy tomato sauce. The results are quite different, and delightful.

3 tablespoons extra virgin olive oil

1 medium-sized zucchini, diced

1 small eggplant, peeled and diced

¼ cup diced onion

¼ cup diced green bell pepper

2 cloves of garlic, minced

1 can (6 ounces) tomato paste

½ cup dry red wine

½ cup sour cream

Salt and freshly ground black pepper

1 can (8 ounces) tomato sauce

1 cup grated mozzarella cheese

1. Preheat the oven to 350°F. Oil a 1½-quart baking dish or 8-inch square pan.

2. In a large skillet, heat the oil over medium-high heat. Add the zucchini and eggplant and sauté until the eggplant is tender, about 15 minutes. Stir in the onion, green pepper, garlic, tomato paste, wine, and sour cream. Heat thoroughly. Add salt and pepper to taste.

3. Transfer the vegetable mixture to the prepared baking dish. Top with the tomato sauce and cheese. Bake for 45 minutes.

4. Serve hot.

Serves 4

Savory Zucchini-Rice Custard

Although custards are usually sweetened and served as dessert, they also have a place prepared with a savory blend of vegetables. Think crustless quiche, and you'll understand why this recipe makes a delicious dish.

4 small zucchini, thinly sliced

¼ cup chopped fresh parsley

¼ cup cooked rice

⅓ cup unbleached all-purpose flour

1 egg

¼ cup sour cream

½ teaspoon salt

⅛ teaspoon cayenne pepper

½ cup freshly grated Parmesan cheese

2 tablespoons butter

1. Preheat the oven to 375°F. Lightly butter a 1-quart baking dish.

2. Bring a medium-sized pot of lightly salted water to a boil. Add the zucchini to the boiling water, and blanch until tender crisp, about 3 minutes. Drain, plunge into cold water to stop the cooking, drain again, and pat dry.

3. Arrange half the zucchini in the baking dish. Sprinkle the parsley and spread the rice over the zucchini. Toss the remaining zucchini with the flour and lay over the rice.

4. In a small bowl, combine the egg, sour cream, salt, cayenne, and ¼ cup of the cheese. Mix well and pour over the zucchini. Dot with butter and sprinkle with the remaining ¼ cup cheese.

5. Bake for 40 minutes, until the custard is set.

6. Allow to stand for 10 minutes before serving. Serve warm or at room temperature.

Serves 4

Zucchini Custard Pudding

The grated zucchini gives this custard a pebbly texture, almost like
rice pudding. However, this pudding is savory.

1 medium-sized zucchini,
grated

1 teaspoon salt

4 eggs

½ cup milk or light cream

¾ cup fine dry bread crumbs

½ teaspoon dried oregano

3 tablespoons freshly grated
Parmesan cheese

2 tablespoons butter, melted

1. In a colander, combine the zucchini and salt. Toss to mix and
   set aside to drain for 30 minutes.

2. Preheat the oven to 350°F. Butter a 1-quart baking dish.

3. In a medium-sized mixing bowl, combine the eggs and milk
   and beat until well blended. Add the bread crumbs, oregano,
   cheese, and butter. Beat until blended. Squeeze any excess
   moisture from the zucchini and fold into the egg mixture.
   Pour the mixture into the baking dish.

4. Bake for 40 minutes, until the custard is set.

5. Let stand for 10 minutes. Serve warm or at room temperature.

Serves 4

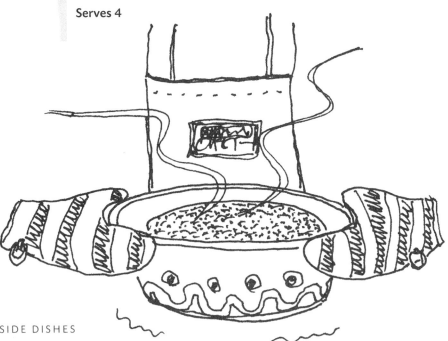

Cheese-Stuffed Zucchini Boats

For some reason, calling these "boats" makes children more inclined
to eat them. Of course, the bacon-cheese filling helps, too.

4 bacon strips

2 medium-sized or 4 small
   zucchini

2 ripe tomatoes, seeded and
   chopped

1½ cups grated Cheddar cheese

   About ½ cup seasoned dry
   bread crumbs

1. Bring a large pot of salted water to a boil.

2. In a medium-sized skillet over medium heat, partially cook the
   bacon until it has colored but is not yet crisp, 6 to 8 minutes.

3. Cut the zucchini in half lengthwise. Blanch in the boiling water
   for 3 to 5 minutes. Drain well. Scoop out the pulp, leaving a
   ¼-inch shell. Chop the pulp and combine with the tomatoes
   and cheese.

4. Place the zucchini on a broiler pan, hollowed-side up. Fill with
   the cheese mixture. Top each squash half with a strip of bacon
   (cut the bacon strips in half if you are using small zucchini).

5. Broil until the bacon is crisp, about 4 minutes.

6. Sprinkle with the bread crumbs. Serve hot.

Serves 4

Stuffing Squash

Stuffed squash may be the first thing a gardener-cook thinks of
when confronted with slightly overgrown squash. It's a good
thought, too. Just halve the squash lengthwise and discard the
pulpy center. You can remove another inch or so of flesh around the
edges of the squash to chop and add to the filling; be sure to leave
¼ inch of flesh to hold the stuffing without collapsing the shell.

But don't wait for overgrown squash. Small squash, particularly
baby pattypans, are particularly appealing as single-serving squash.
Also look for round zucchini — Ronde de Nice and Roly Poly are
popular varieties that are ideal for stuffing.

Stuffed Zucchini with Mornay Sauce

These squash are filled with a rich ham-and-cheese sauce.
This is a wonderful recipe to use with round squash, such as Ronde de Nice or Roly Poly.

MORNAY SAUCE

- 2 tablespoons butter
- 2 tablespoons unbleached all-purpose flour
- 1 cup milk
- 1 egg yolk
- 2 tablespoons light cream
- 2 tablespoons grated Gruyère cheese
- Salt and freshly ground black pepper

ZUCCHINI

- 3 medium-sized regular zucchini, or 6 small round squash
- ½ cup minced onion
- ½ cup minced cooked ham or crumbled bacon bits
- 2 tablespoons butter
- 2 tablespoons freshly grated Parmesan cheese

1. Bring a large pot of salted water to a boil for the zucchini.

2. To make the sauce, melt the butter in a medium-sized saucepan over medium heat. Whisk in the flour and cook for about 3 minutes, whisking constantly. Stir in the milk and mix well. In a small bowl, beat together the egg yolk and cream. Stir in ¼ cup of the sauce, then add the mixture to the sauce. Stir until heated through. Add the Gruyère and stir until melted. Add salt and pepper to taste. Set aside and keep warm.

3. Preheat the oven to 400°F. Lightly butter a large baking dish.

4. If you are using long, straight zucchini, cut the zucchini in half lengthwise. If you are using round zucchini, leave them whole. Blanch the squash in the boiling water for 5 minutes, then drain well.

5. Scoop out the pulp from long, straight zucchini halves, leaving a ¼-inch shell. Cut a small slice off the bottoms of round squash, if necessary, so that they stand up. Cut a 1-inch slice off the tops and scoop out the pulp, leaving ¼-inch shells. Place the shells in the baking dish, hollow-side up. Chop the pulp and add it to the sauce, along with the onion, ham, and butter. Fill the shells with the sauce and sprinkle with the Parmesan.

6. Bake, uncovered, for 20 to 30 minutes, until heated through.

7. Serve hot.

Serves 6

Mushroom-Nut Stuffed Summer Squash

Mushrooms and nuts make a hearty vegetarian filling for squash. The squash is not precooked, so it is important to choose tender, young squash.

3 medium-sized zucchini or 6 small zucchini

3 tablespoons butter

2 cloves of garlic, minced

½ cup chopped mushrooms

½ cup chopped walnuts

1 teaspoon chopped fresh oregano, or ½ teaspoon dried

¼ cup fresh bread crumbs, or more as needed

Salt and freshly ground black pepper

½ cup grated mild Cheddar cheese

1. Preheat the oven to 350°F. Lightly butter a large baking dish.

2. Halve the zucchini lengthwise. Scoop out the pulp, leaving a ¼-inch shell. Finely chop the pulp.

3. Melt the butter in a large skillet over medium-high heat. Add the garlic, mushrooms, and walnuts and sauté until the mushrooms give up their juice, about 5 minutes. Add the chopped zucchini and oregano. Reduce the heat to medium and cook, stirring, until the squash is tender, about 8 minutes. Remove from the heat.

4. Stir the bread crumbs into the skillet and season to taste with salt and pepper. Divide the mixture among the zucchini shells and place the shells in the baking dish. Sprinkle with the cheese.

5. Bake for 25 minutes, until the filling is heated through and the squash shells are fork-tender.

6. Serve hot.

Serves 6

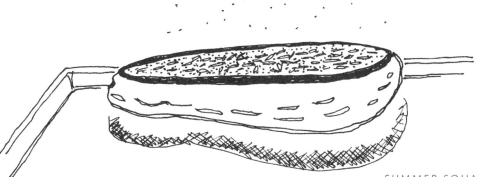

Herb-Stuffed Pattypans

Pattypan squash is shaped like a flying saucer with scalloped edges. It is a terrific vegetable to stuff because it looks so appealing on a plate. This stuffing is simple: bread crumbs seasoned with herbs and sautéed in bacon fat. If you prefer a vegetarian version, omit the bacon, sauté the bread crumbs in olive oil, and substitute a neutral-tasting vegetable broth for the chicken broth.

6 medium-sized pattypan squash

6 strips bacon

1 onion, minced

2 cloves of garlic, minced

1 cup dry bread crumbs

1 tablespoon minced fresh parsley

1 teaspoon chopped fresh basil, or ½ teaspoon dried

1 teaspoon chopped fresh tarragon, or ½ teaspoon dried

1 teaspoon chopped dried rosemary, or ½ teaspoon dried

Salt and freshly ground black pepper

2–3 tablespoons butter, melted

½ cup chicken broth

1. Bring a large pot of salted water to a boil for the squash. Preheat the oven to 350°F.

2. Cut thin lids from the squash. When the water comes to a boil, blanch the squash and lids for 10 to 15 minutes, until tender. Drain well. Hollow out the squash and chop the pulp. Turn the squash upside down to drain. Set aside the lids.

3. Heat a large skillet over medium heat. Add the bacon and fry until crisp, about 10 minutes. Set aside on paper towels to drain. Pour off all but 2 tablespoons of the bacon drippings.

4. Add the onion and garlic. Sauté until softened, about 3 minutes. Add the squash pulp, bread crumbs, parsley, basil, tarragon, rosemary, and salt and pepper to taste. Sauté for 5 minutes.

5. Crumble the bacon and add it to the bread crumb mixture.

6. Butter the squash shells inside and out. Stuff the mixture into the shells. Place the squash in a large shallow baking dish. Add the broth. Cover the squash with their tops.

7. Bake for 20 minutes, until heated through.

8. Serve hot.

Serves 6

Cream Cheese-Stuffed Blossoms

The mild-tasting cream cheese filling allows the delicate flavor of the squash blossoms to come through. This simple recipe can be served as a side dish or an hors d'oeuvre.

1 package (8 ounces) cream cheese, softened

⅓ cup minced onion

2 tablespoons minced chives

Salt and freshly ground black pepper

12 to 14 squash blossoms

1. Preheat the oven to 300°F. Butter a large baking dish.

2. In a food processor or small bowl, combine the cream cheese, onion, chives, and salt and pepper to taste. Mix well. Stuff the mixture into the blossoms and place the blossoms in the baking dish.

3. Bake for 10 minutes or until the cream cheese mixture is heated through.

4. Serve hot or warm.

Serves 6–7

Blossoming

Squash plants bear male and female blossoms. The stem of the female flower eventually begins to swell, which is the squash forming in its initial growth stage. The dried female blossom often must be plucked from the end of the mature vegetable. Male blossoms, having long since met their responsibilities in the pollination process, simply fall off and decay.

When first blooming, squash may produce only male blossoms. Don't fret; this is a common occurrence. Have faith that the female blossoms will appear. Since the female blossoms produce squash, pick only surplus male blossoms for cooking.

Male blossoms (easily identified by their long, slender stems) can be used to make several kinds of dishes. For elegance, dip them in a thin batter and fry. If they are still budding when picked, lightly sauté them in butter. Stuffing possibilities are limited only by your imagination. Sliced blossoms dress up omelettes, pastas, soups, and salads.

Squash Blossom Tempura

Tempura is easy and delicious. In fact, it is my favorite way to enjoy squash blossoms. But — and this is a big "but" — deep-frying makes a mess. However, if you have an exhaust hood over your stovetop and the patience to clean up batter drips and oil spatters, you will be a hero to your friends and family whenever you make this.

1½ cups Tempura Batter (recipe follows)

Oil for deep-frying

16 squash blossoms

16 baby zucchini, cut in half lengthwise

About ½ cup unbleached all-purpose flour

DIPPING SAUCE

6 tablespoons soy sauce

6 tablespoons water

1 tablespoon minced peeled ginger

1 large clove of garlic, minced

1½ teaspoons rice vinegar

1. Make the tempura batter and let it sit for at least 30 minutes.

2. To make the dipping sauce, combine the soy sauce, water, ginger, garlic, and vinegar. Set aside.

3. In a large, deep saucepan, heat 3 to 4 inches of oil over medium-high heat to a temperature of 365°F on a deep-fat thermometer. (If you don't have a thermometer and still want to tackle deep-frying, you can gauge the temperature of the oil by dropping a 1-inch cube of bread into the preheated oil. If the bread browns in 60 seconds, the oil is at 365°F, the ideal temperature for deep-frying most foods.)

4. One piece at a time, dip the blossoms and vegetables into the flour, then into batter. Slip each piece into the hot oil. Fry just a few pieces at a time. Fry until the pieces are golden, 3 to 4 minutes.

5. Drain on paper towels or on wire racks set over a baking sheet. Serve immediately, accompanied by the dipping sauce.

NOTE: The same basic tempura batter, dipping sauce, and method can be used with all manner of vegetables, as well as with shrimp. As long as you are going to the trouble of making tempura, you might as well make a whole meal of it, with many different foods.

Serves 4

Tempura Batter

1 cup unbleached all-purpose flour

2 egg yolks

½ cup flat beer

½ cup cold water

½ teaspoon salt

1. Combine the flour, egg yolks, beer, water, and salt in a blender. Process until smooth.

2. Allow to sit for 20 minutes.

3. Dip the vegetables into the batter and deep-fry until golden brown.

NOTE: To flatten beer, pour it into a bowl and let it sit at room temperature for 1 or 2 hours.

Makes 1½ cups

Blossoms stuffed with spinach and Rice

These blossoms are somewhat more substantial than those in
the previous recipe. The spinach or Swiss chard should be very well drained;
use your hands to squeeze out excess moisture.

1½ tablespoons butter

1 tablespoon chopped onion

2 cups cooked, chopped, and well-drained spinach or Swiss chard

1 cup cooked white rice

1 egg yolk, lightly beaten

½ cup grated Gruyère cheese

Salt and freshly ground black pepper

8–12 squash blossoms

1. Preheat the oven to 325°F. Butter a large baking dish.

2. Melt the butter in a large skillet over medium heat. Add the onion and cook until softened and fragrant, about 3 minutes. Add the spinach and rice; mix well. Stir in the egg yolk, cheese, and salt and pepper to taste.

3. Stuff the mixture into the squash blossoms. Place the blossoms in the baking dish.

4. Bake for 10 minutes, or until the filling is heated through.

5. Serve hot.

Serves 4–6

6. Winter Squash Side Dishes

In an ideal fall harvest season, the winter squash all mature on the vine, and you can enjoy the leisurely process of cooking them whenever the spirit moves you.

There's no question that everyone has a favorite winter squash. Some people look for sweetness, others for moistness. Some people just prefer whatever squash they grew up with (or didn't grow up with). Keep your preferences in mind when you select a squash for the recipes that follow. Even if a particular squash is not recommended for a particular recipe, it probably can be used and will taste great.

Basic Baked Winter Squash

Regardless of the variety, winter squash is delicious baked. After it is baked, you can use the flesh in any recipe calling for cooked squash. Or you can serve it simply, just brushed with butter and sprinkled with salt and pepper. For even more flavor, sprinkle with brown sugar or drizzle with honey or maple syrup during the last 10 minutes of baking.

1–4 winter squash, such as acorn, buttercup, golden nugget, Hubbard, red kuri, sweet dumpling, or turban

Butter (optional)

Salt and freshly ground black pepper (optional)

Brown sugar, honey, or maple syrup (optional)

1. Preheat the oven to 400°F.

2. Cut the squash into halves if small, or into quarters or serving-size pieces if large. Remove and discard the seeds and fibers. Place skin-side up in a baking dish. Add about 1 inch water to the dish.

3. Bake until the squash is tender when pierced with a skewer, 45 to 60 minutes, depending on the size of the pieces.

4. Drain off the water. Turn the pieces flesh-side up, brush with butter, and sprinkle with salt and pepper. If desired, sprinkle with brown sugar or drizzle with honey or maple syrup. Bake for another 10 minutes.

5. Serve hot.

Serves 4

Basic Winter Squash Purée

Like mashed potatoes, winter squash is greatly enhanced by a generous hand with the butter. Also like potatoes, winter squash may be mashed by hand or whipped to a smooth and creamy consistency with an electric mixer. For this preparation, a smooth-fleshed winter squash is preferred.

1 **large buttercup, butternut, or red kuri squash or ½ small Baby Blue Hubbard squash**

4–6 tablespoons butter

4–6 tablespoons maple syrup

3–4 tablespoons half-and-half or light cream

Salt and freshly ground black pepper

1. Preheat the oven to 400°F.

2. Cut the squash into halves if small or into quarters if large. Remove and discard the seeds and fibers. Place skin-side up in a baking dish and add about 1 inch of water to the dish.

3. Bake until completely tender when pierced with a skewer, 60 to 90 minutes, depending on the size of the pieces.

4. Drain off the water. Turn the pieces flesh-side up. Allow to cool enough to be easily handled.

5. Scrape the flesh from the skins into a mixing bowl and discard the skins. Add the butter and mash or beat until smooth. Beat in the maple syrup and half-and-half. Season to taste with salt and pepper.

6. Reheat in a microwave or in the top of a double boiler set over boiling water. Serve hot.

Serves 4–6

Basic Baked Spaghetti Squash

The fun of spaghetti squash lies in its oddball texture. The squash cooks down to a mass of long spaghetti-like strands. Although you can serve it sweetened, as with other winter squash, spaghetti squash lends itself to savory preparations; try topping it with your favorite marinara sauce.

1 large spaghetti squash (about 3 pounds)

4 tablespoons butter

4 cloves of garlic, minced

2 tablespoons chopped fresh parsley

Salt and freshly ground black pepper

1. Preheat the oven to 350°F.

2. Cut the squash in half lengthwise. Scoop out and discard the seeds. Place skin-side up in a baking dish and add about 1 inch of water. Bake until the skin begins to give, about 40 minutes. Let cool slightly.

3. In a small saucepan over low heat, melt the butter. Add the garlic and cook, stirring, until the garlic is fragrant, about 2 minutes. Using a large fork, scoop the squash out of its skin, pulling it into strands. Transfer to a serving bowl.

4. Add the garlic butter and toss to mix. Add the parsley and season with salt and pepper. Toss again and serve.

Serves 4–6

Ginger-Glazed winter squash

A delicate glaze of ginger, brown sugar, and sherry adds another flavor dimension to sweet winter squash.

1–4 hard-shelled winter squash, such as acorn, buttercup, golden nugget, Hubbard, red kuri, or turban, cut in halves, quarters, or serving-size pieces

2 tablespoons butter, melted

2 tablespoons light brown sugar

1 tablespoon dry sherry

1 teaspoon ground ginger

Salt and freshly ground black pepper

1. Preheat the oven to 375°F.

2. Scoop out and discard the seeds and fibers from each squash. Place the squash skin-side up in a baking dish. Add about 1 inch of water to the baking dish. Bake for 30 minutes.

3. In a small bowl, combine the butter, sugar, sherry, ginger, and salt and pepper to taste.

4. Remove the squash from the oven and carefully pour out the water. Turn the squash cut-side up. Brush the flesh with some of the butter mixture. Pour the remaining butter over the squash halves, allowing it to pool in the cavities.

5. Bake until the squash pieces are completely tender, about 25 minutes.

6. Serve hot.

Serves 4

Citrus Squash Bake

Fruit harmonizes beautifully with sweet winter squash,
creating a burst of sunshine on the plate.

1–6 hard-shelled winter squash,
such as acorn, buttercup,
golden nugget, Hubbard,
red kuri, or turban

6 tablespoons butter

6 tablespoons brown sugar

1 tablespoon grated orange zest

½ teaspoon salt

3 oranges, peeled and sectioned

1 grapefruit, peeled and
sectioned

¼ cup golden raisins

1. Preheat the oven to 375°F.

2. Place the whole squash in a large baking pan. Add about ¼ inch of water. Bake for 45 to 60 minutes, until the skins are fork tender.

3. Remove the squash from the oven and cut into serving-size pieces: halves for smaller squash and quarters or serving-size wedges for larger squash. Scoop out and discard the seeds and fibers.

4. Return the squash to the baking pan, cut-side up. Sprinkle each with salt. Fill each cavity with ½ tablespoon of the butter, ½ tablespoon of the sugar, and ¼ teaspoon of the orange zest. Divide the orange and grapefruit sections and raisins equally among the squash pieces.

5. Bake for another 25 minutes.

6. Serve hot.

Serves 6

The View from a Farm Stand

MIKE AND NANCY MERRILL run a small produce business on the outskirts of Middlebury, Vermont. From spring through late fall, they sell a variety of fresh fruits and vegetables, some of which they grow themselves. And what is their best seller?

"Zucchini," says Mike. "We can depend on moving two boxes — that's 40 pounds — every single day."

"And that's not counting the yellow summer squash," adds Nancy.

I commented that it seemed I was seeing zucchini shrink in size over the years. I asked if the size of the average zucchini had gotten smaller since they first started selling it.

"You know, we used to sell big zucchini," Mike commented, holding his hands about 12 inches apart. "People would buy those to slice up and cover with breading and fry. But now it's all about grilling. That's what people want the zucchini for. For grilling."

"And they want them tiny. Little baby zucchini." Nancy holds her hands a finger's distance apart, the pitch of her voice rising. "They'll pay top prices for them. Of course, every once in a while our kids will let the zucchini grow too big and they harvest 'em when they've gotten big, but we put 'em out in a basket and even those will sell."

"Zucchini." Mike shakes his head. "Everyone wants it."

Sweet Baked Acorn Squash

A classic and simple recipe. Try it with any type of squash,
particularly sweet dumplings, allowing one squash per serving.

2 acorn squash, cut in half
   lengthwise

2 tablespoons butter, melted

½ cup milk

½ cup pure maple syrup

1. Preheat the oven to 350°F.

2. Scoop out and discard the seeds and fibers from each squash half. Place the halves cut-side down on a baking sheet. Bake for 45 minutes.

3. Turn the squash cut-side up. Brush the butter onto the flesh of each squash. Combine the milk and maple syrup and pour into each squash half. Bake for another 15 minutes.

4. Serve hot.

Serves 2

VARIATIONS: Instead of using milk and maple syrup, you can fill the cavities with brown sugar, currant jelly, crushed pineapple, mint jelly, applesauce, apple butter, or chutney.

Toasted Almond Squash

A simple and elegant make-ahead squash.

1 **large buttercup, butternut, red kuri, or turban squash or small Baby Blue Hubbard, cut into quarters**

3 **tablespoons butter**

½ **cup maple syrup**

   Pinch of ground nutmeg

⅓ **cup sliced almonds**

1. Scoop out and discard the seeds and fibers from the squash. In a large saucepan, boil salted water. Cook the squash in the boiling water until tender, about 20 minutes. Drain and allow to cool enough to handle.

2. Preheat the oven to 350°F. Butter a 1½-quart baking dish.

3. Scoop the pulp from the skin and discard the skins. Beat the pulp with the butter until smooth. Stir in the maple syrup and nutmeg. Transfer to the baking dish and sprinkle with the almonds. (The squash can be made up to this point, covered, and refrigerated for several days. Add 15 minutes to the baking time if the squash goes into the oven cold.)

4. Bake for about 15 minutes, until the squash is heated through and the almonds are lightly browned.

Serves 4

Glazed Delicata Crescents

Unlike most winter squash, you can slice delicata easily
and enjoy it skin and all. Its flavor is delicate and sweet. Farmers report
a growing acceptance of delicata. Try it, and you will understand why.

2 **medium-sized delicata squash**

3 **tablespoons butter, melted**

1 **tablespoon honey or maple syrup**

1. Preheat the oven to 350°F. Lightly oil a baking sheet.

2. Slice the squash in half lengthwise. Scoop out the seeds and fibers with a spoon. Slice into ½-inch crescents.

3. In a medium-sized bowl, combine the squash with 2 tablespoons of the butter. Toss to coat. Arrange on the baking sheet.

4. Roast for 15 minutes, turning once.

5. Add the honey to the remaining 1 tablespoon butter. Brush the honey-butter mixture over the squash and return to the oven to roast for another 5 minutes.

6. Serve hot.

Serves 4

VARIATION: To make Glazed Sweet Dumpling Wedges, substitute 4 sweet dumpling squash for the delicata. Slice each in half lengthwise. Cut along the ribs to make long wedges. Proceed as directed above.

Winter Squash Fritters

Fritters may be further proof that everything tastes better fried. Here, winter squash is made into a pancake and pan-fried. For people who find winter squash purées too similar to baby food, fritters may be just what they need to develop a better appreciation for this high-nutrition vegetable.

1 medium-sized winter squash, such as buttercup, butternut, or red kuri, halved lengthwise

2 eggs, separated

1 tablespoon minced onion

2 tablespoons milk

½ cup all-purpose flour, or more as needed

1 teaspoon baking powder

Salt and freshly ground black pepper

Vegetable oil, for frying

1. Preheat the oven to 375°F.

2. Scoop out and discard the seeds and fibers from each squash half. Place the squash halves cut-side down in a baking dish. Add about 1 inch of water to the baking dish. Bake for about 1 hour, until the flesh is completely tender. (This can be done up to 1 day in advance and refrigerated, but bring the squash to room temperature before proceeding.)

3. Scoop out the squash flesh and discard the skins. Mash the squash in a medium-sized mixing bowl. Combine the squash with the egg yolks, onion, milk, flour, baking powder, and salt and pepper to taste.

4. In another mixing bowl, whip the egg whites until stiff peaks form. Fold the egg whites into the squash batter.

5. Heat about ⅛ inch of oil in a large skillet over medium-high heat. Drop the batter by the spoonful into the hot oil and fry for 2 to 3 minutes, or until golden brown on the bottom side. Turn once (do not pat down the fritters) and cook on the second side until browned, another 2 to 3 minutes. Drain on paper towels.

6. Serve immediately.

Serves 4

Gingered Winter Squash with Pecans and Cranberries

This winter squash dish has become a Thanksgiving tradition at my house. If oven space is limited, the squash can be roasted a day ahead, then reheated in a microwave and combined with the cranberries, nuts, and crystallized ginger just before serving. Butternut is the squash of choice here because it is so easy to peel.

1½–2 pounds butternut squash

3–4 tablespoons butter, melted

2 tablespoons pure maple syrup

1 teaspoon ground ginger

½ cup pecan pieces

¼ cup dried cranberries or cherries

2 tablespoons white wine or water

2 tablespoons chopped crystallized ginger

1. Preheat the oven to 350°F. Lightly oil a large shallow roasting pan or half sheet pan.

2. Peel the squash, slice in half, and scoop out the fibers and seeds. Cut into ½-inch cubes. Combine the squash, 3 tablespoons of the melted butter, maple syrup, and ground ginger in a large bowl and toss to coat. Arrange in a single layer in the pan.

3. Roast for 30 minutes, until the squash is tender, stirring every 10 minutes or so for even cooking.

4. While the squash is roasting, arrange the pecans in a single layer in a small pan, such as a cake tin. Toast for 8 to 10 minutes in the oven, until lightly colored and fragrant. Set aside.

5. Combine the cranberries with the wine and heat for 30 seconds in the microwave or in a small saucepan over low heat, until the cranberries are softened.

6. When the squash is tender, transfer to a serving bowl. Add the pecans, cranberries, and crystallized ginger. Toss to mix. If the squash is dry, or if you prefer a richer-tasting dish and don't mind the additional butter, add the remaining 1 tablespoon of butter and toss. Serve hot.

Serves 4–6

Candied Pumpkin

If you like your winter squash sweet, this is the recipe for you.
You can use a pie pumpkin or a winter squash, such as acorn, buttercup,
butternut, delicata, banana, sweet dumpling, or Baby Hubbard.

1 **small pie pumpkin or medium-sized winter squash**

¾ cup butter

⅓ cup packed light or dark brown sugar

¼ cup chopped crystallized ginger

1. Preheat the oven to 350°F. Lightly butter a large baking dish.

2. Cut the pumpkin in half and remove and discard the seeds and fibers. Cut the pumpkin into serving-size pieces and place in the baking dish, skin-side down.

3. In a small saucepan, melt the butter over low heat. Stir in the sugar and ginger until the sugar is dissolved. Spoon the butter mixture over the pumpkin pieces. Cover the baking dish with aluminum foil.

4. Bake for about 1 hour, covered, until the pumpkin is tender.

5. Serve hot.

Serves 4

Butternut and Sweet Potatoes Mashed

Did you pack away leftover sweet potatoes *and* leftover winter squash after your abundant Thanksgiving feast? Try making this delicious combination and see if it doesn't please both the lovers of squash and the fans of sweet potatoes.

1 cup cooked and mashed winter squash

1 cup cooked and mashed sweet potatoes

4 tablespoons butter, softened

½ teaspoon salt

¼ teaspoon ground cinnamon

¼ teaspoon ground nutmeg

⅛ teaspoon freshly ground black pepper

1. In a large mixing bowl, combine the squash, sweet potatoes, butter, salt, cinnamon, nutmeg, and pepper. Whip together until fluffy.

2. Transfer the mixture to the top of a double boiler and set over boiling water and heat through.

3. Serve hot.

Serves 4

Dependable Vegetable

Winter squash is an utterly dependable vegetable from the first harvest through a long, cold winter.

Eating winter squash through the winter, avoiding supermarket imports, is a way to eat seasonally and to support sustainable agriculture. But we are so used to variety in our American diets that we need plenty of new preparations to keep our interest high.

When making side dishes with winter squash, keep in mind that you are working with a high-flavor vegetable. It won't lose its character in a crowd of vegetables.

Winter squash can stand up to earthy flavors, such as those of mushroom, goat cheese, and onions.

Acorn Squash with Scalloped Onions

Most winter squash recipes emphasize the sweet nature of the vegetable, but here the vegetable is treated to a savory topping of scalloped onions.

2 medium-sized acorn or deli-cata squash, halved length-wise, or 4 sweet dumpling squash, tops removed

Salt

3 tablespoons butter

1 cup diced onions

2 tablespoons unbleached all-purpose flour

½ cup milk

Ground nutmeg

1. Preheat the oven to 350°F.

2. Remove the seeds and fibers from the squash and discard. Place the squash skin-side up in a baking pan. Add about 1 inch of water. Bake for about 45 minutes, until tender.

3. Remove the squash from the oven and carefully pour out the water. Turn the squash cut-side up. Loosen the pulp with a fork and salt generously.

4. Melt the butter in a small saucepan over medium heat. Add the onion and sauté until softened, 3 to 5 minutes. Stir in the flour to form a paste. Stir in the milk and continue to cook until the sauce is thick.

5. Pour the sauce over the squash. Sprinkle with nutmeg. Bake for 15 minutes.

6. Serve hot.

Serves 4

Spaghetti Squash Cheese Bake

Bacon and cheese is a flavor combination that never loses its appeal. The slightly sweet flavor of spaghetti squash makes a wonderful contrast to the salty bacon and cheese.

1 small to medium-sized spaghetti squash

8 slices bacon

8 ounces Cheddar cheese, grated

Salt and freshly ground black pepper

1. Preheat the oven to 350°F.

2. Cut the squash in half lengthwise. Scoop out and discard the seeds. Place skin-side up in a baking dish and add about 1 inch of water. Bake until the skin begins to give, about 40 minutes. Carefully pour out the water. Set aside to cool slightly.

3. In a large skillet over medium heat, fry the bacon until crisp, turning several times, 8 to 10 minutes. Drain on paper towels. Crumble.

4. Using a large fork, scoop the squash out of its skin, pulling it into long strands. Place in a large mixing bowl. Combine with the bacon, cheese, and salt and pepper to taste. Mix well.

5. Return the mixture to the baking dish and bake until the cheese melts, about 5 minutes.

6. Serve hot.

Serves 4

Noodle Kugel with Butternut Squash

Kugel, which comes from the Yiddish word for "pudding," is a baked pudding. In the Jewish tradition, it can be made with potatoes or noodles, as it is here. Kugel isn't quite sweet enough to serve as a dessert, but it is unusually sweet for a side dish. It is, however, perfect for brunch, that in-between meal. This is a fairly classic version, with grated butternut squash standing in for the more traditional raisins.

1 **pound small-curd cottage cheese**

3 **ounces cream cheese, softened**

1 **cup sour cream**

3 **large eggs, slightly beaten**

2 **tablespoons fresh lemon juice**

⅔ **cup plus 2 tablespoons sugar**

1 **teaspoon pure vanilla extract**

1 **teaspoon salt**

1½ **teaspoons cinnamon**

¼ **teaspoon nutmeg**

3 **cups whole milk**

2 **cups grated butternut squash**

8 **ounces medium (¼-inch) egg noodles**

1. Preheat the oven to 325°F. Butter a 9- by 13-inch baking dish.

2. In a food processor, combine the cottage cheese, cream cheese, sour cream, eggs, lemon juice, vanilla, ⅔ cup of the sugar, the salt, ½ teaspoon of the cinnamon, and the nutmeg. Process until blended. Transfer the mixture to the baking dish. Stir in the milk, squash, and noodles.

3. Bake for 30 minutes.

4. In a small bowl, combine the remaining 2 tablespoons sugar and 1 teaspoon cinnamon. Sprinkle over the noodles.

5. Return the noodles to the oven and bake for an additional 30 minutes, until firm and light brown in color.

6. Serve warm or chilled.

Serves 12

7. Breads and ....

No one is surprised by a zucchini bread or a pumpkin muffin. Zucchini breads are one of the most popular ways to use up excess squash, and pumpkin breads are often served at Thanksgiving, when an apple pie, or even a chocolate dessert, is preferred over the traditional pumpkin pie.

The recipes in this chapter exploit the ability of squash to add life to your baked goods.

Zucchini-Cheddar Biscuits

Zucchini season isn't usually soup season, but nothing goes better with soup than these Cheddar- and zucchini-laced biscuits. It's a good thing you thought ahead and put some grated zucchini in the freezer for recipes such as this one. If you use frozen zucchini, omit the salting step, but do add the salt to the batter.

2 cups grated zucchini

1 teaspoon salt

3 cups unbleached all-purpose flour

1 tablespoon baking powder

2 teaspoons baking soda

½ teaspoon freshly ground black pepper

3 tablespoons cold unsalted butter

1 cup shredded Cheddar cheese

1 large egg

1½ cups buttermilk

1. Combine the zucchini and salt in a colander. Set aside to drain for 30 minutes. Squeeze out any excess moisture and place in a small mixing bowl. You should have about ½ cup zucchini.

2. Preheat the oven to 400°F. Grease a baking sheet.

3. Sift together the flour, baking powder, baking soda, and pepper in a large mixing bowl. Cut in the butter until the mixture resembles coarse crumbs. Add the cheese, egg, buttermilk, and zucchini. Toss with a fork to mix well.

4. Drop the batter by the spoonful onto the baking sheet to make 24 biscuits.

5. Bake the biscuits for 15 minutes, until golden.

6. Serve the biscuits hot out of the oven.

Makes 24 biscuits

Zucchini Trick

The trick with using zucchini and other summer squash in baked goods is to get rid of excess moisture before you start. Most recipes call for grating the squash, salting it, and letting it drain before adding the zucchini to the batter. The zucchini will add days to the storage capacity of the bread and fiber to the diet. If you have frozen grated summer squash, you skip the salting step because the freezing process broke down the cell walls. But the squash will need to be briefly drained. And the batter will need the salt that would have been added to the grated squash. Breads made without salt will taste flat.

Whole-Wheat Zucchini Muffins

Muffins made with whole-wheat flour tend to be drier in texture than
their white-flour counterparts. Not so with the addition of zucchini and honey.

2 cups whole-wheat flour

1 tablespoon baking powder

1 teaspoon ground cinnamon

¼ teaspoon salt

2 large eggs

¾ cup milk

⅓ cup canola oil

¼ cup honey

1 cup grated zucchini

⅔ cup raisins

1. Preheat the oven to 300°F and grease a 12-cup muffin pan.

2. Combine the flour, baking powder, cinnamon, and salt in a medium-sized mixing bowl. Mix well.

3. In a large mixing bowl, beat together the eggs, milk, oil, and honey. Fold in the dry ingredients and the zucchini and raisins. Stir just enough to mix; the batter will be lumpy. Spoon into the muffin pan.

4. Bake for about 20 minutes, until the muffins are firm and a tester inserted in the center of one of the muffins comes out clean.

5. On a wire rack, cool the muffins in the pan for 10 minutes. Turn the muffins out of the pan.

6. Serve the muffins warm or cooled.

Makes 12 muffins

Apple-Carrot-Zucchini Muffins

There's a lot of goodness in these muffins — raisins, coconut, and pecans in addition to apples, carrots, and zucchini. What a great way to start the day.

2 cups unbleached all-purpose flour

1¼ cups sugar

1½ cups coarsely chopped pecans

1 cup grated carrots

1 cup grated zucchini

1 apple, cored and chopped

¾ cup shredded unsweetened coconut

¾ cup golden raisins

1 tablespoon ground cinnamon

2 teaspoons baking soda

½ teaspoon salt

3 large eggs

1 cup vegetable or canola oil

1 teaspoon vanilla extract

1. Preheat the oven to 375°F and grease two 12-cup muffin pans.

2. In a large mixing bowl, combine the flour, sugar, pecans, carrots, zucchini, apple, coconut, raisins, cinnamon, baking soda, and salt. Mix well and make a well in the center.

3. In a second bowl, beat together the eggs, oil, and vanilla. Pour into the well in the dry ingredients. Mix just enough to combine. The batter will be lumpy. Spoon the batter into the prepared muffin pans.

4. Bake the muffins for about 25 minutes, until a tester inserted in the center of one of the muffins comes out clean.

5. On wire racks, cool the muffins in the pans for 10 minutes. Turn the muffins out of the pans.

6. Serve the muffins warm or cooled.

Makes 24 muffins

Zucchini Bread

Many gardeners turn to quick breads when they are overwhelmed by an abundance of zucchini. The virtues of zucchini bread are many: It can be made with freshly grated zucchini or frozen and defrosted (and drained) zucchini, it is quick to make, extra loaves can be frozen and enjoyed later, and, most important of all, it is delicious.

3 cups unbleached all-purpose flour

1 tablespoon ground cinnamon

1¼ teaspoons baking powder

1 teaspoon baking soda

1 teaspoon salt

1 cup canola oil

2½ cups sugar

3 large eggs, beaten

2 cups grated zucchini

1 tablespoon vanilla extract

¼ teaspoon black walnut extract (optional)

1. Preheat the oven to 350°F. Grease two 4- by 8-inch loaf pans.

2. In a medium-sized bowl, combine the flour, cinnamon, baking powder, baking soda, and salt. Mix well.

3. Combine the oil and sugar in a large mixing bowl. Beat until light. Add the eggs, one at a time, beating well after each addition. Stir in the zucchini, vanilla, and black walnut extract, if using. Add the dry ingredients and stir just long enough to combine. Divide the batter between the prepared loaf pans.

4. Bake the loaves for about 1 hour, or until a tester inserted in the centers comes out clean.

5. On wire racks, cool the breads in the pans for 10 minutes. Invert onto the wire racks and cool completely.

Makes 2 loaves

Pumpkin Seed Butter

Pumpkin seed butter is delicious on bread, grilled chicken, or grilled fish.

Combine ½ cup toasted pumpkin seeds, ½ cup chopped fresh cilantro, and 3 cloves of garlic in a blender or food processor and process until combined. Add ⅓ cup softened butter, and salt and freshly ground black pepper to taste. Process to mix. Store in the refrigerator, but serve at room temperature.

Chocolate Zucchini Bread

A bread in name only, this chocolatey, nutty loaf is sweet enough to be dessert, particularly if it is served à la mode. Quick breads are fast to make, easy to store, and always welcome as a housewarming gift, bake sale donation, or make-ahead treat. The recipe makes two loaves — one for enjoying right away and one for giving away or freezing.

1¾ cups sugar

3 large eggs

1 cup vegetable oil

2 cups grated zucchini

1 tablespoon vanilla extract

3 cups unbleached all-purpose flour

½ cup unsweetened cocoa powder

1¼ teaspoons salt

1 teaspoon baking soda

1 teaspoon ground cinnamon

¼ teaspoon baking powder

½ cup chocolate chips

½ cup chopped nuts

1. Preheat the oven to 350°F. Lightly grease two 5- by 9-inch loaf pans.

2. Combine the sugar, eggs, and oil in a large bowl. Beat until well blended. Stir in the zucchini and vanilla.

3. In another bowl, sift together the flour, cocoa powder, salt, baking soda, cinnamon, and baking powder.

4. Add the flour mixture to the zucchini mixture and stir just until blended. Stir in the chocolate chips and nuts. Pour the batter into the prepared pans.

5. Bake the loaves for 1 hour, or until a tester inserted in the centers comes out clean.

6. On wire racks, cool the breads in the pans for 10 minutes. Invert onto the racks and cool completely.

Makes 2 loaves

Zucchini-Bran Squares

These bran squares are a great way to start your morning, especially if you are the type to grab breakfast on the run.

¾ cup (1½ sticks) butter, melted and cooled

¾ cup egg substitute

⅓ cup skim milk

¾ cup bran cereal

½ cup raisins

1¾ cups unbleached all-purpose flour

1 cup sugar

2 teaspoons baking powder

1½ teaspoons ground cinnamon

1 teaspoon baking soda

1½ cups grated zucchini

1. Preheat the oven to 350°F. Grease an 8-inch square baking dish or coat with nonstick cooking spray.

2. Combine the butter, egg substitute, milk, cereal, and raisins in a large mixing bowl. Set aside for 5 minutes.

3. In a small mixing bowl, combine the flour, sugar, baking powder, cinnamon, and baking soda. Mix well.

4. Squeeze the zucchini to remove any excess moisture. Stir the zucchini into the cereal mixture. Add the dry ingredients to the cereal mixture and stir to combine. Spread the batter in the prepared baking dish.

5. Bake the bread for 55 to 60 minutes, until a tester inserted in the center comes out clean.

6. On a wire rack, cool the bread in the pan. Serve warm or completely cooled.

Serves 9

Zucchini-Carrot Bread

You like zucchini bread, and you enjoy carrot cake. This bread combines both vegetables to make a quick bread that is packed with vitamins and fiber.

2½ cups unbleached all-purpose flour

1 tablespoon ground cinnamon

1 teaspoon baking powder

1 teaspoon baking soda

1 teaspoon salt

1 cup vegetable oil

1½ cups packed light brown sugar

2 large eggs

1 cup grated zucchini

1 cup grated carrots

1 cup chopped nuts

½ cup bran cereal

1. Preheat the oven to 350°F. Grease two 8- by 4-inch loaf pans.

2. In a medium-sized bowl, combine the flour, cinnamon, baking powder, baking soda, and salt. Mix well.

3. In a large mixing bowl, combine the oil and sugar. Beat until light. Add the eggs, one at a time, beating well after each addition. Squeeze the zucchini to remove any excess moisture. Add the zucchini and carrots to the sugar mixture and mix well. Add the flour mixture, nuts, and cereal and stir just long enough to combine. Divide the batter between the prepared pans.

4. Bake the loaves for about 1½ hours, until a tester inserted in the centers comes out clean.

5. On wire racks, cool the breads in the pans for 10 minutes. Invert onto the wire racks and cool completely.

Makes 2 loaves

Pumpkin Butter

If you want pumpkin on the table but you aren't a big fan of quick breads, try pumpkin butter. It is especially tasty on whole-wheat toast and English muffins.

Cut a pie pumpkin in half and discard the fibers and seeds. Cut the halves into 2-inch wedges. Place the wedges on a baking sheet and bake in a preheated 350°F oven until the flesh is soft, about 20 minutes. Scrape the flesh from the skin and discard the skin. In a food processor, mash or purée the flesh until smooth. Mix in a dash of salt, a pinch of nutmeg, and honey to taste.

Garden Cornbread

This bread is so packed with vegetables, you can almost regard it as a side dish.
I always bake it in my trusty cast-iron skillet because I like its rustic look, especially
with the cobbled top this recipe produces, but an 8-inch baking dish can also be used.
Preheating the pan in the oven produces a nicely browned bottom crust.

2 cups grated zucchini

1 teaspoon salt

1 red bell pepper

1 tablespoon butter

1 cup stone-ground yellow or white cornmeal

1 cup unbleached all-purpose flour

2 tablespoons sugar

1 tablespoon baking powder

½ teaspoon baking soda

Kernels scraped from 2 ears of corn (about 1 cup kernels)

2 large eggs

¾ cup buttermilk or plain yogurt

¼ cup canola oil

1. In a colander, combine the zucchini and salt. Toss to mix and set aside to drain for about 30 minutes.

2. Under a broiler or over a gas flame, char the bell pepper on all sides for about 10 minutes. Place in a bag or covered bowl to steam for about 10 minutes. Slip off the skin and discard, along with the seeds and stem. Finely chop the pepper and set aside.

3. Add the butter to a large, heavy cast-iron skillet and place it in the oven. Preheat the oven to 425°F.

4. In a large mixing bowl, combine the cornmeal, flour, sugar, baking powder, and baking soda. Mix well. Squeeze the zucchini to remove any excess moisture and add to the cornmeal mixture. Add the bell pepper and corn. Mix until the vegetables are distributed throughout.

5. In a separate bowl, combine the eggs, buttermilk, and oil. Pour the egg mixture into the cornmeal mixture. Working quickly, stir just until well combined. The batter will be lumpy.

6. Remove the skillet from the oven and tilt to swirl around the melted butter to coat the bottom and sides of the pan. Pour the batter into the skillet and smooth the top.

7. Bake for 25 to 30 minutes, until a tester inserted near the center comes out clean.

8. The bread is best served warm, directly out of the skillet.

Serves 6

Zucchini Focaccia

Focaccia is easy to prepare and makes a great accompaniment to a meal of soup or salad. It also makes a delicious bread for sandwiches.

3 cups grated zucchini

1 tablespoon salt

3¾ cups all-purpose unbleached flour

1 cup whole-wheat flour

1½ cups warm (110°F to 115°F) water

1 packet (¼ ounce) or 1 tablespoon active dry yeast

3 tablespoons olive oil, plus additional oil for brushing

Coarse sea salt or kosher salt

1. Combine the zucchini and salt in a colander. Set aside for 30 minutes to drain. Squeeze out the excess moisture.

2. In a food processor or large bowl, combine the zucchini, 3¼ cups of the white flour, and the whole-wheat flour. Pulse, or toss to mix. Measure the warm water into a glass measure, add the yeast, and stir until foamy. Make sure that the yeast is completely dissolved. Stir in 3 tablespoons of olive oil. In the food processor with the motor running, pour the water mixture through the feed tube and process until the dough forms into a ball. Continue processing for 1 minute to knead the dough.

3. Turn the dough onto a lightly floured surface and knead until the dough is springy and elastic, about 5 minutes. As you knead, add as little of the remaining ½ cup unbleached flour as possible; the dough should be easily handled and slightly sticky, not dry.

4. Place the dough ball in a well-oiled large bowl, and turn the dough to coat. Cover and let rise until doubled in bulk, about 1 hour.

5. Preheat the oven to 500°F. Brush two pizza pans with oil.

6. Stretch the dough to fit the pans. Dimple the surface of the dough with your fingertips. Cover and set aside to rise in a warm place for about 30 minutes.

7. Generously brush the top of one of the focaccia with oil so that the oil pools in the dimples. Sprinkle with the sea salt. Bake for 12 to 15 minutes, until the top and bottom crusts are golden. Repeat with the second focaccia.

8. Serve warm or cooled.

Makes 16 wedges

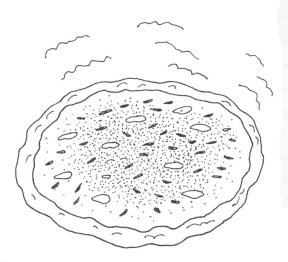

Homemade Pumpkin Purée

Annie Reed Rhoades is the founder of Cooking from the Heart Catering, which provides on-site and off-site catering at the Inn at the Round Barn in Waitsfield, Vermont. She likes to roast her pumpkins to deepen the flavor: "Quarter the pumpkin, scoop out the seeds and fibers, and place the pumpkin pieces in a roasting pan with a little apple cider in the pan. Then roast the pumpkin for about 40 minutes at 400°F." The apple cider is a good tip — it definitely enhances the flavor of the final product.

The next step is to scrape the cooked flesh from the skin and run it through a food processor. If the purée seems watery, drain it in a sieve for about an hour. What's left is cooked pumpkin purée — the same product you get in the can.

Pumpkin Doughnut Muffins

The inspiration for these doughnuts comes from the Downtown Bakery and Creamery in Healdsburg, California, where the morning muffins are brushed with butter, then rolled in a cinnamon-sugar topping to create a fried doughnut effect.

3 cups unbleached all-purpose flour

1 tablespoon baking powder

1 teaspoon baking soda

1 teaspoon salt

¼ teaspoon ground nutmeg

1 cup sugar

½ cup (1 stick) butter, softened

2 large eggs

1¾ cups cooked and mashed pumpkin or winter squash or canned pumpkin purée

¼ cup buttermilk

COATING

¾ cup sugar

2 teaspoons ground cinnamon

6 tablespoons butter, melted

1. Preheat the oven to 350°F and butter a 12-cup muffin pan.

2. Sift together the flour, baking powder, baking soda, salt, and nutmeg.

3. In a large mixing bowl, cream together the sugar and butter. Add the eggs one at a time, beating after each addition. Beat in the pumpkin and buttermilk. Then, beat in the flour mixture until smooth.

4. Divide the batter among the prepared muffin cups. The batter will be stiff; an ice cream scoop does a good job of distributing it.

5. Bake the muffins for 25 to 30 minutes, until they have risen and a tester inserted in the center of one comes out clean.

6. On a wire rack, cool the muffins in the pan for a few minutes.

7. To make the coating, in a shallow bowl mix together the sugar and cinnamon. When the muffins are just cool enough to handle, one at a time, brush them all over with the melted butter, then roll them in the sugar and cinnamon mixture, covering them completely.

8. Serve cooled.

Makes 12 muffins

Pumpkin Math

■ A 6-pound pie pumpkin, baked, puréed, and strained, will yield about 2 cups pumpkin purée.

■ A 15-ounce can of pumpkin will yield 1¾ cups pumpkin purée.

Winter Squash Bread

The next time you find yourself with leftover winter squash, try this bread.
You could also use canned pumpkin purée, but winter squash will yield a lighter loaf.
The sorghum (or honey) ensures that this loaf will stay moist for as long as you
store it (which won't be long at all, given how delicious the bread is).

2 cups unbleached all-purpose flour

1 teaspoon baking soda

½ teaspoon baking powder

½ teaspoon salt

½ teaspoon ground cinnamon

½ teaspoon ground nutmeg

1 cup packed brown sugar

⅔ cup canola oil

2 large eggs

½ cup sorghum or honey

¼ cup milk

1 cup cooked and mashed winter squash or pumpkin

1. Preheat the oven to 350°F. Grease a 5- by 9-inch loaf pan or coat with nonstick cooking spray.

2. Combine the flour, baking soda, baking powder, salt, cinnamon, and nutmeg in a medium-sized mixing bowl. Mix well.

3. In a large mixing bowl, combine the sugar and oil. Beat until light. Add the eggs one at a time, beating well after each addition. Stir in the sorghum, milk, and winter squash. Add the dry ingredients and stir just to combine. Spread the batter in the prepared pan.

4. Bake the bread for about 65 minutes, until a tester inserted in the center comes out clean.

5. On a wire rack, cool the bread in the pan for 10 minutes. Invert onto the wire rack and cool completely.

Makes 1 loaf

Pumpkin Nut Bread

Some people prefer their Thanksgiving pumpkin as bread rather than pie. Here's a fine loaf to set out on your table. The recipe can be doubled easily to make two loaves if you are serving a crowd.

1⅔ cups unbleached all-purpose flour

1 teaspoon baking soda

½ teaspoon baking powder

½ teaspoon ground cinnamon

½ teaspoon pumpkin pie spice

½ teaspoon salt

1⅓ cups sugar

⅓ cup canola oil

2 large eggs

1 cup cooked and mashed pumpkin or canned pumpkin purée

¼ cup milk

½ cup chopped nuts

1. Preheat the oven to 350°F. Grease a 5- by 9-inch loaf pan or coat with nonstick cooking spray.

2. Combine the flour, baking soda, baking powder, cinnamon, pumpkin pie spice, and salt in a medium-sized mixing bowl. Mix well.

3. In a large mixing bowl, combine the sugar and oil. Beat until light. Add the eggs one at a time, beating well after each addition. Stir in the pumpkin and milk. Add the flour mixture and stir just to combine. Fold in the nuts. Spread the batter in the prepared pan.

4. Bake the bread for about 1 hour, until a tester inserted in the center comes out clean.

5. On a wire rack, cool the bread in the pan for 10 minutes. Invert onto the wire rack and cool completely.

Makes 1 loaf

What Is Pumpkin Pie Spice?

Pumpkin pie spice is a pleasing blend of ground ginger, cinnamon, nutmeg, and cloves or allspice. If you keep a well-stocked spice shelf, there's no need to buy the spice blend at the supermarket. Just mix into your batter or pie filling a blend of spices that is pleasing to you (use nutmeg and cloves or allspice more sparingly than the ginger and cinnamon).

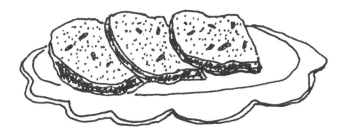

Pumpkin Rice Bread

For those who are allergic to wheat, here's a pumpkin bread made with
rice flour, which can be found at most natural food stores.

2½ cups brown rice flour

1 tablespoon baking powder

1 teaspoon ground cinnamon

½ teaspoon salt

½ cup (1 stick) butter, melted and cooled

½ cup light molasses

2 large eggs

2 cups cooked and mashed pumpkin or canned pumpkin purée

½ cup chopped pecans

1. Preheat the oven to 350°F. Grease a 5- by 9-inch loaf pan, or coat with nonstick cooking spray.

2. Combine the flour, baking powder, cinnamon, and salt in a medium-sized mixing bowl. Mix well.

3. In a large mixing bowl, combine the butter and molasses. Beat until light. Add the eggs one at a time, beating well after each addition. Stir in the pumpkin and beat for 1 minute. Add the flour mixture and stir just to combine. Fold in the nuts. Spread the batter in the prepared pan.

4. Bake for 45 minutes. Cover the loaf with aluminum foil and bake for an additional 30 minutes.

5. On a wire rack, cool the bread in the pan for 10 minutes. Invert onto the wire rack and cool completely.

Makes 1 loaf

Canned or Fresh Pumpkin?

Canned pumpkin purée (not pumpkin pie filling) is one of the best convenience foods I know of. It is a dependably high-quality product that makes a darned good pie, year-round. I always keep a can on hand for making Easy Pumpkin Cake (page 264) at a moment's notice. One can yields 1¾ cups purée, enough for a 9-inch pie.

So why start from scratch? For gardeners, the answer is easy: to make use of what the garden so bounteously provided. Pumpkins and winter squash are incredibly easy to grow, and gardeners are sure to have a surplus. For everyone else, there is the satisfaction of making something from scratch, with the bonus of those irresistible roasted seeds. And don't forget, pumpkin and winter squash can be used interchangeably.

Pumpkin Waffles

Can there be a better choice for a Sunday brunch in the fall?
Pumpkin waffles are delicious served with maple syrup,
applesauce, bananas in yogurt, or spiced pears in syrup.

2 cups unbleached all-purpose flour

2 teaspoons baking powder

½ teaspoon salt

¼ teaspoon ground cinnamon

¼ teaspoon ground ginger

¼ teaspoon ground nutmeg

3 eggs

1¾ cups milk

¾ cup cooked and mashed pumpkin or canned pumpkin purée

½ cup canola oil

½ cup chopped nuts

1. Brush the waffle iron lightly with oil and preheat it.

2. Into a large mixing bowl, sift the flour, baking powder, salt, cinnamon, ginger, and nutmeg. In a separate bowl, beat together the eggs, milk, pumpkin, and oil. Stir the pumpkin mixture into the dry ingredients and mix well. Stir in the nuts.

3. Spread a ladleful or so of batter onto the waffle iron and bake until done, usually 3 to 5 minutes, depending on the iron.

4. Serve immediately.

NOTE: If you are making waffles for a crowd, you can hold them in a 200°F oven for 15 minutes as you make more waffles.

Serves 4

8. Desserts

Pumpkins and winter squash are well-established stars when it comes to desserts. Their sweet flesh adds moisture and flavor to cakes and pies. What would Thanksgiving be without pumpkin pie?

But summer squash should not be overlooked when it comes to dessert. Zucchini that has been peeled, sliced, cooked in lemon juice, and sweetened with sugar and spices can taste remarkably like apple pie filling. This filling can be used in pies, tarts, cakes, crisps — anywhere a pie filling is sought.

Zapple Pie with a Streusel Topping

In the tradition that began with a recipe on the back of a box of Ritz crackers comes this ultimate mock apple pie, made of zucchini. I love to serve this pie to the unwitting and watch their response when I tell them it was made from zucchini. It's delicious, and you can't help smiling as you eat it.

6 cups peeled, quartered, and thinly sliced zucchini (about 2 pounds)

¾ cup sugar

2 teaspoons ground cinnamon

¼ teaspoon ground nutmeg

½ cup plus 2 tablespoons fresh lemon juice

⅓ cup unbleached all-purpose flour

1 unbaked 9- or 10-inch pie shell

TOPPING

½ cup unbleached all-purpose flour

½ cup packed light brown sugar

1 teaspoon ground cinnamon

4 tablespoons butter

1 cup chopped pecans or walnuts

1. To make the filling, in a medium saucepan over medium heat, combine the zucchini, sugar, cinnamon, and nutmeg. Add the 2 tablespoons lemon juice. Stir to mix and cook until tender but not mushy, about 15 minutes, stirring frequently.

2. In a large measuring cup or a small bowl, dissolve the flour in the remaining ½ cup lemon juice. Stir into the zucchini mixture. Continue to cook until the mixture thickens, 2 to 3 minutes. Remove from heat.

3. Preheat the oven to 450°F.

4. To make the topping, combine the flour, brown sugar, and cinnamon in a small bowl. Using a pastry blender or two knives, cut in the butter until the mixture is crumbly. Stir in the pecans.

5. Spoon the filling into the pie shell. Top with half of the streusel topping. Place in the oven and reduce the oven to 350°F. Bake for 30 minutes, until the crust is browned and the filling is bubbling.

6. Sprinkle the remaining topping over the pie. Turn on the broiler. Run the pie under the broiler for about 3 minutes, until the topping is browned.

7. Set the pie on a wire rack to cool. Serve warm or completely cooled. It is best served on the day it is made.

Serves 6–8

Squoconut Custard Pie

I consulted Nancy Merrill when I was digging up unusual zucchini recipes. Nancy generously shared her recipe for a coconut custard pie made with yellow squash instead of coconut. The recipe was originally developed by Nancy's mother, Rose Hudson, and I have adapted it slightly. In the annals of great squash recipes that don't taste like squash, this one is a surely a prizewinner.

3 tablespoons all-purpose unbleached flour

¾ cup evaporated milk

1½ cups half-and-half

1 cup sugar

3 large eggs, lightly beaten

½ teaspoon salt

1 teaspoon coconut flavoring oil or extract

1 teaspoon pure vanilla extract

2 cups grated yellow summer squash

1 unbaked 9- or 10-inch pie shell

¼ teaspoon freshly grated nutmeg

1. Preheat the oven to 425°F.

2. In a medium-sized mixing bowl, combine the flour and evaporated milk. Whisk until the flour is completely dissolved. Mix in the half-and-half. Add the sugar, eggs, salt, coconut flavoring, and vanilla. Whisk until smooth.

3. Pour the custard mixture into the pie shell. Sprinkle the squash over the custard. Sprinkle the nutmeg on top.

4. Bake for 10 minutes. Reduce the oven to 325°F and bake for about 1 hour, until the custard is set but still wobbly and a knife inserted near the center comes out clean.

5. On a wire rack, cool completely. Refrigerate for several hours before serving. This pie is best served on the day it is made.

Serves 6–8

A Leap of Faith

All baking requires of the baker a leap of faith: One puts a batter in the oven and counts on chemistry to transform it into a product of the right texture, consistency, and flavor. Zucchini recipes require an extra leap of faith. No one doubts that chocolate will emerge from the oven tasting delicious, but zucchini? These recipes have been tested and they met with someone's approval. Can zucchini really taste like apple? Can yellow squash really taste like coconut? Take the leap and try it yourself.

Zapple Strudel

Frozen phyllo dough makes strudel easy to whip up. Once again, the zucchini masquerades as apple. I've fooled everyone to whom I've served it.

5½ cups peeled and diced zucchini

½ cup fresh lemon juice

⅔ cup packed light brown sugar

1 tablespoon plus 2 teaspoons ground cinnamon

¼ teaspoon ground nutmeg

1 cup walnuts, toasted

6 double graham crackers

3 tablespoons granulated sugar

12 sheets (each 12 by 17 inches) phyllo pastry, thawed if frozen

¾ cup (1½ sticks) butter, melted

1. Combine the zucchini and lemon juice in a nonreactive saucepan. Bring to a boil over medium-high heat. Reduce the heat and simmer until tender, about 10 minutes. Add the brown sugar, 1 tablespoon of the cinnamon, and the nutmeg. Simmer, stirring, for 1 to 2 minutes, until slightly thickened. Let cool to room temperature.

2. Preheat the oven to 400°F. Line a baking sheet with parchment paper.

3. In a food processor, combine the walnuts and graham crackers Pulse until finely chopped. Stir into the zucchini.

4. Combine the granulated sugar and remaining 2 teaspoons cinnamon in a small bowl.

5. Open 1 sheet of phyllo on a work surface. Brush with some of the butter. Sprinkle about 1 teaspoon of the cinnamon-sugar mixture over the sheet. Top with 5 more sheets of phyllo, brushing each with the butter and sprinkling with the cinnamon and sugar before adding another sheet on top. Spoon half of the filling along the short end of the phyllo, leaving a border of 1½ inches on each end. Fold in the long sides to partially enclose the filling. Roll the phyllo and filling over onto itself to form a roll. Place on the baking sheet seam-side down. Brush with more butter. Repeat to make a second strudel.

6. Bake the strudels for about 25 minutes, until golden. On a wire rack, cool the strudels in the pan.

7. Serve warm or at room temperature.

Serves 16

Winter Squash Pie

You could just as easily call this a pumpkin pie, but making it with winter squash creates a more unexpected dessert. Butternut and Blue Hubbard squash are both excellent choices for this delicious, homey dessert.

1½ cups cooked winter squash or pumpkin purée

1 cup light cream or evaporated milk

3 large eggs, beaten

¼ cup rum

½ teaspoon pure vanilla extract

¾ cup granulated sugar

¼ cup packed light brown sugar

1 teaspoon ground cinnamon

½ teaspoon ground ginger

½ teaspoon salt

1 baked 10-inch pie shell

1. Preheat the oven to 300°F.

2. In a large mixing bowl, combine the squash, cream, eggs, rum, and vanilla. Mix thoroughly. Stir in the granulated sugar, brown sugar, cinnamon, ginger, and salt. Pour the filling into the prepared pie shell.

3. Bake the pie for 1 hour, until the filling is set but still wobbly and a knife inserted near the center of the pie comes out clean. If the edges of the piecrust begin to darken before the pie is done, cover the edges with strips of aluminum foil.

4. Cool completely on a wire rack. Refrigerate for up to 1 day.

5. Serve cold, at room temperature, or rewarmed in a 300°F oven for about 15 minutes.

Serves 6–8

Dress Up Pumpkin Pie

If you love the classic taste of pumpkin pie, you don't want to tamper too much with the pumpkin filling, but you can gild it with a caramel topping.

Mix together 3 tablespoons butter with ⅔ cup light brown sugar. Sprinkle this mixture on top of the pie after it has baked. Broil for 2 minutes. Do not broil it longer, or the topping will become syrupy.

Butternut Custard Pie

Although pumpkin is expected on the Thanksgiving table, butternut squash
makes a darn good pie. Its lovely light orange color makes it the squash
of choice here, but pumpkin or any winter squash can be substituted.

2 large eggs, beaten

2 cups cooked and mashed
butternut squash

1½ cups half-and-half

¼ cup dark corn syrup

¾ cup packed brown sugar

1 teaspoon salt

½ teaspoon ground allspice

½ teaspoon ground cinnamon

¼ teaspoon ground cloves

1 baked 9-inch pie shell

Serves 6–8

1. Preheat the oven to 400°F.

2. In a large mixing bowl, beat together the eggs, squash, half-and-half, corn syrup, brown sugar, salt, allspice, cinnamon, and cloves. Pour into the prepared pie shell. Pour any leftover filling into custard cups.

3. Bake for 10 minutes. Reduce the oven to 350° and bake for 50 minutes, until the custard is set but still wobbly and a knife inserted near the center comes out clean.

4. On a wire rack, cool completely. Refrigerate for several hours before serving. This pie is best served on the day it is made.

Microwave Tip

To speed up cooking a winter squash or pumpkin, cut into halves or quarters, remove seeds and fibers, and place cut-side down in a plastic bag. Poke holes in the bag to allow steam to escape. Microwave at intervals of 5 minutes, until the squash is tender. Carefully remove the squash or pumpkin from the bag; it will be hot, and the escaping steam can burn you.

Easy As Pie

Piecrusts and pastry dough can be tricky, and many good bakers avoid them. Fortunately, some excellent convenience products are available; an example is ready-to-bake piecrusts in the dairy case.

Frozen piecrusts aren't as high quality as fresh-made ones, and they are prone to breaking while still frozen. Refrigerated pie pastry provides a way around this problem. It is packaged as folded disks of rolled-out pie dough. You simply fit the dough into your pan, crimp the edges, and fill. No one will bother to ask whether you made the crust because it will look and taste homemade — buttery, flaky, and tender.

Phyllo dough is another convenience food from the freezer section. It turns strudel-making into kid's play.

Pumpkin Chiffon Pie

The first printed American recipe for chiffon pie was for a "chiffon pumpkin pie," published in 1929 in *The Beverly Hills Women's Club's Fashions in Food.* Whether this recipe below is similar to that original recipe is a question best left to the culinary historians. We know for sure that this version tastes light and delicious.

1 envelope (¼ ounce) unflavored gelatin

½ cup milk

2 cups cooked and mashed pumpkin or canned pumpkin purée

2 large eggs, separated

¾ cup packed light brown sugar

1 teaspoon ground cinnamon

½ teaspoon ground ginger

½ teaspoon salt

¼ teaspoon ground nutmeg

1 teaspoon pure vanilla extract

½ cup whipping cream

⅓ cup granulated sugar

1 baked 9-inch graham cracker crust

Whipped cream, to serve (optional)

1. In a medium-sized saucepan, sprinkle the gelatin over the milk. Set aside to soften for 5 minutes.

2. Add the pumpkin, egg yolks, brown sugar, cinnamon, ginger, salt, and nutmeg. Bring to a boil, stirring constantly. Remove from heat and set aside to cool.

3. When the pumpkin mixture has cooled to room temperature, add the vanilla.

4. Beat the egg whites in a small bowl until stiff peaks form. Fold into the pumpkin mixture.

5. In a large bowl, whip the cream, gradually adding the sugar, until stiff. Fold into the pumpkin mixture. Pour the pumpkin mixture into the crust.

6. Chill until firm, at least 4 hours. Serve with whipped cream, if using. This pie is best served on the day it is made.

Serves 6–8

Pumpkin Ice Cream Pie

Packing ice cream into a crust elevates the ordinary to the extraordinary. Even though this pie requires no special skills and relies on store-bought ice cream, it tastes and looks like a special homemade dessert. The ice cream should be soft enough to work with, but not melted.

1½ cups cooked, mashed, and drained pumpkin or canned pumpkin purée

½ cup packed light brown sugar

½ teaspoon ground cinnamon

¼ teaspoon ground ginger

¼ teaspoon ground nutmeg

¼ teaspoon salt

1 quart vanilla ice cream, softened

1 baked 9-inch graham cracker crust

¼ cup chopped toasted walnuts or pecans

Whipped cream, to serve (optional)

1. In a medium-sized mixing bowl, combine the pumpkin, sugar, cinnamon, ginger, nutmeg, and salt. Mix well.

2. Scoop the ice cream into a large bowl, then fold the pumpkin mixture into the ice cream.

3. Spoon the pumpkin mixture into the piecrust. Use a spatula dipped in water to spread the ice cream smooth. Sprinkle with the nuts and gently press them into the ice cream.

4. Chill in the freezer until firm, at least 4 hours.

5. About 30 minutes before serving, transfer the pie to the refrigerator to soften slightly. Top with whipped cream, if using.

Serves 6–8

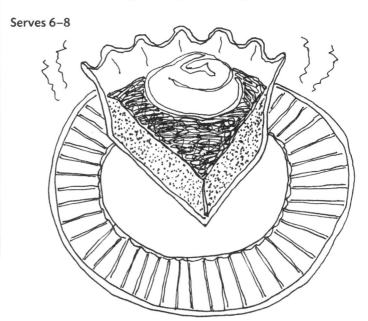

Pick-Your-Own Pie Pumpkins

ALTHOUGH NOT EVERYONE GARDENS, most cookbook buyers cook. And most cooks enjoy making everything from scratch. If cooks are going to go to the trouble of cooking pumpkin from scratch, then they might want to have the pleasure of picking the pumpkin themselves from the field. At least that's what Lori Shea and Bob Hill thought when they decided to raise pie pumpkins as a pick-your-own crop at Clay Brook Farm in Jericho, Vermont.

Bob Hill grew up on a farm in Connecticut where pumpkins were the main fall cash crop. Each weekend in the fall, the farm would host about 1,000 visitors who came to pick pumpkins. It was natural that he and Lori, his wife, planted two acres of pumpkins when they began farming in Vermont. But they discovered that pumpkins were a mainstay crop for many local farmers, and much of their first crop ended up being sold wholesale and shipped to Maryland. Since then, Clay Brook has become a CSA (community-supported agriculture) farm specializing in a diversified mix of vegetable crops and flowers.

But pumpkins remain close to the heart for Hill, and he loves his pick-your-own pumpkin operation: "We get a lot of schoolkids coming out to pick pumpkins. You see their eyes just light up when they get to go pick their own. Little boys especially. They really love pumpkins."

Hill and Shea prefer Baby Bear and Baby Pamela pumpkins for pies, and that is what they grow. "These pumpkins range from 1½ to 3 pounds. New England Pie pumpkins run about 4 to 6 pounds, but they aren't as sweet," explains Shea. They also grow Wee-B-Littles and Jack-B-Littles for table decorations (and mini soup bowls).

I asked Shea for pie-baking advice. She told me to cut one 2-pound pumpkin in half, remove the seeds and bake it at 350°F for 25 to 35 minutes, until it feels soft. The skin will peel off easily.

As for recipes, according to Shea, you can't do much better than the recipe that appears on most cans of pumpkin, so you might as well buy one can and save the recipe.

Pumpkin-Nut Tarts

A topping of orange marmalade brightens these no-bake pumpkin tarts.
Vanilla pudding mix guarantees good texture and eliminates the need to bake the filling.

1½ cups cooked and mashed
   pumpkin or canned pumpkin
   purée
1½ cups milk
 1 package (3 ounces) vanilla
   pudding mix
⅓ cup packed brown sugar
½ teaspoon ground cinnamon
½ teaspoon ground ginger
 8 baked 4-inch tart shells

TOPPING
⅓ cup orange marmalade
¼ cup packed light brown sugar
 1 cup chopped nuts

1. In a large saucepan, combine the pumpkin, milk, pudding mix, brown sugar, cinnamon, and ginger. Bring to a boil, stirring constantly.

2. Pour the pudding mixture into the tart shells. Chill until firm, at least 4 hours.

3. To make the topping, combine the orange marmalade and brown sugar in a small saucepan. Heat, stirring constantly until the sugar dissolves, about 3 minutes. Simmer for 3 minutes. Remove from heat and add the nuts.

4. Spoon the warm topping over the tarts and serve.

Serves 8

Kitchen Sink Cookies

These cookies have everything else in them — oats, dried cranberries,
chocolate chips, walnuts, cinnamon — so why not zucchini?
The zucchini keeps them chewy and moist.

2 cups grated zucchini

1 teaspoon salt

1 cup unbleached all-purpose flour

1½ teaspoons ground cinnamon

½ teaspoon baking powder

½ teaspoon baking soda

½ cup (1 stick) unsalted butter, softened

½ cup granulated sugar

½ cup packed light brown sugar

1 large egg

1 teaspoon pure vanilla extract

1⅓ cups rolled or quick-cooking oats

1 cup semisweet chocolate chips

½ cup dried cranberries, dried cherries, or raisins

½ cup chopped walnuts or pecans

1. Combine the zucchini and salt in a colander. Toss to mix and set aside to drain for 30 minutes.

2. Preheat the oven to 375°F.

3. Combine the flour, cinnamon, baking powder, and baking soda in a medium-sized bowl. Whisk to combine.

4. In a large mixing bowl, combine the butter, granulated sugar, brown sugar, egg, and vanilla. Beat until creamy. With the mixer on low speed, gradually add the flour mixture, beating just until blended. Mix in the zucchini, oats, chocolate chips, cranberries, and nuts.

5. Form heaping tablespoons of the dough into balls. Place 2 inches apart on ungreased baking sheets.

6. Bake for 10 to 12 minutes, until the cookies are light golden brown and appear dry.

7. Cool the cookies on the baking sheets for 1 minute. Transfer to wire racks to cool completely.

Makes 30 cookies

Cookie Keeping

Drop cookies made with grated summer squash or pumpkin are moist and cakelike. Store them in an airtight container for up to 1 week or freeze for up to 3 months.

Zucchini Chocolate Crinkles

The zucchini almost disappears in these delectably chocolatey cookies.

½ cup (1 stick) butter

4 ounces unsweetened chocolate

2 cups sugar

1 cup grated zucchini

4 large eggs

1 teaspoon pure vanilla extract

2½ cups unbleached all-purpose flour

2 teaspoons baking powder

½ teaspoon salt

1 cup chocolate chips

2 cups chopped pecans

1. In the top of a double boiler over simmering water, melt the butter and chocolate, stirring constantly. Transfer the mixture to a mixing bowl and stir in the sugar, zucchini, eggs, and vanilla. Mix well to blend.

2. Sift together the flour, baking powder, and salt into a large mixing bowl. Stir the flour mixture into the chocolate mixture until well blended. Add the chocolate chips and mix well.

3. Chill the batter until firm, at least 4 hours or up to overnight.

4. Preheat the oven to 375°F. Grease two baking sheets.

5. Form the batter into walnut-sized balls and roll each cookie in the chopped nuts. Place 2 inches apart on the baking sheet.

6. Bake for 15 minutes, until the tops of the cookies look dry.

7. Transfer the cookies to wire racks to cool completely.

Makes 48 cookies

Don't Forget the Salt

If you are using frozen grated summer squash, you don't have to add salt to draw the moisture from the squash. When the squash was frozen, the cell walls broke down. As the squash defrosts, it will release its liquid. Just drain in a colander and then squeeze to press out any excess moisture. Add the salt that would have been added to the zucchini directly to the batter; it is needed for flavor.

Zapple Bars

Zucchini stands in for apples in this delicious bar cookie. The bottom is
a classic sugar cookie mixture; the topping is a sweet crumb mixture.
In the middle is zucchini, pretending to be apple.

FILLING

5½ cups peeled and diced zucchini

½ cup fresh lemon juice

⅔ cup packed light brown sugar

1 teaspoon ground cinnamon

¼ teaspoon freshly grated nutmeg

CRUST

2½ cups unbleached all-purpose flour

1¼ cups granulated sugar

½ teaspoon salt

1 cup (2 sticks) unsalted butter, cut into pieces

1 teaspoon pure vanilla extract

1. In a nonreactive saucepan, combine the zucchini and lemon juice. Bring to a boil over medium-high heat. Reduce the heat and simmer until tender, about 10 minutes. Add the brown sugar, cinnamon, and nutmeg. Simmer, stirring, for 1 to 2 minutes, until slightly thickened.

2. Preheat the oven to 350°F. Butter a 9- by 13-inch baking pan.

3. To make the crust, in a food processor combine the flour, sugar, and salt. Add the butter and vanilla. Process until the mixture resembles coarse crumbs.

4. Press half of the crust mixture into the prepared pan. Bake for 10 minutes.

5. Spread the zucchini mixture evenly over the crust. Crumble the remaining crust mixture evenly on top of the zucchini. Bake for 35 to 40 minutes, until golden brown.

6. Cool completely on a wire rack before cutting into bars.

Makes 15 bars

Squash Squares

Although yellow squash is visually prominent in the topping layer,
no one seems to guess that it is there until the name of the recipe
is offered. These cookies are quite sweet, so cut them into small squares.

COOKIE LAYER

½ cup (1 stick) butter, softened

½ cup granulated sugar

1 cup unbleached all-purpose flour

TOPPING

2 large eggs

1½ cups packed light brown sugar

1 cup slivered almonds

1 teaspoon almond extract

1 teaspoon coconut flavoring oil or extract or pure vanilla extract

2 cups grated yellow summer squash

2 tablespoons unbleached all-purpose flour

½ teaspoon baking powder

Pinch of salt

1. Preheat the oven to 400°F. Butter a 9- by 13-inch baking pan.

2. To make the cookie layer, cream together the butter and sugar by hand, with a standing mixer, or in a food processor. Add the 1 cup flour and mix until the dough comes together. Transfer to the baking pan and pat down the mixture to cover the bottom of the pan.

3. Bake for 15 minutes.

4. While the cookie layer bakes, make the topping. In a large bowl, beat the eggs. Add the brown sugar, almonds, almond extract, and coconut flavoring. Stir in the squash. Add the 2 tablespoons flour, baking powder, and salt. Mix thoroughly.

5. When the cookie layer is done, spread the squash mixture evenly on top.

6. Return to the oven and bake for 30 minutes.

7. On a wire rack, cool completely before cutting into small squares.

Makes 28 squares

Zucchini Bars

Think blondies made with lots of good stuff, like raisins and coconut, instead of chocolate chips. There's a healthy dose of fiber in these good-for-you bar cookies.

 4 cups grated zucchini

 1 teaspoon salt

1½ cups lightly packed brown
    sugar

 ½ cup (1 stick) butter, melted

 ½ cup canola oil

 2 large eggs

 2 tablespoons water

 1 teaspoon pure vanilla extract

 ½ teaspoon ground nutmeg

1½ cups unbleached all-purpose
    flour

 ½ cup whole-wheat flour

 1 teaspoon baking soda

1½ cups bran cereal buds

 1 cup shredded coconut

 1 cup raisins

1. In a colander, combine the zucchini and salt. Toss to mix and set aside to drain for 30 minutes.

2. Preheat the oven to 350°F. Butter an 8- by 12-inch baking dish.

3. Combine the brown sugar, butter, and oil in a large mixing bowl. Beat in the eggs. Add the water, vanilla, and nutmeg. Beat well.

4. In a medium-sized mixing bowl, sift together the all-purpose flour, whole-wheat flour, and baking soda. Add to the brown sugar mixture.

5. Squeeze excess moisture from the zucchini. Measure out 2½ cups of zucchini and add to the batter along with the cereal, coconut, and raisins. Spread in the prepared baking dish.

6. Bake for about 40 minutes, until a tester inserted near the center comes out clean.

7. On a wire rack, cool completely before cutting into squares.

Makes 12 bars

Pumpkin Chocolate Chip Cookies

A Halloween variation on America's favorite cookie: chocolate chip. The pumpkin gives the cookies a softer, cakelike texture and adds tremendous flavor.

2½ cups unbleached all-purpose flour

4 teaspoons baking powder

½ teaspoon ground cinnamon

½ teaspoon ground nutmeg

½ teaspoon salt

¼ teaspoon ground ginger

½ cup (1 stick) butter, softened

1¼ cups packed light brown sugar

2 large eggs

1½ cups cooked and mashed pumpkin or canned pumpkin purée

1 cup chocolate chips

1 cup chopped walnuts

½ cup toasted wheat germ

1. Preheat the oven to 400°F. Grease two baking sheets.

2. Sift together the flour, baking powder, cinnamon, nutmeg, salt, and ginger in a medium-sized bowl.

3. Cream together the butter and sugar in a large mixing bowl. Add the eggs one at a time, beating well after each addition. Add the pumpkin and beat to mix thoroughly. Add the flour mixture and beat until well combined. Fold in the chips, walnuts, and wheat germ. Stir until well blended.

4. Drop the batter by the teaspoon onto the baking sheets, spacing the cookies about 1½ inches apart.

5. Bake for 15 minutes, until the tops of the cookies look dry.

6. Transfer to wire racks to cool completely.

Makes about 48 cookies

Raisin-Pumpkin Cookies

Alas, homemade goodies are discarded by worried parents when they turn up in trick-or-treat bags. Pumpkin cookies are perfect for Halloween, so you'll just have to throw a party or send these into the classroom for a Halloween treat.

2½ cups unbleached all-purpose flour

½ teaspoon baking soda

½ teaspoon ground cinnamon

½ teaspoon ground nutmeg

½ teaspoon salt

¼ teaspoon ground ginger

1½ cups packed brown sugar

¾ cup canola oil

1 cup cooked and mashed pumpkin or canned pumpkin purée

1 large egg

½ teaspoon pure vanilla extract

2 cups raisins

1. Preheat the oven to 350°F. Grease two baking sheets.

2. Sift together the flour, baking soda, cinnamon, nutmeg, salt, and ginger in a medium-sized mixing bowl.

3. In a large mixing bowl, combine the brown sugar, oil, pumpkin, egg, and vanilla. Beat well. Add the flour mixture and raisins and mix well.

4. Drop the batter by the spoonful onto the baking sheet, leaving at least 2 inches between the cookies.

5. Bake for 20 minutes, until the cookies are browned.

6. Remove from the baking sheets and cool on wire racks.

Makes about 48 cookies

Pumpkin-Nut Squares

For those who fear making pie dough, here's a wonderful variation.
The crust is sugar cookie dough pressed into a square pan. Pumpkin pie
in a bar cookie is the best of both worlds.

CRUST
1 cup sifted flour
¼ cup packed light brown sugar
5⅓ tablespoons butter
½ cup walnuts, finely chopped

FILLING
1 package (3 ounces) cream cheese, softened
1 large egg
2 cups cooked and mashed pumpkin or canned pumpkin purée
1 can (14 ounces) sweetened condensed milk
½ teaspoon ground cinnamon
⅛ teaspoon ground cloves
⅛ teaspoon ground ginger
⅛ teaspoon ground nutmeg
1 cup hot water
16 walnut halves

1. Preheat the oven to 350°F.

2. To make the crust, combine the flour and sugar in a medium-sized mixing bowl. Cut in the butter with two knives or a pastry cutter. Mix in the nuts. Press into an 8-inch square baking dish.

3. Bake for 20 minutes, until golden.

4. While the crust bakes, beat the cream cheese with the egg. Add the pumpkin, milk, cinnamon, cloves, ginger, and nutmeg. Beat until smooth. Stir in the hot water.

5. Pour the filling into the baked crust. Garnish with the walnuts.

6. Bake for 50 minutes, until firm.

7. Cool on a wire rack. Chill for up to 4 hours in the refrigerator.

8. To serve, cut into 16 squares, each with a walnut half in the center.

Serves 16

Pumpkin-Picking Points

Be sure it's a pie pumpkin you are choosing for your bread or dessert. Avoid both the tiny tabletop decorations and the huge jack-o'-lantern pumpkins. Pie pumpkins have been selectively bred to produce sweet, dense flesh, whereas jack-o'-lantern pumpkins, which have been bred to grow big, have tough skins and watery flesh. Pick ones that feel heavy for their size and have intact stems. Avoid any with a soft spot, because that is where rot will start.

Deep, Dark Chocolate Zucchini Cake

Zucchini's disguise is unusually heavy in this rich cake. No one need know
you have tricked him into eating his vegetable for dessert.

4 ounces unsweetened baking chocolate

½ cup canola oil

2 cups sifted all-purpose unbleached flour

⅓ cup unsweetened cocoa

2 teaspoons baking powder

2 teaspoons baking soda

1 teaspoon salt

½ cup (1 stick) butter, softened

2 cups sugar

3 large eggs

2 teaspoons pure vanilla extract

⅓ cup buttermilk

3 cups grated zucchini or summer squash

Chocolate Frosting

3 ounces unsweetened chocolate, coarsely chopped

3 tablespoons unsalted butter

¼ cup coffee, cream, or milk

1 teaspoon pure vanilla extract

2 cups confectioners' sugar, or more to thicken

1. Preheat the oven to 350°F and grease and flour two 9-inch cake pans.

2. Combine the chocolate and oil. Melt the mixture in a saucepan over low heat or in a microwave set at low heat.

3. Sift together the flour, cocoa, baking powder, baking soda, and salt in a medium-sized mixing bowl.

4. Cream the butter and sugar in a large mixing bowl until light. Add the eggs one at a time, beating well after each addition. Beat in the vanilla and the chocolate mixture. Add the flour mixture and buttermilk and beat just until combined. Fold in the zucchini. Divide the batter evenly between the pans.

5. Bake for 40 minutes, or until a tester inserted into the center of one of the cake layers comes out clean.

6. On wire racks, cool the cake layers in the pans for about 10 minutes. Then invert onto the wire racks, remove the pans, and cool completely.

7. To make the frosting, in a small saucepan over low heat or in a microwave set to low heat, melt together the chocolate and butter. Stir in the coffee and vanilla. In a large mixing bowl, beat the sugar into the chocolate mixture. Beat until you have a spreadable consistency, adding more sugar to thicken or a drop more coffee to thin, if needed. Spread the frosting between the layers and over the sides and top of the cake.

Serves 8–10

Zapple Bundt Cake

If a little mischief is your pleasure, then this cake is for you. Unless you say something obvious, such as "Guess what's in this cake," no one will ever suppose it is made with anything but apples. This is a lovely, lovely cake — moist, gingery, and delicious.

  4 **cups zucchini, peeled, quartered, and sliced**

  ½ **cup fresh lemon juice**

2¼ **cups sugar**

  2 **teaspoons ground ginger**

3¼ **cups unbleached all-purpose flour**

  2 **teaspoons baking powder**

  2 **teaspoons baking soda**

1½ **teaspoons ground cinnamon**

  ½ **teaspoon salt**

  ¾ **cup (1½ sticks) unsalted butter**

  3 **large eggs**

  ¾ **cup buttermilk or plain yogurt**

  2 **teaspoons pure vanilla extract**

1. In a medium saucepan, combine the zucchini and lemon juice. Bring to a boil over medium heat. Reduce the heat and simmer until the zucchini is tender, about 10 minutes. Stir in 1 cup of the sugar and the ginger and simmer for another 2 to 3 minutes, until the mixture is slightly thickened. Remove from heat and cool to room temperature.

2. Preheat the oven to 350°F. Butter and flour a 10-inch fluted tube pan.

3. Sift together the flour, baking powder, baking soda, cinnamon, and salt in a large bowl. Set aside.

4. In a large mixing bowl, beat together the butter and the remaining 1¼ cups sugar until light and creamy. Beat in the eggs, one at a time. Then beat in the buttermilk and vanilla until well blended. Add the flour mixture and beat just until combined. Add the zucchini mixture and beat until combined. Pour the batter into the prepared pan.

5. Bake for about 45 minutes, until a tester inserted in the cake comes out clean.

6. On a wire rack, cool the cake for 10 minutes. Invert the cake over the rack and cool completely.

NOTE: It is important to let the zucchini mixture cool to room temperature before adding it to the batter. If you add it while it is still hot, its heat will activate the baking powder and the batter will rise out of the pan, make a mess, and ruin the cake.

Serves 16

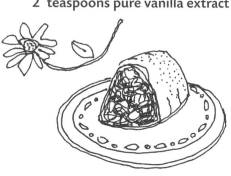

Zucchini Carrot Cake

You could call this a "garden" cake because it has both zucchini and carrots. The zucchini adds moisture and lovely flecks of green, while the carrots pack in nutrition and lovely flecks of orange.

CAKE
- 2 cups grated zucchini
- 1 cup grated carrots
- 1 teaspoon salt
- 1¼ cups unbleached all-purpose flour
- 1 teaspoon baking powder
- 1 teaspoon baking soda
- 1 teaspoon ground cinnamon
- 1 cup sugar
- ⅔ cup canola oil
- 2 eggs
- ½ cup chopped walnuts or pecans

FROSTING
- 1 package (3 ounces) cream cheese, softened
- 3 tablespoons butter, softened
- 2 cups confectioners' sugar
- 1 teaspoon pure vanilla extract

1. In a colander, combine the zucchini, carrots, and salt. Toss to mix and set aside to drain for 30 minutes.

2. Preheat the oven to 350°F. Butter and flour a 9-inch square baking dish.

3. In a medium-sized bowl, combine the flour, baking powder, baking soda, and cinnamon.

4. Using an electric mixer, combine the sugar and oil in a large mixing bowl. Beat until well combined. Add the eggs one at a time, beating well after each addition. Add the flour mixture and beat at high speed for 4 minutes.

5. Squeeze the zucchini and carrots to eliminate any excess moisture. By hand, stir the vegetables and nuts into the batter. Pour into the prepared baking pan.

6. Bake for about 35 minutes, until the top springs back when lightly touched and a tester inserted near the center comes out clean.

7. On a wire rack, cool completely before frosting.

8. To make the frosting, in a medium-sized mixing bowl, beat together the cream cheese and butter. Add the confectioners' sugar and vanilla. Beat until smooth. Spread evenly over the cooled cake.

Serves 8

Zingerbread

Add zucchini to gingerbread and you get zingerbread (rhymes with *gingerbread*).
This is the ultimate in comfort food, filling the house with the warm scent of ginger
as it bakes. It is perfect plain, but it is also terrific with fresh sliced peaches,
applesauce, rhubarb sauce, vanilla ice cream, or whipped cream.

3 cups grated zucchini

1 teaspoon salt

3 cups unbleached all-purpose
flour

4 teaspoons ground ginger

2 teaspoons baking soda

2 teaspoons ground cinnamon

¼ teaspoon ground allspice

¼ teaspoon ground nutmeg

1 cup (2 sticks) unsalted butter,
softened

¾ cup packed light brown sugar

¾ cup light unsulfured molasses

2 large eggs

1 cup hot brewed coffee

1. Combine the zucchini and salt in a colander. Toss to mix and set aside to drain for 30 minutes.

2. Preheat the oven to 350°F. Butter and flour a 9- by 13-inch baking dish.

3. Whisk together the flour, ginger, baking soda, cinnamon, allspice, and nutmeg in a medium-sized mixing bowl.

4. In a large mixing bowl, cream together the butter and sugar. Add the eggs one at a time, and beat until well combined. Add the molasses and beat well; the mixture will appear curdled.

5. Squeeze the zucchini to remove any excess moisture and add to the bowl. Mix just to combine. Add the flour mixture alternately with the coffee, mixing just until combined. Pour the batter into the prepared pan.

6. Bake for 30 to 35 minutes, until the top springs back when lightly touched and a tester inserted near the center comes out clean.

7. On a wire rack, cool the cake in the pan for 10 minutes. Serve hot, warm, or at room temperature.

Serves 12

A "Receipt" for Gingerbread

The first American cookbook featured ginger-bread — without zucchini. It called for "Three pounds of flour, a grated nutmeg, one pound sugar, three small spoons pearl ash dissolved in cream, one pound butter, four eggs, knead it stiff, shape it to your fancy, bake 15 minutes."

The recipe was published in *American Cookery; or the Art of Dressing Viands, Fish, Poultry & Vegetables and the Best Modes of Making Pastes, Puffs, Pies, Tarts, Puddings, Custards & Preserves and All Kinds of Cakes from the Imperial Plumb to Plain Cake Adapted to This Country & All Grades of Life*, by Amelia Simmons, an American Orphan, 1796.

Squice Cake

The yellow squash disappears into the rich, moist spice cake, leaving no one
the wiser for your vegetal sneakiness. Spice cakes should be moist, rich,
and flavorful, and this one exceeds the standard.

3 cups grated yellow squash

1 teaspoon salt

2 cups unbleached all-purpose flour

2 teaspoons baking powder

2 teaspoons baking soda

1 tablespoon ground cinnamon

1 teaspoon ground allspice

¼ teaspoon ground cloves

¼ teaspoon ground nutmeg

1 cup canola oil

2 cups sugar

4 eggs

1 teaspoon grated lemon zest

1 teaspoon pure vanilla extract

¼ teaspoon almond extract

Cream Cheese Frosting (page 264)

1. Combine the squash and salt in a colander. Toss to mix and set aside to drain for 30 minutes.

2. Preheat the oven to 350°F. Butter and flour two 9-inch cake pans.

3. Sift together the flour, baking powder, baking soda, cinnamon, allspice, cloves, and nutmeg in a medium-sized bowl.

4. In a large mixing bowl, combine the oil, sugar, eggs, and lemon zest, and beat until well combined. Squeeze any excess moisture from the squash and add to the mixing bowl, along with the vanilla and almond extracts. Stir in the flour mixture and mix just until smooth. Divide the batter between the cake pans.

5. Bake for 30 to 35 minutes, until a tester inserted near the center comes out clean.

6. On wire racks, cool the cakes in the pans for 10 minutes. Invert onto the wire racks and cool completely.

7. Frost when completely cooled.

Serves 8–12

Zucchini-Bran Breakfast Cake

When is a cake a breakfast cake? When it is high in fiber and low in fat, and therefore healthful enough to start your day, but delicious enough to call cake.

1½ cups bran cereal

1½ cups unbleached all-purpose flour

2 teaspoons baking powder

1 teaspoon baking soda

1 teaspoon pumpkin pie spice

½ teaspoon salt

1½ cups packed brown sugar

1 cup butter, melted

¾ cup egg substitute

2 teaspoons pure vanilla extract

2 cups grated zucchini

1 cup chopped apples

Confectioners' sugar, for dusting (optional)

1. Preheat the oven to 350°F. Butter and flour a 9- by 13-inch baking pan.

2. In a large mixing bowl, combine the cereal, flour, baking powder, baking soda, pumpkin pie spice, and salt. Mix well.

3. In a second large mixing bowl, combine the sugar, butter, egg substitute, and vanilla. Beat until smooth. Stir in the zucchini, apples, and cereal mixture. Spoon the batter into the pan.

4. Bake for 40 to 45 minutes, until a tester inserted near the center comes out clean.

5. Cool on a wire rack. Dust with confectioners' sugar, if using.

Serves 12–15

Butternut-Pineapple Spice Cake

I took my favorite carrot cake recipe and substituted finely grated butternut squash for the carrots. The success of this cake proves that the substitution works. Like many moist cakes, this one is even better on the second day, after the flavors have had a chance to develop. Frosting a cake this good is optional; it certainly isn't necessary.

2 cups unbleached all-purpose flour

2 teaspoons baking powder

1½ teaspoons baking soda

1½ teaspoons ground cinnamon

1 teaspoon salt

¼ teaspoon ground allspice

1 cup canola oil

1 cup granulated sugar

¾ cup packed light brown sugar

4 large eggs

1 teaspoon pure vanilla extract

3 cups finely grated peeled butternut squash

1 cup drained crushed pineapple

1 cup toasted chopped walnuts

Cream Cheese Frosting (page 264) (optional)

1. Preheat the oven to 350°F. Butter and flour a 9- by 13-inch baking pan.

2. Sift together the flour, baking powder, baking soda, cinnamon, salt, and allspice.

3. In a large mixing bowl, combine the oil, granulated sugar, and brown sugar. Beat until well combined. Add the eggs one at a time, beating well after each addition. Add the vanilla. Continue to beat until fluffy. Gradually add the dry ingredients, mixing just until the batter is smooth and blended. Fold in the squash, pineapple, and walnuts. Spoon the batter into the prepared pan.

4. Bake for about 35 minutes, until a cake tester inserted in the center of the cake comes out clean.

5. On a wire rack, cool completely before frosting.

Serves 12–15

Pumpkin Cheesecake

In the style of New York cheesecakes, this pumpkin cheesecake
is rich, creamy, and smooth.

CRUST

1½ cups graham cracker or ginger-snap crumbs (about 22 crackers or cookies)

6 tablespoons butter, melted

¼ cup granulated sugar

CHEESECAKE

1 pound cream cheese, softened

1 cup sour cream

4 large eggs

1 cup packed light brown sugar

1½ cups cooked and mashed pumpkin or canned pumpkin purée

1 teaspoon ground cinnamon

½ teaspoon ground ginger

Pinch of nutmeg

1. Preheat the oven to 325°F.

2. To make the crust, in a medium-sized mixing bowl, mix together the crumbs, butter, and sugar. Press the mixture into a 9-inch springform pan, making a ½-inch rim around the edge.

3. In a large mixing bowl, beat together the cream cheese and sour cream. Beat in the eggs, one at a time. Add the sugar, pumpkin, cinnamon, ginger, and nutmeg. Mix until the batter is completely smooth.

4. Bake for 1 hour. Turn off the heat, open the oven door, and allow the cheesecake to cool to room temperature before refrigerating.

5. Chill completely.

Serves 12

Draining Pumpkin Purée or Winter Squash

For best results, your homemade cooked and mashed pumpkin or winter squash should be as thick as the canned product: stiff enough to hold a spoon upright in it. If your purée seems watery, place it in a sieve and allow it to drain for an hour or so.

Easy Pumpkin Cake

At my children's elementary school, this recipe was passed from mother to mother and from class to class. It has become the cake I am most likely to whip up when a bake sale or potluck dinner catches me unprepared. It is absolutely foolproof.

2 cups unbleached all-purpose flour

2 teaspoons baking powder

2 teaspoons ground cinnamon

1 teaspoon baking soda

1 teaspoon salt

1½ cups sugar

1 cup canola oil

4 large eggs

1¾ cups cooked and mashed pumpkin or canned pumpkin purée (15-ounce can)

Cream Cheese Frosting (recipe follows)

1. Preheat the oven to 350°F. Butter and flour a 9- by 13-inch baking pan.

2. Combine the flour, baking powder, cinnamon, baking soda, and salt in a medium-sized mixing bowl. Mix well.

3. In a large mixing bowl, combine the sugar and oil. Beat until light. Add the eggs one at a time, beating well after each addition. Beat in the pumpkin. Add the flour mixture and beat just until thoroughly blended. Pour the batter into the prepared pan.

4. Bake for 30 to 35 minutes, until the top springs back when lightly touched.

5. Cool completely on a rack before frosting.

Serves 12–15

Cream Cheese Frosting

1 package (8 ounces) cream cheese, softened

½ cup (1 stick) butter, softened

1 teaspoon pure vanilla extract

2–2½ cups confectioners' sugar, sifted

1. In a medium mixing bowl, beat together the cream cheese, butter, and vanilla. Add 2 cups of the sugar and beat until smooth. If the frosting is too thin, add the additional ½ cup sugar and beat until smooth.

2. Spread evenly over the cooled cake.

Makes about 2 cups

Pumpkin-Applesauce Tea Breads

"Tea loaf" is a quaint name for a loaf that is too sweet to be called
a bread but too straitlaced to be called a cake. It makes a great snack,
just the thing to serve with afternoon tea or mid-morning coffee.

3⅔ cups unbleached all-purpose
   flour

2 teaspoons baking soda

2 teaspoons ground cinnamon

1½ teaspoons baking powder

1 teaspoon ground nutmeg

1 teaspoon salt

2 cups sugar

⅔ cup canola oil

3 large eggs

1 cup applesauce

1 cup cooked and mashed
   pumpkin or canned pumpkin
   purée

⅓ cup light molasses

⅓ cup milk

1 teaspoon pure vanilla extract

1 cup chopped walnuts or
   pecans

1 cup raisins or chopped dates

1. Preheat the oven to 350°F. Grease two 5- by 9-inch loaf pans,
   or coat them with nonstick cooking spray.

2. Combine the flour, baking soda, cinnamon, baking powder,
   nutmeg, and salt in a medium-sized mixing bowl. Mix well.

3. In a large mixing bowl, combine the sugar and oil. Beat until
   light. Add the eggs one at a time, beating well after each addition. Stir in the applesauce, pumpkin, molasses, milk, and
   vanilla. Add the dry ingredients and stir just to combine. Fold
   in the nuts and raisins. Divide the batter between the prepared
   pans.

4. Bake for about 1 hour, until a tester inserted near the center
   comes out clean.

5. Cool in the pan for 10 minutes; invert onto wire racks and cool
   completely. Wrap in aluminum foil and store overnight to give
   the flavors a chance to develop.

Makes 2 loaves

Pumpkin-Apple Torte

The flavors of fall — apples, pumpkin, and nuts — are combined in this simple cake. Dress it up with whipped cream or a dusting of confectioners' sugar, or serve it simply with no topping at all.

1 cup cooked and mashed pumpkin or canned pumpkin purée

2 large eggs, beaten

1 cup sugar

¾ cup unbleached all-purpose flour

2 teaspoons ground cinnamon

1 teaspoon baking powder

1 teaspoon ground ginger

½ teaspoon salt

½ cup peeled, chopped apple

½ cup chopped nuts

Whipped cream or confectioners' sugar, for topping (optional)

1. Preheat the oven to 325°F. Grease and flour an 8-inch round cake pan.

2. In a large mixing bowl, combine the pumpkin, eggs, and sugar. Beat well. Stir in the flour, cinnamon, baking powder, ginger, and salt. Stir in the apple and nuts. Pour the batter into the prepared cake pan.

3. Bake for 20 to 25 minutes, until a tester inserted in the center comes out clean.

4. On a wire rack, cool in the pan for 10 minutes. Invert onto the rack and cool completely.

5. To serve, turn the cake top-side up onto a cake plate. Serve plain or top with whipped cream or dust with confectioners' sugar, if using.

Serves 6

Pumpkin Mousse

Who can forget her first taste of mousse, a dessert so rich yet so light it confounds the palate? This version is made with pumpkin rather than the ubiquitous chocolate. It makes a marvelous finale to a fall feast.

2 envelopes (¼ ounce each) unflavored gelatin
½ cup brandy
½ cup packed light brown sugar
½ cup granulated sugar
1 teaspoon ground cinnamon
½ teaspoon ground cloves
½ teaspoon salt
¼ teaspoon ground nutmeg
2 cups cooked and mashed pumpkin or canned pumpkin purée
1 cup milk
2 cups heavy cream

1. In the top of a double boiler, sprinkle the gelatin over the brandy. Let soak for 5 minutes. Place the top of the double boiler over hot water. Add the brown sugar, granulated sugar, cinnamon, cloves, salt, and nutmeg. Stir until the sugar is dissolved. Mix in the pumpkin and milk.

2. Chill in the refrigerator until the mixture thickens, about 1 hour.

3. In a medium-sized mixing bowl, beat the cream until soft peaks form. Using a large rubber spatula, stir ½ cup of the cream into the pumpkin mixture to lighten it, then gently fold in the remaining cream.

4. Lightly oil a 4-cup mold or spray with nonstick cooking spray. Pour the mousse into the mold. Chill for at least 4 hours, up to 24 hours.

5. To loosen, dip the mold into a sink filled with very hot water. Invert a plate over the top of the mold, and turn both over together. The mousse should drop out onto the plate.

Serves 4

Caramelized Pumpkin Custard

If you prefer, you can make this custard in individual custard cups.
Just adjust the baking time accordingly, to about 25 minutes.

1 cup granulated sugar

2 large eggs

1 cup cooked and mashed pumpkin or canned pumpkin purée

½ cup packed brown sugar

½ teaspoon ground cinnamon

¼ teaspoon ground ginger

1 cup milk

**What moistens the lip
And what brightens the eye;
What calls back the past,
Like rich pumpkin pie?**

— John Greenleaf Whittier,
"The Pumpkin"

1. Preheat the oven to 350°F. Butter a 5- by 9-inch loaf pan.

2. Make the caramel by heating and stirring the granulated sugar in a small saucepan over medium heat until melted. Pour into the loaf pan and tilt and swirl to coat evenly.

3. In a medium-sized mixing bowl, beat the eggs with the pumpkin, brown sugar, cinnamon, ginger, and milk, blending thoroughly. Carefully pour the mixture over the caramel. Place the custard pan in a larger pan of hot water.

4. Bake for 1 hour, until the custard is set but still wobbly and a knife inserted near the center comes out clean.

5. Chill for at least 4 hours.

6. To serve, loosen the custard from the edges of the pan with a knife. Invert the pan over a plate and remove the mold. Slice and serve.

Serves 4

Steamed Pumpkin Pudding

Steamed puddings were common early American fare,
and pumpkin was a common early American ingredient.

1½ cups unbleached all-purpose
     flour

½ cup packed light brown sugar

½ cup granulated sugar

1 teaspoon baking soda

¾ teaspoon ground cinnamon

½ teaspoon ground cloves

½ teaspoon ground nutmeg

¼ teaspoon ground ginger

1 cup cooked and mashed
    pumpkin or canned pumpkin
    purée

¼ cup milk

1 egg

5⅓ tablespoons melted butter

2 tablespoons orange juice

¼ cup raisins

1. Lightly grease 6 individual ramekins.

2. Combine the flour, brown sugar, granulated sugar, baking soda, cinnamon, cloves, nutmeg, and ginger in a medium-sized mixing bowl. Mix well.

3. In a large mixing bowl, combine the pumpkin, milk, egg, butter, and orange juice. Add the flour mixture and beat until thoroughly combined. Fold in the raisins.

4. Bring a few cups of water to a boil in a kettle.

5. Divide the pudding mixture among the ramekins, filling each about half full. Cover each ramekin with aluminum foil and tie securely. Place the ramekins on a wire rack in a large pot. Add ½ inch of the boiling water. Cover and steam until the pudding sets, about 15 minutes.

6. Turn off the heat and let the puddings stand in the covered pot for about 15 minutes.

7. To serve, invert onto dessert plates and remove the ramekins.

Serves 6

Pilgrim's Pumpkin Pudding

Pumpkin crème brûlée appears on menus in fine restaurants throughout the fall season. It's a good deal more luxurious than what the Pilgrims had in mind when they whipped up their typical pumpkin dessert. Back then, housewives would remove the top of the pumpkin, scoop out the fibers and seeds, and bake the pumpkin whole. When the flesh was tender, milk flavored with spices and honey was poured in. The resulting pudding was eaten right out of the pumpkin.

pumpkin parfait

If you don't feel like making a dessert from scratch, consider this
easy parfait, which starts with vanilla pudding mix.

1 **package (3 ounces) vanilla pudding mix**

¼ **cup packed lightly brown sugar**

½ **teaspoon ground cinnamon**

¼ **teaspoon ground ginger**

1½ **cups milk**

1 **cup cooked and mashed pumpkin or canned pumpkin purée**

Whipped cream, to serve (optional)

1. Combine the pudding mix, brown sugar, cinnamon, and ginger in a small mixing bowl.

2. Bring the milk to a boil in a medium-sized saucepan over medium heat. Add the pudding mix and pumpkin. Stir to blend thoroughly. Spoon the pudding into serving glasses.

3. Chill thoroughly.

4. To serve, top with whipped cream, if using.

Serves 4

> For pottage and puddings, and
> custards, and pies,
> Our pumpkins and parsnips
> are common supplies.
> We have pumpkins at morning
> and pumpkins at noon;
> If it were not for pumpkins, we
> should be undoon.
>
> — Anonymous (c. 1630)

Butternut-Apple Crisp

Adding butternut squash to apple crisp is a new twist on an old favorite. Ice cream makes a great addition.

3 cups peeled and sliced butternut squash

2 cups peeled and sliced tart apples, such as Granny Smith

1 cup packed brown sugar

1 teaspoon ground cinnamon

⅛ teaspoon ground cloves

2 teaspoons fresh lemon juice

1¼ cups unbleached all-purpose flour

½ teaspoon salt

6 tablespoons butter, softened

⅓ cup chopped nuts

1. Preheat the oven to 350°F. Grease a shallow baking pan.

2. In a large mixing bowl, combine the squash, apples, ½ cup of the brown sugar, the cinnamon, cloves, and lemon juice. Toss gently to mix. Transfer to the baking pan.

3. Bake for 30 minutes.

4. Combine the remaining ½ cup brown sugar, flour, salt, and butter in a medium-sized mixing bowl. Stir together until the mixture is crumbly. Mix in the nuts. Spread evenly on top of the squash and apples.

5. Bake for 40 minutes, until golden brown.

6. Serve warm or cold.

Serves 6

Pumpkin Fudge

No child's life is complete without at least one sticky session of
fudge-making. Perhaps this is the recipe to inspire it.

2 cups sugar

3 tablespoons cooked and
   mashed pumpkin or canned
   pumpkin purée

½ teaspoon pumpkin pie spice

¼ teaspoon cornstarch

½ cup milk, evaporated milk, or
   cream

½ teaspoon pure vanilla extract

1. Grease a 9-inch square baking pan.

2. In a large saucepan, combine the sugar, pumpkin, pumpkin pie
   spice, cornstarch, and milk. Cook over low heat, stirring constantly, until the mixture boils. Still stirring, continue to cook
   until the mixture reaches 236°F on a candy thermometer (a
   small piece of fudge will form a soft ball if dropped in a glass
   of cold water).

3. Immediately remove from the heat. Add the vanilla and beat
   with an electric mixture until smooth. Scrape into the prepared
   pan and let cool.

4. When the mixture is completely cooled and hardened, cut into
   squares. Fudge is best eaten fresh, but it can be wrapped well
   and kept in the refrigerator for several weeks.

Makes 1 pound

9. Pickling, Preserving & Freezing

When faced with an overabundance of perishable zucchini and summer squash, the obvious solution is to freeze or can the excess. Here's a sampling of recipes to help you do so — deliciously.

Pickles & Preserves

For more than a few years, making pickles was a big undertaking for me — mountains of vegetables, stacks of jars, steam to the rafters. These days, my pickle-making is much slower-paced. I prefer recipes that call for small quantities. The advantages of working with small quantities are numerous. You can preserve the limited quantities a small garden produces each day, using very fresh produce to create superior pickles. Or you can take advantage of a great bargain at the farmer's market, without buying a whole bushel. Working in small quantities allows you to experiment with flavors. If it turns out you don't really like a particular recipe, there won't be multiple jars to haunt you. And working in small quantities does not require a large block of time.

When choosing squash for making pickles, think small. Overgrown zucchini and summer squash have large seeds and pulpy centers. If you pickle them, your pickles will be mushy. A young, firm squash will have very small seeds and tender skin, resulting in a superior pickle.

Ingredients

Vinegar is a key ingredient in making fresh-pack pickles. As long as the vinegar has a 50-grain strength or 5 percent acetic acid, it can be used safely to make pickles. This includes most commercial vinegars, as well as most homemade herb vinegars that use commercial vinegars. White distilled vinegar is most commonly used because it doesn't compete with the distinctive flavors of the herbs and spices used to make pickles and because it is very inexpensive. Cider vinegar imparts a rich, fruity flavor that is occasionally desirable, particularly with sweet pickles; however, be sure that it has 5 percent acetic acid. In experimenting with various wine and balsamic vinegars, I have found that they discolor the brine and muddy the flavors, so I generally stick with distilled white vinegar.

Use only whole herbs and spices to avoid clouding the brine. Dill is the queen of herbs for pickles. Sprigs of immature dill can be used interchangeably with mature dill heads. If you find yourself ready to make pickles but unable to locate fresh dill, substitute a tablespoon of dill seed for each dill head. The "pickling salt" used in many recipes is simply table salt without the additives that can make a pickling liquid cloudy. It is sold in supermarkets.

The full flavor of a pickle doesn't develop for some 6 weeks, at which time the herbs and spices have infused the pickling brine fully. So what goes in the jar may be less tasty than what comes out. This is another good reason to work in small quantities. Keep notes on the recipes you use; next time around you may want to increase the amount of herbs, decrease the sugar, or use a different full-strength vinegar. What you must *not* do is alter the proportion of vinegar to other liquids in the brine. If a pickle is too sour, increase the amount of sugar; otherwise, you risk spoilage.

Processing

The acidity of the vinegar reduces the likelihood that naturally occurring yeast, molds, and bacteria will spoil your pickles, but unless you have the space to refrigerate your pickles, you should process the jars in a boiling-water bath to seal them. This also inactivates organisms that cause spoilage and enzymes that affect the taste, color, and texture of the vegetable. Unfortunately, processing also cooks the pickles, which makes them less crisp and fresh-tasting. So the challenge is to keep your pickles crisp while following all the safety guidelines established by the U.S. Department of Agriculture.

Start with fresh, firm young squash, freshly picked if possible. If you are harvesting from your own garden, do not pick in the heat of the day. Store the vegetables in the refrigerator or on ice in insulated coolers. Smaller, younger squash tend to be firmer and make better pickles.

Zucchini and other summer squash benefit from a brief brining in salt water. The salt draws the water from the cells, resulting in a firmer pickle. Just rinse off the excess salt under cold running water before packing the jars. Another trick is to use a food processor to uniformly slice the vegetables. Summer squash have a crunchy skin and a softer center. The smaller the squash and the thinner the slice, the greater the proportion of crunchy skin to soft center, and the more pleasing your pickle will be.

Once you've assembled all your ingredients and selected your recipe, there are no great cooking challenges. The vinegar brine is made up and heated to boiling on the stove in nonreactive cookware or in a microwave. The jars are packed and then processed for 10 to 20 minutes in a boiling-water bath to seal.

The boiling-water bath can be a large 7-quart or 9-quart canner that you buy at a hardware store. Or it can be a large saucepan that is tall enough to allow the jars to sit on a metal rack and be covered by 2 inches of water, with at least 1 inch of space to spare. If you don't have a metal rack that fits into the saucepan, set each jar on a metal screwband set on the bottom of the pot.

The jars to use for preserving are also sold at hardware stores. The tops, sold separately, are two-piece metal screwbands (which can double as a rack for the jars) and a flat metal lid. The jars and metal screwbands can be reused, but the metal lids should be purchased new each year.

Equipment

A few gadgets make life easier. A food processor saves a great deal of time, and because it produces uniform-size pieces, it helps you make a superior product. A jar lifter for removing jars from the boiling-water bath is necessary if you aren't using a conventional canner with rack. A timer keeps you on schedule. A sharp paring knife and a chopping board are musts, as is a colander for draining and the usual assortment of measuring spoons, cooking spoons, and ladles. A set of Pyrex measuring cups will be tremendously useful and will reduce spills and messes. If preserving is likely to become part of your culinary repertoire, you will find a wide-mouth canning funnel that fits inside canning jars well worth its low cost; it aids in packing jars and helps prevent messes.

Finally, you will need labels for your jars. Even if the product is easy to identify, it is a good idea to date the jar. That way, you can be sure to use the oldest jars first. You can often find labels where canning jars are sold, but freezer tape works just as well.

The steamy part of pickling is the processing of the jars. All sorts of shortcuts have been developed by harried cooks, including use of the microwave and the oven. The only safe shortcut is to store unsealed jars in the refrigerator and use them quickly. Since this isn't a practical storage solution, you will probably want to seal the jars in a boiling-water bath (see Canning Basics, below).

Canning Basics for Pickles and Marmalade

1. Preheat the canner filled with water. Wash jars, screwbands, and lids with hot, soapy water, and rinse them well. Follow the manufacturer's directions for preparing the lids, usually by placing them in a saucepan with water to cover and bringing the water to a simmer (180°F), then removing the pan from the heat and leaving the lids in the water until you are ready to use them. Sterilize jars by immersing them in boiling water for 10 minutes. Some dishwashers have a sterilizing cycle. Heat extra water in a kettle.

2. Pack the jars tightly, trying not to squash the vegetables. Pour in hot brine to cover, allowing the specified amount of headroom (the space between the rim of the jar and the top of its contents). Remove any air bubbles that have been trapped inside by running a wooden or rubber spatula around the inside. Add more brine to cover the vegetables, if needed.

3. Use a clean, damp cloth to wipe the rim of the jars. Place the lids on the jars. Secure with a metal screwband, hand-tightened into place.

4. Set the jars on a rack in the preheated canner. The water should be very hot but not boiling, or the jars may break. Add more water from the preheated kettle, if necessary, to cover the tops of the jars with about 2 inches of water. Cover the pot. Turn the heat to high and bring the water to a boil. Begin timing your processing once the water is boiling.

5. When the processing time is up, immediately remove the jars from the canner and set them where they can cool undisturbed for at least 12 hours. Never tighten the screwbands after the jars have been processed.

6. As the jars cool, a metallic popping sound tells you a jar has sealed. The center of a sealed jar will be slightly depressed. After the jars have cooled, remove the screwbands and test any questionable seal by lifting the jar by its lid. Unsealed jars should be stored in the refrigerator and used quickly. Store sealed jars in a cool, dry place.

Refrigerator and Freezer Pickles

Refrigerator and freezer pickles are increasingly popular ways to preserve excess zucchini, because they don't require slaving over a hot stove in the heat of August. Nor do they require any special equipment.

You can substitute zucchini for cucumbers in any recipe you find for refrigerator or freezer pickles, but here are a few tips to guarantee a good product.

- Although you are probably making pickles to use up extra zucchini, you will get the best results if you use young, firm zucchini. If your squash is overgrown, consider making a relish (pages 286 to 288) rather than a freezer pickle.
- Slice the zucchini as thin as possible, using a food processor or mandoline. The skin of the zucchini is much firmer than the flesh. If you slice the zucchini thick, you are liable to end up with a tough outer ring of skin and a mushy, or nonexistent, center.
- The first step is to combine the zucchini with salt and set it aside to drain. This removes excess moisture from the zucchini, resulting in a more pleasing texture.

Dill Chips

Crunchy and full of flavor, these classic pickle slices are delicious on sandwiches. This recipe makes 1 pint of pickles. Multiply the recipe to accommodate the volume of zucchini you want to work with. Zucchini or cucumbers can be used in this recipe.

2–2¼ cups thinly sliced zucchini

1½ teaspoons pickling salt (or more to taste)

Water to cover

1 sprig fresh dill or 1 tablespoon dill seeds or 1 dill head

1 clove of garlic

½ cup distilled white vinegar

Boiling water

1. In a large bowl, combine the zucchini and 1 teaspoon of the salt. (If you are making more than 1 pint, increase the salt up to a total of 2 tablespoons only.) Toss to mix well. Add cold water to cover. Let stand for 2 to 3 hours.

2. Drain the zucchini. Taste a slice and rinse if the flavor is salty to you.

3. Heat water to boiling in a kettle. Pack the clean, hot jar(s) with the dill and garlic. Add the remaining ½ teaspoon salt to each jar, if desired. Pack the cucumbers up to the shoulder of the jar. Add the vinegar and top off the jar with the boiling water, leaving ½ inch of headroom. Using a plastic or wooden spatula, remove air bubbles. Wipe the rim with a clean cloth and seal.

4. Process in a boiling-water bath according to the directions on page 279 for 10 minutes at an altitude of up to 1,000 feet; for 15 minutes at 1,001 to 6,000 feet; and for 20 minutes above 6,000 feet.

5. Let cool undisturbed for 12 hours. Label the jar and store it in a cool, dry place. Allow 6 weeks for the full flavors to develop.

Makes 1 pint

Brined Squash Pickles

The old-fashioned way to make pickles was to ferment them in a salt brine. The method is time-consuming, but the results are simply delicious. In this recipe, the pickles are first salt-brined, then canned in a sweet syrup.

9½ pounds small zucchini (or a mixture of squash and cucumbers), cut into 3- or 4-inch spears

6 pounds cauliflower, broken into florets

1½ cups pickling salt

12 cups water

12 cups sugar

8 cups distilled white vinegar

8 sticks cinnamon

1. In a clean large bowl or pickling crock, combine the zucchini and cauliflower. Leave at least 4 inches of space at the top of the crock.

2. Cover with water. Drain the water into a saucepan and bring to a boil. Remove from heat and add the salt. Stir to dissolve. Cool to room temperature. Pour the salted water over the vegetables.

3. Using a weighted plate, cover the vegetables to keep them in the brine.

4. Let stand for 1 week; the ideal fermenting temperature is between 70°F and 75°F. Fermentation will be much slower at cooler temperatures.

5. Check the pickles daily and skim off any foam that forms. After 7 days, drain. Discard the brine. Cover the vegetables with hot water and let stand for 24 hours.

6. Combine the 12 cups water, sugar, vinegar, and cinnamon. Bring to a boil. Drain the vegetables and pour the hot syrup over them. Cool to room temperature, cover, and let stand for 24 hours.

7. For the next 3 days, drain the vegetables daily, reserving the syrup. Bring the syrup to a boil and pour over the vegetables. Cool to room temperature, cover, and let stand for 24 hours.

8. On the fourth day, bring the vegetables and syrup to a boil and pack into hot 1-pint glass jars, leaving ½ inch of headroom. Using a plastic or wooden spatula, remove air bubbles. Wipe the rim with a clean cloth and seal.

9. Process in a boiling-water bath according to the directions on page 279 for 15 minutes at altitudes up to 1,000 feet; 20 minutes at 1,001 to 6,000 feet; and 25 minutes over 6,000 feet.

10. Let cool undisturbed for 12 hours. Label and store in a cool, dry place. Allow 6 weeks for the full flavors to develop.

Makes 6 pints

Make-Your-Own-Pickle Recipes

If you want to experiment with your own recipes, figure that you will need 2¼ to 2½ cups of sliced summer squash. Plan to soak them in a salt brine to remove excess moisture (which is how they will come to fit in a pint jar). You will need approximately ¾ cup of pickling brine for each jar (this will vary, depending on how tightly the jar is packed). Include at least ½ cup vinegar in the brine **per jar** for safety and flavor. Although you can experiment with different types of vinegar, I think that distilled white vinegar gives the best results. Use 1½ teaspoons of pickling salt per jar. Sugar is optional; 2 to 3 tablespoons will make a sweet pickle. A sliced onion or a clove or two of garlic combines nicely with most flavorings. A few black peppercorns or dried hot peppers add zing. Add 1 or 2 teaspoons of whole spices to each jar, or 1 to 2 sprigs of fresh herbs. Celery seed, dill seed, fresh dill, mustard seed, and mixed pickling spices all are good choices for zucchini pickles.

Christmas Pickles

The red and green colors of the pickles inspired the name of this recipe.
The pickles make a lovely addition to a holiday relish tray.

20 green cherry tomatoes

5 or 6 small zucchini, cut into
3- to 4-inch spears

2 red bell peppers, cut into rings

4 heads fresh dill or 4 teaspoons
dried dill seed

4 cloves of garlic

4 whole cloves

3 cups water

1 cup distilled white vinegar

2 tablespoons pickling salt

1. Pack all of the vegetables into four clean, hot glass 1-pint jars, leaving ½ inch of headroom. To each jar, add 1 head dill, 1 clove of garlic, and 1 clove.

2. Combine the water, vinegar, and salt in a nonreactive saucepan and bring to a boil. Pour over the vegetables, leaving ½ inch of headroom in each jar. Using a plastic or wooden spatula, remove air bubbles. Wipe the rim with a clean cloth and seal.

3. Process in a boiling-water bath according to the directions on page 279 for 15 minutes at altitudes up to 1,000 feet; 20 minutes at 1,001 to 6,000 feet; and 25 minutes over 6,000 feet.

4. Let cool undisturbed for 12 hours. Store in a cool, dry place. Allow 6 weeks for the full flavors to develop.

Makes 4 pints

Rainbow Pickles

Maybe "rainbow" is an exaggeration, but the colorful mix of
squash and vegetables is pleasing to the eye and palate.
These pickles take several days to make.

8 cups mixed zucchini and yellow summer squash, cut into 3- to 4-inch spears

2 onions, cut into rings

1 red bell pepper, cut into strips

2½ cups distilled white vinegar

1½ cups sugar

¼ cup pickling salt

2 tablespoons dried dill seed

1 tablespoon mixed pickling spices

2 teaspoons mustard seed

1. In a large shallow bowl, combine the squash, onions, and bell pepper. Add ice and water to cover. Set aside for 15 minutes.

2. Combine the vinegar, sugar, salt, dill seed, pickling spices, and mustard seed in a large nonreactive saucepan and bring to a boil. Let cool to room temperature.

3. Drain the vegetables and pour the pickling syrup over. Refrigerate for several days.

4. Pack into clean, hot 1-pint jars, leaving ½ inch of headroom. Using a plastic or wooden spatula, remove air bubbles. Wipe the rim with a clean cloth and seal. Store in the refrigerator for up to 2 weeks, or process in a boiling-water bath according to the directions on page 279 for 15 minutes at altitudes up to 1,000 feet; 20 minutes at 1,001 to 6,000 feet; and 25 minutes over 6,000 feet.

5. Let cool undisturbed for 12 hours. Label and store in a cool, dry place. Allow 6 weeks for the full flavors to develop.

Makes 4 pints

Hot Dog Relish

Hot dog relishes can be sweet, dilled, or mustardy — and they aren't just for hot dogs. This version belongs in the sweet category. It is terrific on a grilled Cheddar cheese sandwich.

2 cups distilled white vinegar

2 cups sugar

4½ teaspoons salt

1½ teaspoons freshly ground black pepper

1½ teaspoons ground cinnamon

¾ teaspoon ground cloves

9 cups finely chopped zucchini

4 small onions, finely chopped

2 apples, peeled and finely chopped

2 green tomatoes, finely chopped

1. In a large nonreactive kettle, combine the vinegar, sugar, salt, pepper, cinnamon, and cloves. Bring to a boil. Add the zucchini, onions, apples, and green tomatoes. Simmer uncovered, stirring frequently, until thick, about 30 minutes.

2. Pack the relish into four clean, hot 1-pint jars, leaving ½ inch of headroom. Using a plastic or wooden spatula, remove air bubbles. Wipe the rim with a clean cloth and seal.

3. Process in a boiling-water bath according to the directions on page 279 for 10 minutes at altitudes up to 1,000 feet; 15 minutes at 1,001 to 6,000 feet; and 20 minutes over 6,000 feet.

4. Let cool undisturbed for 12 hours. Store in a cool, dry place. Allow 6 weeks for the full flavors to develop.

Makes 4 pints

Grand-Scale Zucchini Relish

Roll up your sleeves and prepare to take charge of the zucchini harvest. This recipe
makes 8 pints of a relish that is delicious on hot dogs, burgers, and sandwiches.
Note that the vegetables are combined with salt and left to stand overnight.

10 cups minced zucchini

5 cups minced onions

1 cup diced celery

3 green bell peppers, diced

2 red bell peppers, diced

1 cup pickling salt

6 cups sugar

5 cups distilled white vinegar

3 tablespoons celery seed

3 tablespoons cornstarch

1 tablespoon dry mustard powder

2 teaspoons ground turmeric

1. In a large bowl, combine the zucchini, onions, celery, and bell peppers. Add the salt and toss to mix. Set aside for 12 hours or overnight.

2. Drain the vegetables in a large colander. Rinse thoroughly under cold running water and drain again. Press a bowl down on top of the vegetables to force out as much liquid as possible.

3. In a large nonreactive pot, combine the sugar, vinegar, celery seed, cornstarch, mustard, and turmeric. Mix well. Add the vegetables and bring to a rolling boil. Reduce heat and simmer for 20 minutes, until thick.

4. Pack into clean, hot 1-pint jars, leaving ½ inch of headroom. Using a plastic or wooden spatula, remove air bubbles. Wipe the rim with a clean cloth and seal.

5. Process in a boiling-water bath according to the directions on page 279 for 10 minutes at altitudes up to 1,000 feet; 15 minutes at 1,001 to 6,000 feet; and 20 minutes over 6,000 feet.

6. Let cool undisturbed for 12 hours. Store in a cool, dry place. Allow 6 weeks for the full flavors to develop.

Makes 8 pints

Curried Squash Relish

A friend of mine made this relish and took third place at the Tunbridge World's Fair, held in September each year in Tunbridge, Vermont. The fair doesn't really draw in the whole world, but the squash relish really is a prizewinner. Serve it with crackers and cheese as an appetizer, or as a condiment with chicken, fish, or beef. It is particularly attractive made with yellow squash, but zucchini can be substituted.

4 **pounds yellow summer squash**

4 **red bell peppers**

2 **onions**

3 **cups dark brown sugar**

3 **cups cider vinegar**

3 **tablespoons curry powder**

2 **teaspoons mixed pickling spices**

½ **cup cornstarch**

½ **cup water**

Salt and freshly ground black pepper

Cayenne pepper (optional)

1. Grate, grind, or finely chop the squash, peppers, and onions. A food processor works well.

2. In a large nonreactive saucepan, combine the vegetables, brown sugar, vinegar, curry, and pickling spices. Bring to a boil.

3. Make a paste with the cornstarch and water in a small bowl. Briskly stir the cornstarch mixture into the boiling relish. Boil until the syrup appears almost clear and the mixture has thickened, about 5 minutes. Season to taste with salt, pepper, and cayenne, if using.

4. Pack the relish into eight clean, hot 1-pint jars, leaving ½ inch of headroom. Using a plastic or wooden spatula, remove air bubbles. Wipe the rim with a clean cloth and seal.

5. Process in a boiling-water bath according to the directions on page 279 for 10 minutes at altitudes up to 1,000 feet; 15 minutes at 1,001 to 6,000 feet; and 20 minutes over 6,000 feet.

6. Let cool undisturbed for 12 hours. Label and store in a cool, dry place. Allow 6 weeks for the full flavors to develop.

Makes 8 pints

Pumpkin Pickles

We don't generally think to pickle pumpkins because they have
such a long shelf life and the purée freezes so well. But if you like pickles
and the process of making them, these will add welcome variety to the larder.

8 cups peeled and cubed
    pumpkin

2½ cups distilled white vinegar

2½ cups sugar

4 sticks cinnamon

1 teaspoon ground cloves

1 teaspoon pickling spices

1. Over boiling water, steam the pumpkin cubes until tender but not mushy, about 15 minutes.

2. In a large nonreactive saucepan, combine the vinegar, sugar, cinnamon, cloves, and pickling spices. Bring to a rolling boil. Reduce heat and simmer for 10 minutes.

3. Add the pumpkin cubes and simmer for 4 minutes.

4. Pack into clean, hot 1-pint jars, leaving ½-inch headroom. Using a plastic or wooden spatula, remove air bubbles. Wipe the rim with a clean cloth and seal.

5. Process in a boiling-water bath according to the directions on page 279 for 5 minutes at altitudes up to 1,000 feet; 10 minutes at 1,001 to 3,000 feet; 15 minutes at 3,001 to 6,000 feet; and 20 minutes above 6,000 feet.

6. Let cool undisturbed for 12 hours. Store in a cool, dry place. Allow 6 weeks for the full flavors to develop.

Makes 4 pints

Zucchini Marmalade

Zucchini marmalade is proof that if you add enough sugar to any ingredient,
it will be tasty. But if you think making a sweet preserve from raw zucchini
is too weird, you should taste an uncooked Seville orange,
the original — and truly sour — marmalade fruit.

6 cups trimmed and sliced small zucchini

1 can (13½ ounces) crushed pineapple, drained

1 teaspoon grated lemon zest
Juice of 2 lemons (about 6 tablespoons)

1 package (1¾ ounces) powdered fruit pectin

5 cups sugar

2 tablespoons crystallized ginger

1. In a large saucepan, combine the zucchini, pineapple, lemon zest, and lemon juice. Bring to a boil. Reduce heat and simmer uncovered for 15 minutes, until the zucchini is tender but not mushy.

2. Stir in the pectin. Bring to a boil. Stir in the sugar and ginger. Bring to a rolling boil. Stirring constantly, continue boiling for 1 minute.

3. Remove the marmalade from the heat. Skim off any foam. Ladle into clean, hot half-pint jars, leaving ¼ inch of head-room. Using a plastic or wooden spatula, remove air bubbles. Wipe the rim with a clean cloth and seal.

4. Process in a boiling-water bath according to the directions on page 279 for 5 minutes at altitudes up to 1,000 feet; 10 minutes at 1,001 to 6,000 feet; and 15 minutes above 6,000 feet.

5. Let cool undisturbed for 12 hours. Label and store in a cool, dry place.

Makes 5 half-pint jars

Freezing

Many delicious dishes can be prepared easily and quickly from frozen vegetable combinations.

When the copious bounty of the squash patch becomes threatening, make several batches of a zucchini-vegetable mix and stack them away in the freezer. Make a list of what you are storing and where; perhaps tape this list to the freezer itself, so that anytime you need a vegetable mix, it can be located easily, already partially cooked and ready to pop into a pot or baking dish at a moment's notice.

Freezing Summer Squash

Before you decide to freeze summer squash, be very clear on how you will use it all up. There's no point in investing the time in stocking the freezer if the frozen foods will never be used. Grated squash can be frozen without much effort. Just grate the squash with a food processor or by hand, using the large-hole side of a box grater. Pack it into freezer containers or plastic bags in convenient 1- or 2-cup quantities, label, and freeze. Squash prepared this way can be used in any recipe calling for grated squash. Defrost the squash in a colander, and the excess moisture will drain away. You can omit the salting step that many recipes call for, but be sure to add the salt to the batter.

Sliced squash should be blanched in boiling water for 3 minutes and then cooled in a cold-water bath for 3 minutes. Pat the squash dry, then pack in freezer containers and freezer bags. A lot of texture is lost in the freezing process, but the squash can be added to stews and soups, where a crisp texture is not required. Use home-frozen vegetables within 8 to 12 months for best quality and nutrient retention.

Freezing Winter Squash & Pumpkin

Of all vegetables, winter squash is the easiest to freeze and produces the most fresh-tasting results. But fresh squash has a shelf life of several months in cool storage. The only reason to freeze it is to have it ready as a convenience food, or if you have more than you will use up in a few months.

To freeze, cut the squash or pumpkin in halves or quarters. Remove and discard seeds and fibers. Steam over boiling water, or bake with 1 inch water in a baking dish at 350°F for 45 to 60 minutes, until completely tender. Separate the flesh from the skin; discard the skin. Mash or purée the flesh. Pack into freezer containers and freeze.

Basic Zucchini-Vegetable Mix

Mixed vegetables are convenient for adding to soups and casseroles.

2 tablespoons butter or extra virgin olive oil

1 cup diced celery

1 cup minced onion

2 cups chicken or vegetable broth

2 cups sliced or diced carrots

2 cups sliced or diced zucchini or other summer squash

1 cup corn kernels

1 cup chopped green bell pepper

Salt and freshly ground black pepper

1. Melt the butter in a large skillet over medium-high heat. Add the celery and onion. Sauté until softened, 3 to 5 minutes. Add the broth and carrots. Simmer for 20 minutes.

2. Add the zucchini, corn, and bell pepper to the skillet. Simmer for 10 minutes.

3. Season to taste with salt and pepper. Cool briefly. Pour into freezer containers, leaving ½ inch of headroom for expansion. Freeze for up to 3 months.

Makes about 8 cups

Zucchini Mix in Tomato Sauce

Frozen tomato sauce with zucchini in it can be defrosted and
used as an instant pasta or pizza sauce.

3 pounds ripe tomatoes, chopped

2 tablespoons extra virgin olive oil

¼ cup minced onion

1 cup chopped celery

5–6 cups diced or sliced zucchini

1 tablespoon sugar or honey

1½ teaspoons salt

1. Force the chopped tomatoes through a food mill or coarse sieve to remove the seeds and skins.

2. In a large skillet, heat the olive oil over medium-high heat. Add the onion and celery. Sauté until softened, 3 to 5 minutes. Add the zucchini, tomato purée, and sugar. Simmer, stirring frequently, until the sauce is reduced by about one quarter and thick, about 25 minutes.

3. Add the salt. Remove from the heat and cool briefly. Ladle into freezer containers, allowing ½ inch of headroom in the container for expansion. Label and freeze for up to 3 months.

Makes 8 cups

Summer Squash Italiano Mix

This interesting mix of vegetables can be used to make soup or pasta sauce.
It is also delicious served on its own as a vegetable side dish.

2 tablespoons extra virgin olive oil

2 cups sliced or diced yellow summer squash

1 medium-sized onion, chopped

2 cups Romano beans (flat beans), cut into 2-inch pieces

1 cup cooked or canned chickpeas

1 red bell pepper, chopped

2 cups chicken or vegetable broth

½ cup sliced or chopped green olives

Salt and freshly ground black pepper

1. In a large skillet, heat the oil over medium-high heat. Add the squash and onion. Sauté until softened, 3 to 5 minutes.

2. Add the beans, chickpeas, bell pepper, and broth. Simmer until the vegetables are tender, about 10 minutes.

3. Add the olives. Season to taste with salt and pepper. Cool briefly. Ladle into freezer containers, leaving ½ inch of headroom, and label. Freeze for up to 3 months.

Makes about 5 cups

Puréed Soup Base

To make soup, combine 1½ cups milk with each pint of purée. Add 1 cup chicken or vegetable broth. Season to taste and serve the soup hot.

- 6 tablespoons butter or extra virgin olive oil
- 3 large onions, thinly sliced
- ¼ cup water
- 18 cups thinly sliced zucchini or other summer squash
- 2 green bell peppers, thinly sliced
- 3 cloves of garlic, minced
- 2¼ teaspoons salt
- ½ teaspoon freshly ground black pepper
- 1 cup minced fresh parsley, basil, or tarragon

1. Heat the butter in a large skillet over medium-high heat. Add the onions. Sauté until softened, 3 to 5 minutes. Add the water, zucchini, bell pepper, garlic, salt, and pepper. Cover and cook over low heat for 3 minutes, until the vegetables are completely tender. Remove from the heat and add the herbs.

2. Purée the mixture in a food processor, blender, or food mill. Pack in 1-pint freezer containers, leaving ½ inch of headroom, and label. Freeze for up to 3 months.

Makes about 5 pints

Freezer Bread and Butter Zucchini Chips

In recent years, many cooks have been making freezer pickles to avoid the heat and hassle of canning. This recipe can be made with either cucumbers or zucchini. It is very important to slice the zucchini as thin as possible. A food processor or mandoline yields the best results.

  4 cups thinly sliced zucchini
  1 onion, thinly sliced
1½ teaspoons salt
1¼ cups distilled white vinegar
 ½ cup sugar
  1 teaspoon ground turmeric
 ½ teaspoon celery seed
 ¼ teaspoon black pepper

1. Combine the zucchini, onion, and salt in a large bowl. Toss to mix and set aside for at least 2 hours. Drain but do not rinse.

2. In a nonreactive saucepan, combine the vinegar, sugar, turmeric, celery seed, and black pepper. Heat just enough to dissolve the sugar. Pour over the zucchini mixture. Toss to mix.

3. Pack the zucchini and brine into freezer containers, leaving about 1 inch of headroom. Label and freeze for up to 6 months.

4. Defrost in the refrigerator for at least 8 hours before serving.

Makes about 4 cups

Appendix 1

Play Zucchini Bingo

To some people, cooking is child's play. For those who like to play in the kitchen, here is a new form of bingo. The resulting jackpot is a casserole, just like Mom used to make.

To start, melt 2 tablespoons butter in a large skillet over medium-high heat. Add 1 cup sliced zucchini and 1 sliced onion. Sauté until just barely tender, about 3 minutes. Next, make a selection from each category to make a prizewinning dish. For example, B-3, I-9, N-4, G-7, O-8 creates an Italian-style casserole with spinach noodles, veal, cheese, and tomatoes. Recipes for the sauces in column N follow. Combine all in a casserole dish and bake at 350° F for 30 minutes.

B	**I**	**N**	**G**	**O**
Vegetables 1 cup, chopped	**Meat** ½ pound, cooked	**Sauces** 1 cup	**Base** 1 cup, cooked	**Top** ½ cup
1. Peas, celery	1. Chicken, chopped	1. Béchamel	1. Spaghetti squash	1. Bread crumbs
2. Tomatoes, mushrooms	2. Ground lamb	2. Mornay	2. Rice	2. Bread crumbs, cheese
3. Tomatoes, eggplant	3. Turkey, chopped	3. Fresh Tomato	3. Barley	3. Crushed potato chips
4. Summer squash, celery	4. Ground pork	4. Sour Cream	4. Noodles	4. Cracker crumbs
5. Tomatoes, corn	5. Tuna	5. Sour cream–Tomato	5. Macaroni	5. Grated Swiss
6. Tomatoes, green peppers	6. Ham, chopped	6. Chicken Velouté	6. Spaghetti	6. Grated Parmesan
7. Green peppers, carrots, celery	7. Bacon, crumbled	7. Mayonnaise Casserole	7. Spinach noodles	7. Grated Romano
8. Peas, mushrooms	8. Ground beef	8. Cheese	8. Acorn squash shells	8. Grated mozzarella
9. Green peppers, celery	9. Ground veal	9. Custard	9. Scooped-out zucchini shells	9. Grated Cheddar
10. Green peppers, mushrooms	10. Ground pork sausage or Italian sausage	10. Tomato-Cheese	10. Bulgur	10. Grated Gruyeré

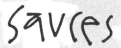

Sauces

The sauces that follow are designed to be used to make a Zucchini Bingo casserole. Some of them can also be used to dress up a simple plate of squash.

Béchamel Sauce

2 tablespoon butter
2 tablespoons all-purpose flour
1 cup warm milk
   Salt and freshly ground black pepper

In a small saucepan, melt the butter. Whisk in the flour until smooth and cook for about 30 seconds. Whisk in the milk and cook until thick and bubbly, 3 to 5 minutes. Season with salt and pepper to taste.

Makes about 1 cup

Mornay Sauce

1 egg yolk
1 cup light cream
2 tablespoons butter
2 tablespoons unbleached all-purpose flour
   Salt and freshly ground black pepper
   Freshly grated Parmesan cheese

1. In a medium-sized bowl, beat the egg slightly. Add the cream and beat until thoroughly blended. In a small saucepan, melt the butter. Whisk in the flour until smooth and cook for about 30 seconds. Whisk in the cream mixture. Add salt, pepper, and Parmesan cheese to taste.

2. Cook until thick and bubbly, 3 to 5 minutes.

Makes about 1 cup

Fresh Tomato Sauce

3 tablespoons extra virgin olive oil
½ cup minced onions
2 pounds tomatoes, seeded and chopped
1 clove of garlic, minced
1 bay leaf
1 tablespoon chopped fresh marjoram, or
   1 teaspoon dried
1 tablespoon chopped fresh oregano, or
   1 teaspoon dried
1 tablespoon chopped fresh parsley, or
   1 teaspoon dried
1 teaspoon sugar
   Salt and freshly ground black pepper

1. In a medium-sized saucepan, heat the oil over medium-high heat. Add the onion and sauté until softened, 3 to 5 minutes. Add the tomatoes, garlic, bay leaf, marjoram, oregano, parsley, sugar, and salt and pepper to taste.

2. Simmer until thick and reduced, about 20 minutes.

Makes about 2 cups

Sour Cream Casserole Base

½ cup sour cream
1 can (10¾ ounces) condensed cream soup (cream of chicken, cream of mushroom, or cream of shrimp)

Mix together the sour cream and soup.

Makes 1½ cups

Sour Cream–Tomato Casserole Base

½ cup sour cream
¾ cup tomato purée
½ teaspoon paprika

Mix together the sour cream, tomato purée, and paprika.

Makes 1¼ cups

Chicken Velouté

2 tablespoons butter
2 tablespoons unbleached all-purpose flour
1 cup chicken broth
1 egg yolk
1 tablespoon cream
1–2 tablespoons dry sherry (optional)
   Salt and freshly ground black pepper

1. In a small saucepan, melt the butter. Whisk in the flour until smooth and cook for about 30 seconds. Whisk in the broth. Beat the egg yolk with the cream and whisk into the sauce. Add the sherry, if using. Add salt and pepper to taste.
2. Cook until thick and bubbly, 3 to 5 minutes.

Makes about 1¼ cups

Mayonnaise Casserole Sauce

¾ cup shredded sharp Cheddar cheese
½ cup mayonnaise (can be reduced-fat mayonnaise)
¼ cup chopped onion
1 tablespoon fresh lemon juice
   Salt
   Chervil

1. Combine the cheese, mayonnaise, onion, and lemon juice.
2. Add salt and chervil to taste.

Makes about 1½ cups

Cheese Sauce

2 tablespoons butter
2 tablespoons unbleached all-purpose flour
1 cup milk
½ cup grated Cheddar cheese
   Salt and freshly ground black pepper

1. In a small saucepan, melt the butter. Whisk in the flour until smooth and cook for about 30 seconds. Whisk in the milk. Add the cheese and salt and pepper to taste.
2. Cook until thick and bubbly, 3 to 5 minutes, stirring until the cheese is melted.

Makes about 1½ cups

Custard Sauce

2 eggs
1½ cups milk
   Salt and freshly ground black pepper

1. In a medium-sized bowl, lightly beat the eggs. Mix in the milk and salt and pepper to taste.

Makes about 1½ cups

Tomato-Cheese Sauce

½ can (10¾ ounces) condensed tomato soup
1 cup shredded sharp Cheddar cheese
1 tablespoon tomato paste
½ cup milk

1. In a small saucepan over medium heat, combine the tomato soup, cheese, and tomato paste. Heat, stirring, until the cheese is melted. Stir in the milk.
2. Continue to cook, stirring frequently, until the sauce is heated through, about 5 minutes.

Makes about 2 cups

Appendix 2

Metric Conversion and U.S. Equivalents

Unless you have finely calibrated measuring equipment, conversions between U.S. and metric measurements will be somewhat inexact. It's important to convert the measurements for all of the ingredients in a recipe to maintain the same proportions as the original.

GENERAL FORMULA FOR METRIC CONVERSION

Ounces to grams	multiply ounces by 28.35
Grams to ounces	multiply grams by 0.035
Pounds to grams	multiply pounds by 453.5
Pounds to kilograms	multiply pounds by 0.45
Cups to liters	multiply cups by 0.24
Fahrenheit to Celsius	subtract 32 from Fahrenheit temperature, multiply by 5, then divide by 9
Celsius to Fahrenheit	multiply Celsius temperature by 9, divide by 5, then add 32

APPROXIMATE METRIC EQUIVALENTS BY VOLUME

U.S.	Metric
1 teaspoon	5 milliliters
1 tablespoon	15 milliliters
¼ cup	60 milliliters
½ cup	120 milliliters
1 cup	230 milliliters
1¼ cups	300 milliliters
1½ cups	360 milliliters
2 cups	460 milliliters
2½ cups	600 milliliters
3 cups	700 milliliters
4 cups (1 quart)	0.95 liter
1.06 quarts	1 liter
4 quarts (1 gallon)	3.8 liters

APPROXIMATE METRIC EQUIVALENTS BY WEIGHT

U.S.	Metric
¼ ounce	7 grams
½ ounce	14 grams
1 ounce	28 grams
1¼ ounces	35 grams
1½ ounces	40 grams
2½ ounces	70 grams
4 ounces	112 grams
5 ounces	140 grams
8 ounces	228 grams
10 ounces	280 grams
15 ounces	425 grams
16 ounces (1 pound)	454 grams

Metric	U.S.
1 gram	0.035 ounce
50 grams	1.75 ounces
100 grams	3.5 ounces
250 grams	8.75 ounces
500 grams	1.1 pounds
1 kilogram	2.2 pounds

U.S. Measurement Equivalents

A few grains/pinch/ dash, etc. (dry)	Less than ⅛ teaspoon
A dash (liquid)	A few drops
1 teaspoon	60 drops
3 teaspoons	1 tablespoon
½ tablespoon	1½ teaspoons
1 tablespoon	3 teaspoons
2 tablespoons	1 fluid ounce
4 tablespoons	¼ cup
5⅓ tablespoons	⅓ cup
8 tablespoons	½ cup
8 tablespoons	4 fluid ounces
½ cup	4 fluid ounces
10⅔ tablespoons	⅔ cup
12 tablespoons	¾ cup
16 tablespoons	1 cup
16 tablespoons	8 fluid ounces
⅛ cup	2 tablespoons
¼ cup	4 tablespoons
¼ cup	2 fluid ounces
⅓ cup	5 tablespoons plus 1 teaspoon
½ cup	8 tablespoons
1 cup	16 tablespoons
1 cup	8 fluid ounces
1 cup	½ pint
2 cups	1 pint
2 pints	1 quart
4 quarts (liquid)	1 gallon
8 quarts (dry)	1 peck
4 pecks (dry)	1 bushel
1 pound	16 ounces

Sources

Clay Brook Farm
802-899-3743
www.claybrookfarm.org

Cook's Garden
800-457-9703
www.cooksgarden.com

High Mowing Seeds
802-472-6174
www.highmowingseeds.com

Lewis Creek Farm
Hank Bissell and Cecilia Elwert-Bissell
802-453-4591
www.greenmountainaccess.net/~lcfarm

Local Harvest
831-475-8150
www.localharvest.org

Oakville Chamber of Commerce
360-273-2702
www.oakville-wa.org

Okemo Valley Regional Chamber of Commerce
802-228-5830
www.okemovalleyvt.org

Pleasant Hill Farm Market
Mike and Nancy Merrill
formerly of Middlebury, Vermont
no longer in business

Poughkeepsie Farm Project
845-473-1415
www.farmproject.org

Southern Exposure Seed Exchange
540-894-9480
www.southernexposure.com

Index

Other Storey Titles You Will Enjoy

Apple Cookbook, by Olwen Woodier.
More than 140 recipes to put everyone's favorite fruit
into tasty new combinations.
192 pages. Paper. ISBN 978-1-58017-389-6.

The Big Book of Preserving the Harvest, by Carol W. Costenbader.
A revised edition of a classic primer on freezing, canning, drying,
and pickling fruits and vegetables.
352 pages. Paper. ISBN 978-1-58017-458-9.

Maple Syrup Cookbook, by Ken Haedrich.
Recipes both sweet and savory that feature maple syrup
and its wonderful earth, tangy qualities.
144 pages. Paper. ISBN 978-1-58017-404-6.

Mom's Best Crowd-Pleasers, by Andrea Chesman.
The latest in a best-selling series — a relaxed approach to
feeding casual gatherings of every size.
208 pages. Paper. ISBN 978-1-58017-629-3.

Pickles & Relishes, by Andrea Chesman.
Quick-and-easy recipes to turn bumper crops into
mouthwatering pickles and relishes, using little or no salt.
160 pages. Paper. ISBN 978-0-88266-744-7.

Pumpkin, by DeeDee Stovel.
A wide-ranging collection of recipes, from soups to desserts
and everything in between that use this nutritious orange super food.
224 pages. Paper. ISBN 978-1-58017-594-4.

Serving Up the Harvest, by Andrea Chesman.
A collection of 175 recipes to bring out the best in garden-fresh
vegetables, with 14 master recipes that can accommodate
whatever happens to be in your produce basket.
516 pages. Paper. ISBN 978-1-58017-663-7.

These and other books from Storey Publishing are available
wherever quality books are sold or by calling 1-800-441-5700.
Visit us at *www.storey.com.*